Praise for Wayne T. Morden's Golf Shorts and Plus Fours

Hole No. 7: "Anger is a part of being human . . . how one deals with it defines him as you so aptly describe. The one constant is the ability to let anger go once it's grabbed onto you. Some are better at it than others. Thanks for your thoughts on this . . . they were on point."

-Tom Watson, eight-time major championship winner

Hole No. 11: "It was delightful reading and your depiction of the Pebble Beach experience was classic (and very much appreciated I might add . . .). Both Bill Perocchi and I thoroughly enjoyed the read. The comparison to St Andrews is a terrific debate. Thanks for making it so appealing. Our sincere best wishes to you in bringing this to many readers and golfers throughout the world."

-RJ Harper, Senior Vice President, Golf at Pebble Beach Company

Hole No. 9: "This is the best side-by-side presentation and analysis I've seen."

-George Peper, currently editor, *LINKS Magazine*, was editor in chief of *Golf Magazine* for twenty-five years and is the best-selling author of fifteen previous books

Hole No. 6: "Thank you very much for sending us the St Andrews chapter of your manuscript which I found very enjoyable. It sounds like Jimmy also looked after you and we are delighted he brought you home under 80! The Verma Cuppers certainly seemed to enjoy themselves and you did well to 'run' on the West Sands, albeit in slow motion, after your experiences the day before! We are delighted you enjoyed the experience of

St Andrews and can certainly detect from your writing your appreciation of the history surrounding the Home of Golf. We hope these memories will last you for many years, but also that you will return and enjoy our courses again in the future."

-John Grant, Director of Golf, St Andrews Links Trust

Hole No. 17: "Golf's rich history is part of its endless charm. Wayne Morden knows that history, and his appreciation for it comes through in his idiosyncratic stories."

-Lorne Rubenstein, Curator, Royal Canadian Golf Association, Editor, *SCOREGolf* Magazine, Golf Columnist, *The Globe and Mail,* and author of many books on golf

Hole No. 6: "Thank you for your note and the excerpt from *Golf Shorts and Plus Fours: Musings from a Golfing Traditionalist,* which is entertaining indeed—you have a wonderful style reminiscent of Jerome K. Jerome's *Three Men in a Boat*! I am forwarding this to our Alumni Office, which will no doubt be as delighted as I am to read of the bonds you describe so well among our alumni."

-Daniel R. Woolf, Professor of History, Principal and Vice-Chancellor, Queen's University, Kingston, Ontario

Hole No. 18: "The points you make are all very important and go to the core of the game's success."

-David Roy, Managing Secretary at Crail Golfing Society in Fife Scotland.

Hole No. 17: "Thanks for sending me "Hole No. 17"—it is very good. I can't wait to see the book. Stop by City Hall when you are in Charleston."

-Joe Riley Jr., Mayor of Charleston, South Carolina

Hole No. 14: "Thank you for the email and it is always nice to read a new perspective on the experience our resort provides. I am glad to hear you all enjoyed our resort above all!"

-Michael Chupka Jr., Head Golf Professional, Pacific Dunes at Bandon Dunes Golf Resort

Hole No. 15: "Thanks for getting in touch and sharing your chapter on business golf. You have a wonderful, engaging writing style. Also very good advice for anyone new to business golf. The beginning sounded like you were generalizing, but then you clarified that not all business golfers expect to play 'customer golf.' I really liked the section on how to interpret specific behaviours. As I read, I got the feeling that it was a labour of love and something that your father would have enjoyed."

-Judy Anderson, *BizGolf*

Golf Shorts
and
Plus Fours

GOLF SHORTS
AND
PLUS FOURS

Musings from a Golfing Traditionalist

WAYNE T. MORDEN

iUniverse, Inc.
Bloomington

Golf Shorts and Plus Fours
Musings from a Golfing Traditionalist

iUniverse books may be ordered through booksellers or by contacting:

iUniverse
1663 Liberty Drive
Bloomington, IN 47403
www.iuniverse.com
1-800-Authors (1-800-288-4677)

ISBN: 978-1-4697-3140-7 (sc)
ISBN: 978-1-4697-3141-4 (hc)
ISBN: 978-1-4697-3142-1 (ebk)

Library of Congress Control Number: 2011963576

Printed in the United States of America

iUniverse rev. date: 01/10/2012

For my father, Terry Morden, alias Sam Morgan. You died too young at 57 but you are still in my mind, the self-acclaimed "Best Putter in Oxford County." I miss your great expressions; however, I mostly miss you. As you would brightly exclaim, "Carry on!" So I have.

ACKNOWLEDGMENTS

There are many people that I would like to thank for contributing to the book you are about to savour. It was a long process to write the many versions but the final product is well worth the effort. These influential people range from strangers to close friends and family. Some read individual chapters while others read complete and different drafts of *Golf Shorts and Plus Fours*.

I appreciate all those who provided the quotes found on the cover and inside the book. I selected applicable "holes" for each of them to read and they were kind enough to find the time to get back to me. I would especially like to thank George Peper for his encouragement while I was writing my book and for helping me to coordinate the meeting of the Verma Cuppers with Gordon Murray at St Andrews. Thank you too Gordon for your hospitality at the St Andrews Club and for suggesting Jimmy to carry my bag on the Old Course.

To those who constructively reviewed different drafts of my entire book, I would like to mention the following: Donna Bull, Steve Bull, Peter Callahan (thanks for setting me on my writing path too, buddy!), Gerard Chiasson, Ross Genge, Greg Haddow, Barry Hennigar, Pat Hinnegan, Rick Kaleta, Debbie Karns, Ron Luckman, Gary Keeler, Tess Moore, Steve Roy, Jim Slomka, Ian Tetro, and Johanna Swenson.

Thank you to Grant Fraser for all his guidance while I wrote my book and for connecting me to Barb Chambers to edit my book. Not many people like Barb could grasp my quirky way of writing and understand my use of *Star Wars* terminology on the golf course. Masterful job Barb—you were the perfect fit!

My Verma Cup comrades need to be mentioned because they have made trips to Scotland and Ireland most memorable. I would like to highlight my close friends Tom "Chief" Stanton, Martin "Scugog" Stewart, and Andrew "Bags" Merrick. I have shared many travels and adventures with them both on and off the course. I owe them much for enhancing my experiences at golf's great places, for giving me their thoughts about the book, and most importantly, for being there when I needed them.

I would like to mention Rob Mason, the General Manager and Head Professional and others at my home club of Craigowan. Rob read my book and had great input for me to consider. This club has a special place in my heart and is where my dad got me first smacking a sawed-off four-wood at 5 years of age. Dad, I think of you all the time. I wrote a book of which you would be proud. "Don't leave your putt short, son . . ."

Thank you to Steve Cohen, David Currie and Hilton Tudhope at the Shivas Irons Society and Bob Brown and Jim Corbett at Keepers of the Game. Both organizations believe in upholding the same values and traditions that I do for the fine game of golf. Keep it up . . . just like I will.

I must commend the iUniverse team for coordinating the editorial, production, and marketing of this book. They helped me turn my thoughts and this dream of mine into a tangible reality so passionate golf readers can enjoy it all over the world.

And I have a final thank you to my 82-year-old mother Doris and my wonderful wife Alison. With her glasses snugly fit, Doris tackled *all* the versions of my book. We had great chats about it in Woodstock over coffee and dinner, interspersed with conversations about politics and the changing world. She has been a great supporter of my endeavour. Alison, the Number One female in my life, you were always there for me during the long hours of work in my cave. Doubts never crept into your mind because you knew I would complete this monumental task. Sacrifices have to be made to undertake such a large project and I thank you profusely for standing by me, always. A writer needs such fuel to succeed in finally getting a book published. This is for you, Roc, and our future trip to New Zealand.

CONTENTS

Outward Half

Inward Nine

Playoff Holes

Golf Shorts and Plus Fours: Musings from a Golfing Traditionalist

Are you ready to play a rollicking par-69, 18-hole golf course and a trio of playoff holes that is full of quirky doglegs, uphill brutes, questionable par 4s, and laughable shorter holes? *Golf Shorts and Plus Fours: Musings from a Golfing Traditionalist* is just a tad different type of course than you are used to, but you will find it quite enjoyable and enticingly playable. Passionate golfers, curious golfers, and worldwide golfers will connect with all the "holes" I roll out in my design.

My vivid, personal storytelling transports you on journeys to the Holy Trinity of golf: St Andrews, Pebble Beach, and of course, the Masters. Penetrating subjects like avoiding folded arms, respect for the game, Ryder Cup, debates on golfing greatness, plastic golf balls, and mystery golf trips also dot this undulating landscape. Whether perused in the comfort of your spacious den, warm bedroom, or on a cramped plane, readers will find this an adventurous ride. Scan, study, and lock this golf tome away where it is easily accessible for future examination. Learn about this great game and laugh at your leisure!

It is only fitting that I start this pre-round warm-up with a question. Golf has been a lifelong pursuit of mine and I feel that I am in a strong position to speak on behalf of amateur lovers of the game. I asked myself an important question: What is it that avid golfers would want to know about? Here is the net result of this query.

Forget about technical jargon involving swing plane and mechanics of the hip thrust when you read this book. *Golf Magazine, Golf Digest,* and other applicable manuals will be more helpful to solve these mysteries and improve your skills. Frankly, these technical aspects of golf do not interest me, although I respect others who indulge in such research in order to improve the quality of their game. Let's talk about other important and memorable material for you intrigued golfers. You will discover lessons and truth, and my stories will resonate and unleash your own fond memories of this beautiful game. Storytelling is compelling to all of us.

I satisfy my curious nature by posing stimulating questions to pave the way for zealous players to discover some of golf's great travels and destinations, commonalities, and debates. I draw upon the history of the game and the many characters who have participated. Amusing anecdotes and seemingly off-the-wall arguments from my own recollections and experiences also punctuate this read. After all, if you are not laughing about golf subjects raised in conversation or when playing, then you are missing the obvious point of enjoying this wonderful game.

My slant in this book is clearly a traditionalist or purist one. The Masters has created a wonderful tournament event with memories of the past when people were treated as honoured guests and politeness was in abundance. I, too, hearken back to a past where individuals acted with class on the golf course through proper etiquette and when respect for the game was put on the highest pedestal. I'm of the opinion that our society and golf has slipped recently in this regard. Perhaps it is my utopian hope that by beating this traditionalist drum, golfers may pause and reflect on the state of their game and individual behaviour can improve. Golf should definitely stand on a higher plane than other games and sports.

How best to create my "course" so you can relate? I compiled these short and longer written pieces into par-3, par-4, and par-5 holes. The short stories are par-3s, medium length pieces are par-4s, and the longer ones are par-5s.

I even added three playoff holes following the end-of-round drinks in the nineteenth hole for those keen on playing a few additional holes. Hopefully, you will enjoy your golf day further by playing them after refreshing cocktails, medium chicken wings, and clubhouse sandwiches toasted on brown.

This eclectic mixture of holes is a unique Wayne T. Morden-designed and—branded golf course. Read at your own pace. Also, if you like, please feel free to read the holes out of sequence and make your own customized course. Each hole offers its own beauty and challenges.

There are numerous breaks provided during your golf round so you can enjoy a visit from the Cart Girl. She will gladly provide you with an assortment of thought-provoking trivia refreshments for your edification and enlightenment. I thought these snacks and drinks could give you a welcome breather before heading to the next hole for your tee shot. Nineteenth-hole breaks with even more trivia are also included after each half of the course. See them as added fuel to further enhance the satisfaction of your round.

I beseech you to please hold off on using the Internet to find answers to these trivia ticklers unless you are absolutely stumped. You wouldn't dare cheat on the golf course with an illegal mulligan or a crafty and shuffling foot wedge in the rough if you respect the game, would you? The answers to all of these brainteasers are found at the back of the book. I have also listed some good books for you to read. And what would this book be without me providing a cheat sheet of Waynerisms and other lingo? This list has been included just after the *Star Wars* hole found early in the round. Stash it in your bag for quick access so you can intelligently utter Ewok, Chewie, Temple of Doom, and the like with your friends and psychological enemies.

What are my golf credentials, you might ask?

- My golfing career began when I was 5 years old and, at one time, our whole family of six played simultaneously. My parents felt that it was the best way for them to get me out of their way at home and, as my father (Terry Morden) would say, "to keep me out of the pool hall."
- I caddied as a tyke and dutifully worked in a pro shop for 4 years as a teenager, sometimes having to take those blasted iron covers off old Lynx Predator clubs to shine the grooves and clean the antiquated persimmon woods. I was even at our club when my uncle, Bill Parkes, an excellent man and golfer, died of a heart attack on the 18th hole at the ripe young age of 50. This is not something you easily forget and you appreciate that life is fleeting. Golf when you have the chance.
- My lowest score is 65 on a par-71 course at Craigowan (my home course) including a 29 on the front nine with six birdies. I have shot several other scores in the 60s. I have also shot 75, 85, 95, and 105 (and I am sure 115 when I was a small fellow). This is quite a large span in golf scores, don't you think?
- I played varsity golf for 2 years at Queen's University in Kingston, Ontario. Sinking a pressure putt in sudden-death overtime to

make the team in my first year of trying was surely a character builder. My knuckles remain white from that occasion. And thank you, Gerard, for providing me with motivation to make the team after your snickering and sarcastic comment following my lousy front nine at Glen Lawrence on Day 1 of the Qualifying. I am glad we ended up having fun together at exotic destinations like Fonthill, Conestoga, and Guelph, buddy!

- My years of golf have seen some victories in junior and men's tournaments. Mind you, I have also felt the chokehold when competing for trophies. I've certainly experienced the best of both worlds. I have felt the pain, brother . . .

- I have been subject to the enormous sting of being disqualified or "DQ'd" as we loved to say, during a junior tournament when I was 15. I failed to finish out a putt because of my ugly, adolescent temper. From the Thrill of Victory to the Agony of Defeat. Thank you Jim McKay and *Wide World of Sports*. I felt like that poor tumbling skier from the infamous opening sequence of that 1970s television program.

- It has been my pleasure and privilege to play some of the best golf courses in North America, Scotland and most recently, Ireland. They include: Pebble Beach, Spyglass, and PGA West in California; Pacific Dunes, Bandon Dunes, and Pumpkin Ridge in Oregon; Pinehurst No. 2 in North Carolina, The Ocean Course at Kiawah Island, South Carolina; Whistling Straits in Kohler, Wisconsin; The National in Woodbridge, Ontario and Hamilton Golf Club in Ancaster, Ontario; Troon North in Arizona; the Old Course at St Andrews, Gullane No. 1, and Carnoustie in Scotland; and Ballybunion, Waterville, Lahinch, Tralee, and Old Head in Ireland. If I get struck by lightning like Lee Trevino (he luckily survived but suffered a bad back), I can die with a smile on my face, knowing that I have played many of golf's finest venues.

- My golf game has transitioned through many stages to what I aspire to be—an enlightened golfer: first as a bratty juvenile who liked to entrench clubs in the ground; to the obsessive type where low score is the be-all and end-all; to the inner Zen-meister who sees comradeship and the serenity of golf as being the raison d'être for playing the game. At which stage of this golfing cycle do you reside?

Welcome to a refreshingly new, wonderful brand of golf course. Hitch up your pants like Arnie would and step up to the opening tee. Indulge. Think. Enjoy. Chuckle. Hopefully by the end of playing it, ***Golf Shorts and Plus Fours: Musings of a Golfing Traditionalist*** will expand your mind, increase your perspective, transport you to your own world of why you love golf, and finally, make you view golf in a different way. Play for the joy of it and always uphold its integrity.

Please feel free to email me with your thoughts at <u>wayne.morden@ rogers.com</u>. I certainly would like to hear your comments about how golf has impacted your life and made you chortle.

And what better way is there to usher in the beginning of the spring golf season and playing my golf course than to offer the first hole about the Masters . . . .

May the Force be with you on a Yoda bounce!

Cheers, Wayne T. Morden ("the Commish")

THE CODE OF PRINCIPLES BY WHICH ALL GOLFERS SHOULD ABIDE ON THE COURSE

Play honours off tee blocks (except business golf). Note especially: Never hit off in front of a person who has earned the right through a birdie on the preceding hole.

Genuinely compliment a good shot taken by your competitor or partner. I don't hear this enough from players.

Doff your headgear upon completion of the round when shaking hands. This shows respect for the match, your competitor and the game. Watch the class Tiger displays with this gesture upon completion of his round.

Repair your ball mark on the green and fix an extra one. There is nothing worse than putting on greens where players do not take pride in its upkeep. Pockmarks are unacceptable.

If you are able and have a chance to walk courses do so rather than ride a gas/electric cart. You "feel" your golf game much better playing in this traditional fashion and it is good exercise.

Replace or seed divots and rake traps.

Don't step in someone's line on greens unless permission is granted.

Determine the stakes and rules of the game (e.g., strict competition, customer golf, Nassau bets, fun, etc.) before you tee off.

Don't talk too much about your own game. No one cares.

Enjoy a drink, food, or quick chat following the round in the 19th hole. This time allows you to enjoy a recap of the day and brings closure to the round before going back to the life of stress, screaming kids, and other worries.

If you hit into a group by mistake (not on purpose—like the cell phone case I will explain later), make sure you apologize.

No "helicopter" hurling, throwing, or slamming of your clubs. I know Tiger occasionally engages in such theatrics but just because he does, doesn't mean you should.

Arrive at the course a minimum of 15 minutes before your tee-off time. Rushing from the parking lot with spikes flailing is not the way to respect your group or the game.

Do not talk or walk while players are hitting or putting. Stand still.

Buy the first round of drinks and say "Cheers" to your mates!

OUTWARD HALF

HOLE No. 1, PAR 5. WHAT IS IT LIKE TO ATTEND THE MASTERS THEATRE?

There is green—and then there is Augusta green. Witnessing the unfolding drama of The Masters firsthand has always been a lifelong dream of mine. And I am pretty sure that I speak on behalf of any other passionate golfers; that they too have this as a top priority on their golfing wish list. One only has to mention that he or she attended the Masters, and awestruck individuals will quickly congregate around that person to get the inside story. I never imagined that I would be one of the lucky few to live this dream until an historic meeting with my friend Tom "Chief" Stanton.

He specifically asked me to visit him at his Oakville home so he could discuss something of great importance to me. Once I arrived, I was given orders to plunk my butt down in the leather chair in his den so he could share his news. Such a statement carried an ominous ring to it, especially since Chief also happens to be my doctor. Fortunately his message was quite the opposite of what I'd expected. He simply said that I was going to Augusta. My heart skipped a beat and then I offered silence. Chief's ever-broadening smile told me that this was not a joke. I steepled my hands as though in a peaceful trance, grinning and beaming with unbridled glee.

My good pal was able to procure these tickets through a patient who had contact with a ticket holder. Providentially for us, and perhaps unluckily for this gentleman, he was not able to attend. Chief jumped at the opportunity and merrily asked if he could take them off his hands. My friend was going to treat his three fellow Chewie Open competitors to a wonderful trip to the Masters. The Chewie Open is our annual golfing trip to various destinations and resorts in the United States. This extravaganza involves a 4-or 5-day tournament of intense stroke play involving psychological warfare and some choice sarcastic quips. But at Augusta, we would all individually focus on watching others battle their own unique inner demons and unpredictable weather events.

After confirming that this was no hallucination, I began to think of myself joining the exclusive and tiny club of "patrons" who walked the hallowed grounds of this southern gem. No longer would I have to remain content to watch this major championship solely on television. The tinkling piano music and soothing sounds of Jim Nantz at CBS would be replaced with the silent and actual sightings of Tiger, Phil, and other great PGA players. My "bucket list" item of watching The Masters live would be fulfilled in 2010!

Chief, you may take possession of my first-born if I ever decide to start a family with my wonderful wife Alison. I am forever in your debt. And that year's Masters had the added colour of seeing the return of four-time green jacket winner Tiger Woods who was playing in his first competition after a 5-month self-imposed exile from golf. Ticket valuations had skyrocketed as a result. Would his game be rusty and how would the patrons receive him? I was keenly interested to see how Tiger would cope with this embarrassing situation and if he could continue to hit the beautiful shots of previous Masters.

Whether Tiger liked it or not, he was now a celebrity with a bull's eye stuck on his back. He now resided in the disreputable category and was not merely an enigmatic golfer who could keep things extremely close to his vest. People in general, not only golf junkies, knew far more about his personal life than he'd ever wanted or imagined. Gossipy *Entertainment Weekly* Hollywood types would have an almost insurmountable task in penetrating this tightly controlled environment in order to gain further sordid details of his affairs. Their fortress-like mentality could successfully resist such intrusive outside interference. No doubt that Mr. Woods understood only too well Augusta National's unique and uncompromising way of doing things. Also, his past successes on the venerable site made it a natural choice for his golf game resurrection and, possibly more important, the resurrection of his brand.

A distinct buzz about his appearance permeated the air as though we were witnessing the return of the prodigal son. Many aficionados of the Masters hoped Tiger's return would not diminish the importance of the tournament itself. Augusta executives would not allow it. He had his press conference on Monday to make his sincere apologies. I personally found Tiger's script to be less than satisfactory. Masters Chairman Billy Payne then took a surprising swing at Tiger during Wednesday's opening speech. This action surprised many people, as this platform is usually subdued and uneventful. Mr. Payne discussed Tiger's egregious behaviour and how he'd let down everyone, including kids and grandkids, with his failure to act as a proper role model. It sounded like a firm but smartly worded lecture from a loving uncle to a nephew, as though he stated: "Please clean up your act and have a positive character change because we all want to see you again as our hero." Golf purists and the other Green Jackets were no doubt nodding their heads in agreement. It was (and still is) very interesting to see the lines of discussion being blurred between a man's private life, including character traits, and his profession, which is the sport of golf. We would see how this would pan out in the near future . . .

The Friday I was preparing to fly to Charlotte began inauspiciously. Alison was expecting delivery of our new, luxurious and heavy Montauk couch. Furniture needed to be shifted. Not the light stuff of course, but the unwieldy and bulky kind. First we moved, rather clumsily, the wooden cabinet to the corner of the living room. Next, the daybed's metal understructure had to be meticulously folded and marched into our dilapidated garage. Rats scurried and snakes slithered as we trundled into this hotbed of wild creature activity. Finally, we hoisted the heavy island in our kitchen once, then twice and finally, a third time (doesn't everything work in threes?) to accommodate the movers who shuffled the couch through the kitchen's sliding French doors. On the last move of the island I finally put my enormous foot down with Alison and said, "Hun Bun, this is my absolute last move." After her intense glare subsided and she unfolded her arms, I breathed a monstrous sigh of relief that my back had not given out on me. I could just imagine my lurching, Quasimodo-like movements as I staggered down the steep hill on the 10th hole at Augusta and then back up the incline to reach this Notre Dame Cathedral green.

I arrived in Aiken, South Carolina late Friday night via a convertible Ford Mustang after enjoying a fine filet mignon in downtown Charlotte with two of my friends, Martin "Scugog" Stewart and Andrew "Bags" Merrick. Chief had planned to join us for dinner but we were late in arriving. Luckily we caught him before he hopped into his rental car outside the restaurant to bolt to the airport. A quick and animated 5-minute debrief in his typical booming voice got our juices going about the Masters. He described Augusta as being even more beautiful than anticipated. We placed lanyards with the plastic Masters passes over our necks as though crown jewels were being bestowed upon us for the weekend rounds. "DO

NOT LOSE THESE PASSES AT ALL COSTS." There was no grey area around these words of advice.

Scugog had already walked the first two rounds with Chief. But due to diligent research he was able to land a ticket via eBay for Sunday. He would have to deal through a shady outfit working out of a rented house a mile away from Augusta National. This was great news; our friend was attending the final round with us. It floored me that he'd actually acquired the ticket. I was under the impression you could not access Masters tickets so easily, except at a steep extra cost. Masters tickets have always been revered as being extremely difficult to acquire—the Holy Grail of sporting event admissions. Gold, my friends. Here is another case of the power of the Internet and enterprising entrepreneurs coming to the aid of golfing fans!

The Comfort Inn in Aiken, South Carolina was no Taj Mahal but the three of us squeezed into our compact room. Rooms for Masters Week were going for a pretty premium in the surrounding area but we were not too far from Augusta National to make it inconvenient. Scugog drew the short straw to sleep on a cot. The Cotman could have the bad back on my behalf (you may recall that I'd avoided it earlier in the day at home). We are apparently selfish, evil friends, since Martin has had two back surgeries. Flicking on the Golf Channel, we watched some of the highlights of the day to prepare us for the Masters spectacle. Tired, we all flaked out until we heard Bags' irritating watch alarm.

Andrew and I woke up at 6:30am all fired up. My roommates were not impressed with my constant coughing from my lingering cold and the slight sucking-in of drapes from my snoring. A couple of tossed pillows and ample nudges in my direction were not-so-subtle reminders that they too wanted to get a good night's sleep before our big day. Before partaking of a rather pedestrian continental breakfast with plastic utensils in the main reception area, we passed two people reclined on their front seats in their white car just outside our hotel room. That seemed odd enough until we noted the engine was still running (I wonder for how long?). A quick peek inside determined they were not stiffs. I am pretty sure they were not dreaming of the green jacket presentation but simply staying warm during this cool South Carolinian spring.

Off we went for the approximately 30-minute drive that included crossing the Savannah River to Augusta, Georgia. The 200,000-person city resides just inside the state of Georgia next to South Carolina and is the second-largest one in Georgia after Atlanta. For all those sightseeing folks, there is a fine statue of the hometown funk and soul singer "I feeeeeel good!" James Brown.

You can't help but notice the severe contrast between Augusta, the city, and Augusta National, the golf course. Shifty locals wandered Broad Street and pawnshops, strip joints, and other shops of dubious nature dominated the downtown core. I am certain there are some good areas in the city to appreciate but you don't see them on the road to the golf course. We took this scenic route of the city's underbelly then passed several churches before merging on to Washington Road. Many strip malls and gas stations lay along this next stretch and you wonder how this can possibly be the way to the Masters. But lo and behold, what appears to be Augusta National Golf Club suddenly appears as if by magic on the left.

The private course's grounds cannot be seen from the road but visitors can certainly sense its presence. Magnificent Magnolia Lane leads from Washington Road to the clubhouse and is practically hidden from view. Thick bushes act as brawny centurion guards, blocking prying eyes along its entire perimeter. After crossing Eisenhower Drive and then Berckmans Road, we turned left to free Augusta parking. There is a large parcel of land dedicated for parking and Masters personnel obligingly directed us to a spot. Usually parking is a pain in the butt for such major sporting events but not here. Free parking only a block away from the patron entrance—unheard of!

This enticing gesture of free parking symbolized our first exposure to The Masters and the tremendous appreciation for its customers, its patrons. Already you are in Masters mode on your first touch point. This is a fantastic strategy set by this tournament and is very much planned and intentional. Numerous examples of customer appreciation and service would rule throughout our two days. In a sense, we were going back in time to a kinder and gentler world where humans were treated with the utmost respect. The meticulous preparation and outstanding organization of this event remains overwhelming and all-encompassing. Each and every detail regarding better experiences at food areas, faster moving restroom lines, and golf viewing is examined and scrutinized by the Masters decision-makers to make this a first-class affair. By the end of Sunday, the Masters would emphatically show me true southern hospitality and the best-run sports event that you could imagine.

Before reaching security at the gates, individuals pass through turnstiles. Security before entering Augusta's grounds is extremely tight. Patrons have to pass through airport-type screening machines and badges are checked for their authenticity. Don't dream of carting in your electronic gadgets, backpacks or cameras. They will promptly confiscate them and fellow patrons will chuckle at you for not doing your homework. Cajoling or sweet-talking will not do you any good. Homework was something I certainly did before making this historic trip.

The plastic badges are a piece of art and a great keepsake. I examined the top right hand of the badge more closely and noted the surreal "$200.00 NOT FOR RESALE NO REFUND." This brought a huge snicker since those in the know understand that the real value and cost of the ticket is exponentially higher. What I held in my hand was like a mint-condition rookie Mickey Mantle baseball card. The number of your ticket is located in the top left and there is a nice oval-shaped picture of Magnolia Lane and the clubhouse. Masters 2010 April 8th-11th completed the front of the badge.

On the rear of the badge there is a lot of legalese but I want to outline **TWO LARGE PARTS THAT ARE CAPITALIZED IN BOLDFACE:**

CELL PHONES, BEEPERS, AND OTHER ELECTRONIC DEVICES ARE STRICTLY PROHIBITED ON THE GROUNDS AT ALL TIMES. CAMERAS ARE STRICTLY PROHIBITED ON TOURNAMENT DAYS. VIOLATION OF THESE POLICIES WILL SUBJECT THE TICKET HOLDER TO REMOVAL FROM THE GROUNDS AND THE TICKET PURCHASER TO THE PERMANENT LOSS OF CREDENTIALS.

FAILURE TO OBSERVE ANY OF THE TERMS OR PROVISIONS HEREOF MAY RESULT IN THE TICKET HOLDER'S REMOVAL OR EXCLUSION FROM THE TOURNAMENT AND THE ORIGINAL PURCHASER'S PERMANENT LOSS OF CREDENTIAL(S). THIS AGREEMENT SHALL BE GOVERNED BY GEORGIA LAW.

Is this clear enough? The words "permanent loss" mentioned twice captures your attention. Badges need to be taken out of their transparent plastic holders for presentation to the security people. Next, the ubiquitous green collapsible chairs with the yellow Masters logo are to be removed from their carrying cases. I would not say that the frontline security agents were the most polite of people but it is not an easy task to frisk and check thousands of people as they enter. Other security people at the end of the line were more welcoming in this not overly uncomfortable process. Bags looked kind of shell-shocked after this initiation to the tournament. I steered my shaky friend towards an unforgettable experience. I was elated to get through this preliminary routine so I could be ready for my grand entrance to Augusta!

Now we were in . . . . Take a moment to breathe in its significance to you as a human, golfer, and fan of the game. The golf Garden of Eden lay before us. I guess the forbidden fruit would be to streak across the ninth fairway yelling to Tiger, "You da Man!" Except biting that apple was certainly not in the cards for me. Permanent banishment from The Masters for the rest of your earthly life is a hu-u-u-ge price to pay. I only had to reread the dire warnings on the back of my badge as a reminder. Chief would have a lot of 'splainin' to do to the wonderful man who had provided us with the tickets. Plus, I think a fracture of a long-lasting friendship that began on my first day at Queen's University in 1983 was too costly for the momentary thrill of indulging in such reprehensible behaviour.

Because we were attending the weekend rounds, tee-off times did not begin until 10:45am. The cut line had reduced the playing field substantially following Friday's round. I liked that we had the opportunity to soak up the ambience of the course and visit some of the storied places before rushing off to see drives and iron shots. Reading books with intriguing storylines of the tournament and researching Masters' history was most helpful in preparing for this day.

Arriving within its confines allows you to finally physically experience the sites that were previously etched only in your imagination. My analysis of the Masters would be threefold: view how immaculate and tricky Augusta is, appreciate how well this tournament is set up in order to cater to the patrons, and finally, size up the Masters as an event and as a brand. Is it really that spectacular?

Bags and I hungrily grabbed the tee-sheet pairings from the nifty bird feeder-type-holder. These sheets would allow us to cleverly navigate the course and catch up to those players we wanted to see at particular times of the day and on specific holes. After a cursory look at this vital information we peered to our left to see the impressive new practice range. This 18-acre marvel was just opened for its first Masters tournament in

2010. The old, narrow practice range was on the other side of Magnolia Lane and this antiquated facility included a net to capture high rising balls heading toward Washington Road. As late as 2009, the new elaborate practice grounds we saw this weekend in 2010 had been a parking lot for Masters patrons. The current 70-acre lot that we parked at has replaced it and was acquired by Augusta National to serve just this function. I would say it was quite a fair exchange.

Players will love practicing shots on the two separate 400-yard-long fairways. Trees are placed strategically on the range so golfers can hit creative shots. Beautifully manicured bunkers and sloping greens mimic the look of the course. "Observation Stands" are provided for interested people so they can watch their favourite players. There is also an area where players sign autographs. The old range could no longer satisfy the professionals and their explosive new equipment—big-headed drivers, sleek hybrids, (now) non-squared groove irons, and high-tech golf balls. Augusta can host a golf tournament like no other course. First class.

Upon further reflection, I should have spent more time watching players practice. It really is something special to see these top-calibre athletes interact with their caddies and manufacture inventive shots that they may not necessarily hit during the tournament. I found though, that you could not get very close to this action with the growing throngs of spectators. By contrast, you could practically touch the players when they were on the course. In fact, we almost ran into 6' 3" Ernie Els on the 18th tee as we were coming up the hill from the 10th green. The "Big Easy" seemed even bigger when he loomed a mere 2 feet away. The intimacy of seeing players in close proximity at the Masters distinguishes itself from my other experiences of watching professional sporting events—hockey, football, and baseball games—in person.

The next stop on this dream visit was the pavilion on our left showcasing trophies and mementos of the Masters. The short walk was only minutes from the range. While 99% of the tourists jockeyed for position to buy a ton of trinkets and gifts from the souvenir shop across the way, Bags and I instead chose this small place with the cozy atmosphere to soak up the Masters tradition.

Under a protected glass case sits the mammoth trophy and its small replica brother that is awarded to the winner. One would need a wheelbarrow to cart that original trophy through the gates! I hadn't realized it was so large. Pictures and brief stories of past Masters champions are presented in a classy way. Interestingly and maybe a bit disturbingly, a television sales representative was hawking his wares and announcing to anyone who was listening that there are many benefits of purchasing a new 3D television he was displaying. I thought the silver-haired Green Jackets would have frowned upon this type of commercialism. Needless to say, make sure you add the pavilion to your hit list as one of your early first visits. The souvenir shop, though worthwhile, can wait.

Our first exposure to the multitude of concession stands took place 30 seconds down the way on our left-hand side, across from the first set of washrooms that we saw. Bags and I joined the short winding line of people examining simple fruit, coffee, and small snack selections. We moved very quickly and proficiently. The two of us each grabbed a coffee and utilized one of the tables where others were gathered having their first drinks and breakfasts of the day. The sun's rays seeped through the trees and blue skies prevailed. The weather was going to be perfect—unlike prior years in which rain wreaked havoc upon Georgia's landscape.

Now even more energized about the Masters, we strolled for a minute and rounded a corner to the right through a subdued group of patrons. We viewed the giant scoreboard towering by the first hole fairway. Our eyes shifted from this structure on the right and the two of us then stared straight ahead. This was the Kodak moment (although pictures are not allowed during the tournament rounds, I am sorry to remind you). A vast panoramic landscape appears, stretching through the first fairway and beyond to several other holes. What a great first and lasting impression of the Augusta National Golf Course!

The hilliness and contouring of the course become immediately evident. Television does not do justice to how difficult this course will be to traverse and how treacherous these greens are for amateurs and professionals alike. Augusta's tricky greens continue to hold their own against technology improvements and are a perfect bulwark to this equipment siege. And the magnificent and almost surreal green colour of the grounds is something to behold, especially when outlined by pure, dazzling white sand traps and gigantic pine, oak, and magnolia trees. Dogwoods and azaleas are found sprinkled throughout the course, which used to be a nursery owned by the aristocratically named Belgian Baron Louis Mathieu Edouard Berckmans before being purchased by Bobby Jones and Clifford Roberts in 1931. Berckmans Road is named after this fine gentleman.

We wound left and strode up a steep hill, already feeling our hamstrings and calves being tested. Looking to your left you find the pro shop's rear entrance. A clever Bobby Jones sundial stands sentinel. No access will be allowed to us—or any other member of the great unwashed. Special badges must be acquired to go beyond this point and into the building. The magnificent 150-year-old oak tree resides in the same area behind the distinguished clubhouse, the largest on this ex-nursery land. Engaging player interviews take place here during Masters Week.

Admire this handsome tree and then examine the charming clubhouse. Outside, tables rest inside a roped-off area and the more fortunate members of society sit quietly sipping their iced teas, lemonades and other drinks with higher octane additives. The rope that separates the Haves and the Have-Nots tells you, "Don't even think of entering this area or you will receive a friendly tap on your shoulder."

The time was now ripe to have a healthy look at the quaint two-floor Butler Cabin located at the end of the clubhouse. The winner's tradition of slipping on the green jacket is performed for television crews in this building shortly following Sunday's round. The jacket transfer from one champion to the other is a most worthy ritual fans enjoy watching. They then provide a more extended green jacket ceremony to the public, out by the eighteenth green. Television viewers see the green jacket presentation before the patrons who are actually attending the Masters. Kind of weird in a way . . .

Off to the Par-3 course we go, behind Butler Cabin. This fantastic piece of real estate is seen on television during the Wednesday tournament. Sons and daughters of the players hoist small golf bags for their proud fathers. Sometimes the little guys and girls even participate in shots and putts. There are many smiles on people's faces during this Par-3 competition and friendly bantering takes place among players, their families and patrons. You do not see such informality when the Thursday round begins. Business turns serious.

The whammy or curse is on though, for those players willing to win the Par-3 tournament. No victor of this tournament has ever gone on to win the green jacket that same year. "After you dear sir, no, after you my esteemed soul, you can sink that birdie to win this grand event!" Although as it will turn out, the winner this year (Louis Oosthuizen) will go on to win the 2010 Open Championship at St Andrews with brilliant and clinically accurate precision. It was a good omen winning this Wednesday competition at Augusta for the South African and not a bad feather in one's cap to win at the Home of Golf!

Bags and I sauntered by some of the holes and imagined ourselves striking daunting wedge shots into tucked-away pins on these miniscule greens. Lurking water frames some of the holes. Interestingly, there was a paved path along one end that would allow you to walk down to more distant holes on the Par-3 track. We chose not to pursue this course of action but it was a nice touch for the Masters to give the opportunity for the lucky few to see a very private part of their golfing property.

Our next move was to sweep left around Butler Cabin and forge to the front of the clubhouse. Regal Magnolia Lane beckoned us. This of course is the grand entrance for players and VIPs coming off Washington Road. We lucked out when we encountered a fairly substantial line-up formed by delighted patrons. At first the two of us were confused as to what the purpose of the line was. Then we found out—young Masters employees were snapping pictures of individuals at the front of the clubhouse. I waffled at joining this line but my wise friend was adamant.

My friend Ron told me that lines move quickly and with enviable efficiency at the Masters. He was absolutely right and there was a great sense of pride in the organizers with respect to making this happen. Even a Green Jacket asked a patron how long he had been waiting in line for his photo. This considerate gesture, I surmise, was not just to make pleasant small talk but to truly express interest and determine if the Masters needed to improve this aspect of their tournament experience. The care for the customer was right there for me to see. Incredibly, this was a free service offered by the Masters. Other sporting events would charge a hefty premium and many attendees would gladly pay for the privilege. But not here. That is not the way the Masters wants to do things. Again, like in the case of the free parking, the hosts want to leave an indelible mark on patrons when they return to the real world. They hope people will spread the word that this is an event like no other and Augusta succeeded spectacularly well.

We only had to wait a quite tolerable 20 minutes. I passed the time easily by having an informative conversation with a cigar-chomping Allentown, Pennsylvania Republican. The chat ranged from his concerns about Canadian health care, his love of the older Oakland Raiders (he was amazed to hear that I knew more about Jack "They Call me Assassin" Tatum, Ted "The Stork" Hendricks, and the other mean guys than he did), and the mess America found itself inside of Iraq and Afghanistan. I found myself impressed with his grasp on the state of Canadian, American, and world affairs. Ohhhhh, the people you meet when you spark a conversation with a stranger! Finally Bags and I were called, so we could grace their camera with our dazzling smiles.

Awaiting our arrival in front of the clubhouse was the famously branded yellow Masters flagstick. You are probably familiar with that iconic flag—yellow with the green outline of Georgia and the tall green flagstick including a red flag. "2010 Masters" with the small, circled "R" trademark at the bottom right adorns the version I purchased from the souvenir shop later on in the weekend. It presently looks mighty fine on my bookshelf in my man cave at home. The friendly camera crew positioned both of us correctly and took some shots before handing each of us plastic Masters cards with log-on and pass code information to view the pictures conveniently online.

Magnolia Lane's full-length drive stretched before us to Washington Avenue. Patrons were prohibited from wandering further down this drive. A police car was not-so-subtly tucked away on the right side along the tree line to prevent any incursions. No, we would humbly enjoy the short time on this stage before exiting stage right to wonder what was next on this fantastic voyage through Augusta's grounds. I would highly recommend making the effort to get your picture taken because this is the only way to see famous Magnolia Lane and you will have a lasting keepsake of your visit outside of Augusta's clubhouse. Thank you, Bags, for being so obstinate and thank you, Green Jackets, for thinking of this special addition to Masters' memories.

We strolled back by the Par-3 course then swung up a small hill to examine the meticulously crafted white cabins. There are ten of them. The President's Seal, including the iconic eagle, is found on the Eisenhower cabin and is the first one you see. Dwight D. "Ike" Eisenhower was a member at Augusta and club members created this plaque after he became President. President Eisenhower, the same man who was Commander-in-Chief of the Normandy invasion in World War II, also had a tree named after him on No. 17 because he clumsily managed to hit it so many times. Grand success in politics and war does not necessarily translate into victory over wood at Augusta!

We purposely strolled clockwise to soak in these beauties until we finally ended up at Bobby Jones cabin. An imposing security guard posted here questioned us as to how we had been able to enter this supposed closed-off perimeter. We stuttered a bit and said there was nothing like a rope barrier preventing us from doing this tour. After properly playing the apology card that I have used many times in my life, he let us on our way, but only grudgingly. Got away with that one and it was worth it . . .

This most famous amateur golfer promptly retired from the game after brilliantly winning the Grand Slam in 1930 (U.S. Amateur, U.S. Open, British Amateur, and Open Championship). This beloved Georgian went out at the pinnacle of his career when he was a youthful 28 years of age. Mr. Jones' next exciting challenge was to construct the ultimate golf course at Augusta National. He certainly had a great practical education in playing many fine links and non-links golf courses around the world. He had a sense of what he wanted and insisted that it be special. And we know what resulted, don't we?

Jones' No. 1 cabin overlooks the 10th fairway and is where he stayed. Bags and I eyed people inside the cozy but not ostentatious cabins and as they exited through the front and rear doors. Imagine the influence and money these people wield to be so fortunate and stay in these places during the week of the Masters.

After thoroughly enjoying some of the surrounding treasures of Augusta's premises, it was now time to venture down the roller-coaster 10th hole to begin the inaugural tour of the course. It was absolutely gorgeous to start from this perspective! As we paced down the 10th hole and its dramatic drop in elevation, we came to appreciate this very tough hole. 3-D television will be a brilliant tool to do justice to its inclines and declines. Mike Weir and Angel Cabrera recently won playoffs here.

A strategically driven ball to catch the slope on the left-hand side will give the players a shorter shot. The second shot is uphill and is all carry. The large green has a wicked slope from back to front with a substantial sand trap guarding the front right. But then again, these greens are all incredibly sloping and lightning fast. Think putting on billiard tables.

We wandered around the 10th green for a few minutes to envision shots coming in and then walked down a slope behind the green. Up the hill we hiked to the 11th tee and I stood behind the tee. Neat perspective of the drive from here . . . The driving area is parked in a secluded corner of Augusta and only a few people are able to be squeezed into this corner to view these shots.

The evocatively named Amen Corner commences at this spot. The great golf writer Herbert Warren Wind came up with this term to describe Arnold Palmer's exciting play on a stretch of holes at the 1958 Masters and it was lifted from a jazz record titled, *Shouting at Amen Corner.* This magical section of Augusta covers three terrific golf holes.

The first in this triumvirate is the very long and difficult par-4 11th hole. Trees protect both sides of the fairway off the drive. Out of a chute it comes (the 18th tee is even more dastardly) and the tee-shot needs to be long and straight to approach the green with a second shot. After shaking our heads in amazement, we walked down a substantial hill and chatted with a course marshal who had been working there for over 20 years. The elderly gentleman was in charge of protecting the fairway from any ruffians who might get the notion to sprint across. They would definitely have to go through him first. While speaking with him about Rhode Island and picking his brain about Augusta, an older woman mistakenly tried to travel across the fairway. His quick cat-like reflex dispelled that notion and the humbled lady was ushered on her way in the proper direction.

We continued along the right-hand side in the "second cut" of the tree line. Using the word "rough" in Masters' terminology is a no-no. This is too much of a negative term for the Green Jackets. They have created a new class of words to be used at Augusta National. The second cut is barely noticeable to impact golf shots and not anywhere near as penal as the stuff we play in at home or worse yet, in the U.S. Open. Second cut is a relatively recent addition to the golf course.

A pond resting to the left of the green is a stark reminder for players not to flirt anywhere near this side. Just ask Raymond Floyd how despondent he felt when he hooked his shot into this ball collector with a splash and subsequently lost his playoff with Nick Faldo in 1990. Sportscasters and golfers often comment that when a ball goes left of the pin on its approach shot in to No.11, it was a mistake.

Par is an extremely good score on this hole and many shots are purposely sent right of the green. Too bad you are unable to get closer to this green (like No.12) for a better understanding and appreciation of its undulations. Television does a better job of covering the greens on these two holes than when you are there in person.

Bags was famished and getting a little edgy. We needed our energy for the busy day. As we wheeled towards the grandstand overlooking the 11th green and the 12th tee we came across one of the first signs of how this course was perfectly set up for tournament golf. Deliberately hidden behind the stands was our first exposure to an on-course concession stand. By design, these structures will not be seen during Masters coverage. They blend perfectly into the background, unassuming. We had heard prior to our arrival that pricing of food and drink was very inexpensive. Boy, is it affordable. Was I living back in 1985?

I grabbed a tasty ham and cheese sandwich for $2.50, a thirst-quenching sweetened iced tea for $1, a chocolate chip cookie enclosed in its Masters packaging for $1, and finally a $1.50 pimento cheese sandwich—the delicacy of the Masters. I could not prevent myself from keeping the wrapper of this packaged treat for its long list of prized ingredients. What the heck is in this well-advertised southern states sandwich?

It tastes like a Cheese Whiz sandwich but with a bit more pizzazz (Bags would concur). The pimento cheese sandwich is surprisingly quite delicious and I enjoyed a couple more over the two days. It comprises of an eclectic mix of ingredients that includes Swiss cheese, American cheese, mayonnaise, pimento, and paprika on white bread. Now doesn't this potent concoction just fire you up enough to knock over anyone standing in your way of nabbing one!

The next move was to sit in the grandstand and enjoy our early lunch. We knew that this was a primo spot to watch the golfing heroes on moving day Saturday. All was quiet now but the 12th hole was going to be gridlock hell come final groups on both days of the weekend. As mentioned, the vantage point of this viewing area was quite distant from the 11th and 12th greens. You could vaguely see the shot going in to the 12th green and there was an impersonal distance that separated individuals from the feeling of this shot. We decided that that there would be better and different spots on the course that would enable us to see the shots more clearly.

The 12th hole, and second hole of Amen Corner, is a short but diabolical par-3. The circling wind is hard to judge even when players think they can discern its direction from the flapping flag. Although hope should not be a strategy, sometimes players only have this dubious thought to determine the proper club selection. Unfortunately there is no available gizmo to make pros more comfortable and confident when hitting this shot. If I could borrow Winston Churchill's well-known quotation from 1939 describing Russia, it may very well apply to this extremely tricky shot into the 12th green: "It is a riddle, wrapped in a mystery, inside an enigma."

This shaky uncertainty causes under-clubbing into the water or sand trap, and over-clubbing into the pine straw and shrubbery surrounding the rear part of the green. Just having the ball come to rest anywhere on the green brings a huge sigh of relief. Many players and media members rank this as one of the most difficult and competitive par-3 holes in the world.

Unfortunately, patrons cannot sit around this green, only the tee, since this space is neatly tucked away in the far corner of Augusta along with the 13th tee. Players may appreciate its privacy, though, as a welcome oasis from their relentless gazes. Perhaps this enables them to vent any bubbling frustrations out of the range of patrons' curious ears.

Time to move down No.13 fairway . . . Bags and I both spoke with a spotter who monitored drives coming from this tee. He was a rotund man with a shock of white hair and a bald patch. The seated gentleman was squeezed into a two-yard-square roped-off area in the right-hand side second cut. His occupation in this small habitat was to count the shots and he told us that he was forbidden to speak with the golfers even if he got plunked in the pumpkin by an errant 300-yard drive. This would be a long day for him. I hoped he had sunscreen to use . . .

The shorter par-5 13th is the perfect risk/reward hole for the participants. We admired the dynamic 13th green as we approached its right hand side. All along this hole there are great sightlines to watch incoming shots. Eagle and especially birdie scores are in abundance during the week on this extreme dogleg left hole.

An accurate and long drive sets up whether the green can be reached in two. A slight mis-hit or chunk and Rae's Creek will gobble up the ball to the left and across the fairway short of the green. Rear sand traps catch balls and force players to blast down the quick green, scaring the bejeebers out of them. Watching players have the guts to go for the green in two on the 13th hole is one of the most popular and dramatic shots to experience at the Masters or anywhere in the world for that matter. There is a special roar that results when patrons know there is a chance of eagle. Standing or sitting by the 13th green and hanging around the 12th tee have traditionally been two of the busiest spots. It would be no different this year.

Our ensuing strategy would be to swing around the 14th tee. Later in the day we would position ourselves near this hole's green—a fantastic secret spot the three of us would highly recommend others to seek out. In the meantime, we walked towards the 15th fairway and green. This par 5 also offers eagle and birdie chances, and water book-ended the front and the back of this green. I looked to the shimmering green fairway. This hole possessed a worthy memory for all Masters historians that I wanted to share and that many of you have heard about.

The 15th fairway bore witness to the "shot heard 'round the world." The mind-numbing 2 marked on the scorecard. The almost unobtainable albatross (imagine seeing a unicorn before accomplishing such a feat in your golfing career). This refers to the incredible double eagle that Gene Sarazen jugged into the hole with the Turfrider four-wood from a very long 235 yards at the 1935 Masters. Bobby Jones fortunately witnessed this momentous occasion since he was positioned near the green. Good timing indeed! Such a highly skilful yet lucky result propelled "The Squire" into a playoff the following day and the ensuing victory for the green jacket. How despondent do you think Craig Wood felt when he had already finished his round and had a 3-stroke lead until this miraculous shot? Do you honestly think Wood slept well that night knowing that the gods were surely aligned against him? Eagle roars (but not double eagles) would be heard at this hole later in the weekend.

The 16th hole popped into view and what a gorgeous par-3! There is great history at this spot. Think of the Nike swoosh on Tiger's ball when he famously chipped in for birdie on the last day in 2005. The ball had initially dangled on the precipice of the hole and teased the universe before finally dropping. And who can forget the time when Jack drained his short birdie putt in 1986 after nearly acing his memorable shot. Patrons who attended that day still say that the roars for this 46-year-old's 30 on the back nine were the loudest in Masters history.

The area found to the left of the green and pond fronting the hole is one of the other top positions at Augusta from which to watch the action. Nearby concession stands and restrooms make it comfortable for people to stay for long durations. This is definitely a spot you should spend time at. Shots have to fly over the shimmering water and when the pin is tucked in the front left part of the green, balls can disappear for aces. We would witness a magical hole-in-one on Sunday.

The 6th green could be seen nearby to our left so Bags and I walked over to this downhill par-3. Television viewers do not often get to see this scenic hole because the Masters has traditionally minimized coverage of the front nine. Patrons were just starting to settle down behind the green so we gladly joined the party. Beautiful flowers in full bloom sat on the embankment just below the supremely elevated tee area. Angel Cabrera and Robert Allenby were the first players off in the morning and we viewed them hitting their iron shots into No. 6. The official tournament and the maiden shots of the first players we saw were underway!

There are roped-off areas by the majority of the greens that are set up for chair placement. This is where we sat for Cabrera's and Allenby's shots. No standing spectators are allowed in this area, as they would be positioned behind. Smoking is not allowed within these roped-off areas; nevertheless, there were a lot of cigar smokers puffing away throughout the course. Later that day, Bags would be amused to see a large man get caught red-handed while smoking a cigar by No. 10 green in a roped-off zone. The look of horror on his face was priceless when a Masters official tapped him on the shoulder. The giant promptly rose from the chair in record time and departed silently into the day, knowing that this was not the time to challenge authority. Yes Sir and No Sir are the only viable answers to these Masters men with their influence and power.

The Australian, Allenby, led off and we saw his ball plunk at the front and then leak down the treacherous green on to the fairway. The patrons sounded a united groan. The back-right pin position resting on a small crest would leave him with a devilish chip to get close. Cabrera followed with a great shot. His ball landed softly and rolled only a few inches to finish pin-high approximately 15 feet away. Allenby ended up with a double bogey and slumped shoulders for his efforts. Cabrera made an easy par after a close miss for birdie. These shots highlighted the differences in getting the proper distance control on these greens; and also, that professional golfers are human and can make doubles too.

Cabrera, the defending Masters Champion and proud Argentinean, squeaked into the weekend rounds by the narrowest of margins—exactly on the cut line by draining a clutch putt on the last hole. Augusta National can do that to players of his talent. Lose concentration for the slightest second and you can book your flight early to watch your favourite sitcom rather than stressing yourself out on moving day Saturday. So if the hurtful joke for hockey players missing the playoffs is to be banished to the links, what is the equivalent mockery for golfers missing the cut? Is it skating at your local rink with amateurs?

We headed up the slope towards the 6th tee and winded around the par-4 5th hole. This par-4 had few spectators and also receives little television coverage. I did appreciate the drive more on this hole once we arrived at the grandstand by the 4th green. It has to carry over a hill with a large sand trap to the left. The two of us enjoyed watching some shots coming into the 4th green, a long par-3, from the grandstand sitting to the left of the green. This was a priority viewing area so we had to wait in line at the bottom of the stairs for ten minutes before some left to give us room to sit. From this angle we could see the drives off No. 5 as well as bunker shots and putts on No. 4.

An important strategic question to ask yourself while attending the Masters is as follows: Do you set up shop at one spot all day and see every player come through or do you wander around and check out different holes and players? A couple of young Southerners planted their keesters down by the 16th hole all 3 days. After I asked them what they thought of their position at this location, the young men responded by saying they felt right on top of the action and loved the viewing angles. We decided to meander and see different holes, different shots, and different players.

I think a mixture of both strategies is best with a heavier emphasis on walking the course. There are too many neat perspectives and places to stand and sit throughout the course to limit your viewpoint to one hole. You also just sometimes happen upon some action or see a player up close who's just come out of the blue (like seeing Els at the 18th and Tiger strolling down the 2nd fairway for my first sight of this superstar). But be aware that your quads and feet will cry with pain by the end of Day 1 at the Masters. Make sure you wear comfortable golf spikes or running shoes. Seeing a clueless male with black dress shoes and several uninformed females in high heels and sandals caused me to shake my head. How stupid can you be? These failed students of the Masters had conducted no homework. I want to reiterate that Augusta is one heck of a hilly and tough course to navigate. Do not underestimate this fact.

What was the typical patron for the Masters and his attire? Middle-aged white males with sunblock, hats, shorts, golf shirts, and running shoes or golf shoes predominated. It was as though there was a finely crafted template created with this look. They tended to be carting retractable chairs around the course. Some had binoculars but not as many as I thought. Since you have to walk a lot you do not want to saddle yourself with heavy equipment. There were probably more females in the patron audience than I expected and they seemed to come well-prepared for the day's enjoyments and challenging hikes.

Speaking of the Masters chair . . . . The purchase of a lightweight, green Masters foldable chair from the souvenir shops is a must and can be carried quite easily using its shoulder strap. Whoever invented the design of this $39 item was brilliant. Thousands upon thousands would be sold during the week and they were everywhere among patrons. The quick set-up of the chair provides you with a necessary break from standing in trees, by tees, and in fairways or second cut. You will be glad to have this change of pace.

After sitting at the No. 4 grandstand for a half an hour, Bags and I headed to No. 2. My esteemed colleague soon had a brush with greatness after almost being decapitated by a screaming Titleist on this par-5 hole. We just arrived at the right-hand side of the 2nd hole about 280 yards out from the tee when Robert Karlsson sliced his drive. A distant-sounding "Fore!" allowed Bags to usher a well-timed duck of the noggin. Because of this unforced error, the circumstance enabled us to be one of the first on the scene to surround his golf ball. I had always seen people on television scurrying around players when they go in the trees and wondered what it would be like. Now I had a front row seat in this Masters theatre. What other sport or game could you engage in such intimate action? Great stuff . . .

The lanky 6' 5" Swede spoke in accented English with his Limey caddie (no Swedish chitter-chatter was evident) to analyze options. This man was a two-time participant in Ryder Cup competitions and has won in Qatar, Dubai and Wales, so Karlsson was no slouch of a player. He had a pretty fair opening between trees to punch his ball out after having a big television camera with its hydraulic lift removed. Karlsson eliminated this choice of shot briskly even though it would have been the prudent play to rescue par. But the angle of the shot would have left him with a much longer third shot into the green. Instead, our Scandinavian friend chose the more dangerous approach. Karlsson was trying to expertly thread it through two trees in close proximity that were stationed just to his right only a few yards away. Was he going to make this happen?

He made a weaving movement with his left hand to emphasize the shot pattern he wanted to execute. His brain was calculating percentages of success. Next, he took some practice swings, stood behind it, fidgeted a bit more, lingered some more—then struck the ball. Bags' eyes bulged in fascination and I admiringly watched the wizard-like Karlsson launch the ball with a magnificent up-shoot trajectory fired just inches beneath a large branch. The snappish shot travelled about 230 yards. What a gutsy play to try the risky shot. One clunk of a branch and bogey would have been a distinct possibility.

Following this creative and miraculous result, we then witnessed him hitting a short wedge into the 2nd green before barely missing his very makeable birdie putt. That technician-like shot proved the immense talent that these PGA players have over mere mortals like we are. What a great bird's-eye view of a fine shot!

This was the most intimate encounter we had with the golfers over the two days. Something like this experience with Karlsson provides a powerful tactile sensation that sitting on a couch cannot duplicate. It was a great case study of a professional golfer undergoing his thought process with the help of his trusted caddie sidekick. I will always remember this Augusta moment vividly.

The number of patrons multiplied as the day progressed. It was still pretty early in the day and already Masters chairs were plunked down around the greens to assure prime viewing spots. Clapping and groaning sounds had begun in the distance.

We wandered nonchalantly across No. 2 fairway and perched ourselves along the left hand side of No. 8 where the drives were coming to rest. There were only sporadic numbers of fans in this area. After I chatted with a seated Masters volunteer about college football, we found ourselves adjacent to Nick Watney's caddie (this player finished with a furious charge in the final round and is a rising star). I could reach out and touch him. He had arrived much in advance of his boss and the caddie was chatting amiably with a fan. I noticed that caddies are often striding quite far ahead of their players, lugging heavy and bulky bags. Watney's ball was resting only 3 yards away from the rope line and he soon joined his bag carrier. This is another lengthy par-5 and the uphill lie creates an awkward second shot. It is hit blindly and needs to draw around trees. Most end up to the right of the green for a delicate wedge or pitch shot.

After watching Watney hit a pretty good shot, we walked towards the 8th tee. There was enough room at the tee to see the big drives being launched. I lucked out later in the day when I returned here to see Tiger and his 6-foot frame approach only a few feet away. He doesn't look much different than what you see on television. After having seen some erroneous pull draws into the tree line from preceding groups, the Anointed One crushed his drive. His ball exploded off his Nike driver. A sand trap is strategically placed around 280 yards out on the right-hand side to capture those who flirted with the hazard. Tiger's flight had a high trajectory with a flawless, subtle draw that seemed to float before perfectly clearing the sand trap's left-hand side. His drive finished in the middle of the fairway. Of all the shots I viewed from this angle, his was the best struck and as long as Phil's shot and just ahead of Freddie's. Yes, I saw Picasso execute his best art and no clubs were tossed theatrically. He was on his best behaviour.

Our first exposure to loud roars came later in the day while we were positioned along the left hand side of the 14th fairway near the green. The first roar to reverberate was the one we heard from our left at the nearby 12th green and then soon another one followed from our right at the 13th green. This symphony of sounds reminded me of the Imax Sensurround experience that I had when watching the Redux version of *Apocalypse Now*. Your left ear heard the choppers' blades and explosions while your right ear focused on Wagner's famous Ride of the Valkyries. In Augusta's case it was the competition between Freddie and Phil and determining who the roar was for. Guessing with your fellow patrons was a constant game—"Was that an eagle for Freddie or a pitch-in birdie from Phil?" It was a great feeling to share your thoughts with your Masters comrades-in-arms.

This positioning by the 14th green would turn out to be our favourite spot to catch the action and witness great shots. Few patrons had selected this position on the course and I do not understand why it was not more popular. It gives a great viewing angle of approach shots coming into the green. Go there if you attend the Masters. You can then pivot and see tee shots whiz by your ears from the 15th tee. Action would be relentless in this area over the next 2 days.

Here is only a sampling of the flurry of shots and scores that we saw from the leaders in Saturday's round at this spot: Mickelson's mind-boggling eagle from the middle of the fairway (h-u-u-ge roar with my arms fired in the air) when he sent the ball spinning to the right in to the middle of the cup, Freddie's birdie, Ricky Barnes making an impossible chip in for birdie, Anthony Kim with a birdie and Tiger with a birdie. These players licked their chops when they saw the accessibility of the pin. That was an impressive run of quality shots over a short period of time!

After a few other brief stops around the course, Day 1 at The Masters ended and Bags and I were exhilarated. You can debate whether we picked the right hole or player to watch but a single point needs to be accentuated—how great is it to be here! We saw Woods, Mickelson, Westwood, and Couples. We examined Mike Weir, Retief Goosen, Chad Campbell and others at close range. They do not look much different in person than what we imagined, but boy, could they explode their shots! As mentioned earlier, what is noticeable is the way they try to land shots pin-high. Weight of the shot can have a higher priority than the line although they absolutely know being below the hole on some of these greens is vital. They judged distances with incredible accuracy and this is what sets them apart from the average golfer. The approach shots in to the14th hole brought this home to me.

We unfurled our chairs and sat on the right-hand side of the 10th fairway to reflect on the day's activities and soak in this feeling of rapture. What a beautiful evening after a wondrous day. Our bright smiles and state of bliss told the story. We looked down the sloping fairway and admired the pure white sand trap sitting by the green. The symmetry of this picture is mind-boggling. How could a course be so immaculate? Already groundskeepers and volunteer help were walking down the fairway as a coordinated group with buckets of sand to repair divots. I counted around eight of them. No blemishes on this beautiful landscape would be left for the Green Jackets to see. I must say that I have gone to many sporting events but this one left me in awe. Lee Westwood sat on top by one stroke over Mickelson. Tiger, Freddie, K.J. Choi, and Anthony Kim all lurked a few strokes back. Sunday at The Masters was sizing up to be a d-a-a-n-n-dy!

It was extremely prescient of us to let the traffic dwindle before tackling Washington Avenue. We were already late for our steak dinner reservation in Aiken but we had a legitimate excuse, don't you think? Sweaty and high from my first Masters experience, we gathered Scugog at the pedestrian Day's Inn and carried him over to Primehouse Steak. All of us indulged in a frosty pint or two, a wonderful Cabernet, and a juicy steak. The selection of food and drink were great complements to the earlier indulgence of pimento and cheeses, pink lemonades, and hearty chocolate chip cookies at the course. The conversation was jovial as we exchanged thoughts of Augusta's spectacle. Usually I have time to read books and reflect during my daily routine in life. But it was go, go, go all day today so they pressed me to finish up and we headed back to our crunched-in hotel quarters. The final round at the Masters was approaching . . .

Sunday was going to be a hectic day, so the three of us decided on getting to Augusta around 7:45am. I was nice enough to give Scugog the front seat in the Mustang while I played martyr myself with the cramped quarters in the back. It was quite chilly first thing in the morning.

Bags and I hopped out of the car at a plaza parking lot and I had to shake my leg to regain bloodflow. This location was conveniently situated across from the golf course. Scugog then took the prized red car to go and pick up his eBay ticket from a nearby location.

As we prepared to cross the street, we heard another car's horn honk and saw Scugog squeal his tires in front of us and cut off this irate American while turning right on a red light. We chuckled, knowing that Scugog is an impatient soul and was on a mission to get his Masters ticket. Who can fault a man who is excited about seeing this major championship? He was worried that some unsavoury types might stiff him. Bags and I wondered if we might have to fish his cement-booted body out of the Savannah River.

Patrons were congregating outside the gates just before opening bell. This was a different scenario than yesterday when we swiftly entered the grounds through security. What the heck was the logjam? A solitary policeman on Berckmans Road attempted to calm the growing swell of people. He anxiously told us there was a "computer glitch" and that this needed to be fixed before allowing anyone into the tournament. Mumbling echoed throughout the patrons but I did not sense panic . . . yet.

I scanned the surroundings and locked onto some shifty-eyed and nervous security personnel standing by the turnstiles. They were examining the burgeoning group and checking out the mood of the as yet well-behaved patrons to see if they might turn ugly and charge the gates. I wondered if they imagined themselves as serving a similar role like French dragoons did when protecting the ancient regime from the discontented lower masses just before the Storming of the Bastille in 1789. Somehow I did not think it would be necessary for them to wrestle a 50-year-old preppy named Biff who was equipped with a Lacoste golf shirt, knee-cut-high shorts, Adidas running shoes, a Masters cap, and a retractable chair, *s'il vous plait*. Anyways, who in their right mind would even risk losing their Masters pass forever and ever? The beheading of the King (not Arnie Palmer) could wait . . .

This inconvenient delay was an ironic twist, since the Masters prides itself on impeccable efficiency and will sometimes minimize the use of technological tools to maintain tradition. The Green Jackets would be quite annoyed at this disruption of service to their respected paying patrons. Main scoreboards found on the course are still changed manually and I think it is a great tribute to convention. Individuals tasked with changing the scores often dramatically linger just that extra bit to ratchet up the suspense before posting that new birdie score. Spectators react with cheers and moans based on updated postings of popular players.

Hundreds of restless patrons stood helplessly, eager to get inside the gates and claim the popular spots throughout the course for the final-round viewing. Gaining this valuable real estate would be extremely competitive. Bags, Scugog and I created a plan to set up chairs at the pivotal 16th and 18th greens and we needed to move pronto. That meant taking a Machiavellian ends-justify-the-means approach by possessing two chairs each. I hope the Masters committee does not think of us as dishonourable for bypassing the one-chair policy, but it was obvious other patrons had a similar battlefield strategy.

Finally, the gates were opened after a half-hour delay and people quickly moved towards security. People were chattering and pumped for action. The backlog was not too inconvenient and we entered Augusta's premises in reasonable time. It was necessary for us to purchase those extra chairs and the souvenir shop was filling with harried people, even this early in the morning.

Initially, we scurried quickly to the 18th green to scrutinize the situation. It should not have surprised us that the area was already packed with chairs. Obviously we were not the only geniuses around this Georgian town. Bags made a smart managerial decision and bee-lined to a spot several rows back from the right sand trap. The CBS camera already set up for the coverage would act as our lighthouse beacon to guide us upon our return later in the day when the area would be inundated with a thrilled audience. This selection seemed to give us a smart perspective of players taking their final shots and putts. I had a sneaking and uneasy feeling, however, that seeing the final groups in the dying moments of the tournament would be much more difficult than the present sightline since only chairs existed (no large bodies blocking the way). My thoughts would prove to be prophetic when I missed seeing the final putt because of this enormous collection of humans.

We then strolled down towards the 16th green area with our other chairs. A Masters official suggested placing a chair on top of the steep hill.

This vantage point had its benefits but the slope would force me to put stress on the legs and hamstrings to hold this position. Also, we couldn't quite see the teeing area. Bags and I decided to grab some spots three rows from the pond. Again, other patrons had beaten us to the punch. And I thought we had done our due diligence to get to these positions. Based on what we saw, others probably had lined up by 6:30am. It was going to be entertaining to see shots coming into this green and it would be extremely packed!

Now that our seating had been established we hiked up a few holes to meet Scugog at the Oak Tree by 9:30am. Hopefully he had met with success in gaining his ticket. We trekked by No. 8 green and saw a television commercial being shot by an unknown teaching pro. His putting prowess impressed the interested watchers who applauded. This was added value that you would not see on television.

Then up the difficult 9th fairway we trudged past an attractive young female flaunting a provocative top, cut-off jeans, and stiletto heels. This was incredible to see and it indicated a total lack of respect (or education) about this golfing shrine but I should not have been surprised. She looked pained to be at the Masters and I am sure on-course officials were displeased to see her wearing this highly inappropriate outfit. I noted, however, that although this is a pristine and proper private golf course only opened up to the public for the Masters, there did not seem a wardrobe police enforcing a stringent dress code. Kind of ironic, actually. However, preventing a person from entering because of a fashion faux pas would have been a nightmare to monitor and control. Better to let them in and enjoy the show.

The 9th green hearkened back to memories of Greg Norman's limp approach shot that barely reached the front of the green before rolling precipitously back down in to the fairway. The slope going from back to front is nasty. The Great White Shark's mis-hit was one of many in his repertoire on Sunday of the 1996 Masters. These errors contributed to his utter collapse, as he ultimately shot a 78. It was painful to watch such futility especially from one of the greats of his era. His score was a whole 15 strokes higher than his sparkling opening day 63! Wow. Speaking of Eisenhower, this day, not June 6, 1944, may have been The Longest Day. Norman lost a whopping 6-stroke lead to Nick Faldo. Faldo won with a fantastic 67 (which is often forgotten as everyone focuses on Norman's score), gaining 11 strokes on his Australian foe and cementing the victory of a third green jacket for the Englishman. The Shark would not be the only one to wilt under the strain of attempting to capture the green jacket. Just ask Ed Sneed or Kenny Perry.

Scugog was found pacing back and forth in front of the tree wondering if his buddies were going to show. We gathered the antsy one and prepared for the execution of our strategy for Sunday at the Masters. What a ring this has to it . . . Sunday at the Masters.

You could see the growing multitude vying for great viewing angles. The atmosphere felt more electric today. The Masters does not announce its patron attendance (because it doesn't have to) but I am sure approximately 40,000-50,000 attend the final round. Don't expect that you are going to see clear shots like you do when watching CBS coverage on television. Be content with being part of a special event that will excite your senses—especially sound and sight. In fact, I met a fellow Canadian from Owen Sound, Ontario on the 8th hole on Saturday who had annual passes to the Masters. He was choosing to miss the final round this year because he preferred to golf in South Carolina and then watch the last couple of hours on television. His argument was that he had seen it enough times on Sunday and that it was just too busy on the course. Man, what a spectacle to miss! I guess when you have season's tickets to the Masters, rather than having only one crack at the experience, priorities may shift . . .

I was very impressed with how well the patrons behaved during the two rounds. Imagine being with thousands of people and all you can hear is a bird chirp. The group as a whole seemed to possess a collective inherent DNA, as they knew when to be absolutely still and quiet once a player was ready to hit his shot or make his putt. Such manners and politeness made me proud and renewed my faith that humans could be respectful and exemplify proper etiquette. They could have been golfers or non-golfers, male or female. I only witnessed one out-of-order yell, which was in support of Phil. A female admirer on the 10th green shouted it, causing the unimpressed Westwood to back off his putt. This flagrant transgression annoyed us (by gosh, I am part of the Patron tribe) and many evil eyes were cast upon this culprit. This should not have occurred and I could see her friend start drifting away so she too would not be caught in her wake if she were ejected from the tournament. Other than that, I can attest that this was one heck of a well-behaved group of thousands.

Security personnel on the course were almost invisible. I am sure there were some watching this docile group but you wouldn't know it. Even at the teeing area you did not see the usual suspects with pith helmets dating back to the Boer War who hold those plastic or Styrofoam signs high and mighty with "Quiet Please." As mentioned above, people seemed to know when to stay silent, so there was simply no need for these protectors. I did note however, that Tiger did have a security person on each side of him carrying an earpiece. These serious, sunglasses-wearing men scowled as they marched swiftly alongside him on the fairway just inside the ropes. They swivelled their heads alertly, scanning for any potential troublemakers as though they were secret service agents for President Obama. He was the only one that had such an entourage or an obvious one. Yes, if security was there on the course it was not at all obvious—outside of Tiger's.

One of the holes Scugog wanted to see was the very long and difficult 4th hole, a par-3. The three of us were able to slither into spots by the tee. We enjoyed watching the players launch 240-yard-long irons and hybrid clubs onto this green. The pin was tucked into an impossibly difficult spot in the right rear of the green, on top of a shelf. This viewing angle caused me to strain my neck because I had to look around others to see the ball flights. What a feat to make par! Even the pros struggled to hit the shot close to the hole. The front sand trap snatched quite a few of the shots. Standing so close to this action made us feel like we were participating in each player's strike of the golf ball.

Ornery Sergio Garcia trudged wearily up the hill after three-putting the 3rd green. This hole is a short par-4 that requires a positional iron drive followed by a short approach shot. Although some of the longer hitters will try and drive it (one player actually made Mike Weir back off his putt as the ball bounced up close to the green). Bogeys should not be counted at No. 3 although there is a runoff on the back that will leave a most delicate touch back to the hole if overshot. Patrons gave Garcia weak applause as he approached the tee and he, impolitely, did not even acknowledge this gracious gesture. He looked absolutely miserable. Sergio then slumped onto a bench a mere few yards away from where I stood. He bowed his head in disgust and fiddled with his glove and shoes. I have a term for this disappointing feeling after finishing a bad hole: grinding. "Grinding" is a time-out provided to those players who have just suffered a bad hit, or missed an easy putt. They are entitled to this "alone time" to try and reduce the seething and mental anguish of this misfortune. Once time has expired (defined as anywhere between 30 seconds and 5 minutes) the sufferers have to contribute to the usual banter and conversations with other colleagues in the group.

The swashbuckling Spaniard seems to have lost his way and he lacks that passionate fire and youthful exuberance he once displayed early in his career. Who can forget the fantastic contest he presented to Tiger as a 19-year-old rookie at the 1999 PGA Championship played at Medinah Country Club? He hit that memorable shot near the root of a tree, fearing he would break his wrist. After escaping such a dire result he giddily scampered down the fairway and scissor-jumped in the air to find his ball running to the back of the green. He salvaged par and eventually lost to Tiger by only one stroke. Tiger thrives on such competition but this particular rivalry with Sergio did not take root.

Pundits were expecting major championships out of Garcia after this barnstorming beginning. The hope was that he would follow in the footsteps of his Spaniard brethren, the late Seve Ballesteros and Jose-Maria Olazabal. Unfortunately he has become a pretender and sometimes publicly complains too much about bad breaks going against him. This further damages his reputation and makes him out to be a whiner. His frequent putting woes have not helped his game much either. Such major championships have eluded him and he came agonizingly close at the Open Championship hosted at Carnoustie in 2009. A late bogey cost him a victory to Harrington. He does have the capability once in awhile, however, to exhibit a flashy and entertaining game for us to enjoy. Fans of Sergio would be happy to see some of his long lost smiles while gaining successes in 2011.

The adidas gear he was wearing at the Masters made him into a walking billboard for the brand and the white stripe on his black pants made him look like he was wearing track pants. I wonder what the Green Jackets felt about this apparel selection at Augusta. Hey, where was that other person with the cut-off jeans so we can chain them together to show others what not to wear in a golf setting!

An older man in white Masters coveralls was proudly guarding the 6th tee from inside the ropes. He seemed to be comfortable and in his element, spinning yarns with patrons about working at the Masters for 25 years. His demeanour reminded me of that Festus character from *Gunsmoke* who hobbled with a pronounced limp. The slow Georgian drawl replaced Festus' husky, wild, wild western accent. No chaw in his cheek, either. I am sure you could pick his brain for some standout memories.

Luckily, we saw something that just came out of the blue. A streak of fortune. I noticed that Steve Williams, Tiger's caddie, was wandering around the area in stealth mode, writing down yardages. He was dressed incognito in a t-shirt and shorts but I knew it was him. The famous caddie obsessively kept his head down to continue his numerous calculations and he obviously wanted to avoid distractions. One patron tried to strike up a conversation with him but he acted as though this person did not exist. Then he was off like a shot, striding gracefully and purposefully down the tree-line between the 2nd and 3rd holes to do more homework. His mission was to try and give his boss the exacting edge to collect his fifth green jacket. Tiger is a man driven by perfection. He would be demanding of his loyal accomplice and there was no time for him to waste. The brushed-off patron would have been devastated by this non-exchange with Mr. Williams. His story to his friends and grandchildren about his experience might go something like this: "I chatted with Stevie Williams but it was like speaking to a brick wall, but the New Zealander seemed awfully nice . . ." And I am sure he *is* nice but he is also a millionaire, having earned the money for doing such intense work for Tiger. Respect him for doing his job and doing it very well.

We departed from No. 4 and checked out some shots on No. 2 fairway before continuing on our way up to No. 7 green. This green is absolutely evil. I know when they lengthened this par-4 by more than 40 yards it made approaches of balls much tougher to stick on the green, since it was originally designed to accept higher lofted clubs. Sand traps guard the front and the rear, and the pin was tucked delicately on the right hand side. Tiger would drain an eagle from the fairway later in the day when we were sitting at another hole. What a fantastic turnaround for him after starting with three bogeys on the first five holes of the final round.

As we watched shots coming in, it became obvious that players would find it tough to get the ball close. Goosen especially hit a good shot only a few yards to the right onto the fringe and it just sat there on the peak of the hill, ready to drop. The South African egged on the shot with his flippant hand gesture in the hope that it would telepathically trickle the ball down left toward the hole. Mysteriously, it sat there like a stubborn mule. The gods above did not obey his request. Players absolutely had to be spot-on with their yardage or bogey was a distinct possibility.

Off we headed to see a couple of tricky putts on No. 9, the tee-shots of Kenny Perry and Cabrera off No. 1 (funny to see them teeing off so early on the final round since they duked it out so admirably late in the round and into a playoff at Augusta last year) and then down to beautiful No.10 before ending up in Amen Corner. We enjoyed some inexpensive food and drink. Bags picked up the tab for all three lunches for less than $20. He was flabbergasted that you could nosh on such quality food and drink in the year 2010 for such an insignificant sum. "Cheap dates," he thought. I then chatted up a University of Georgia Bulldog booster at one of the stand-up tables about his views on alumnus QB David Greene and Defensive End David Pollack. The time was now ripe for us to enjoy a short stint at No.12 because this was going to be the epicentre of the action.

We proceeded to walk along the par-5 13th and set up in the bleachers by the green. As mentioned earlier, this is a fantastic viewing angle to capture second and third shots coming into the green. You can also just barely see drives sail by from the 14th tee if you rise up in the grandstands. Sitting down at this juncture was a smart decision as my legs and feet were very sore from all the gallivanting around the course. The adrenaline of being at the Masters however, could easily neutralize any lingering pain in the legs as the day approached its crescendo.

Scugog was pressing us to venture out to see the final groups. After initially hesitating to commit to this request because of our exhausted lower extremities, Bags and I decided to make a go of it with him. Scugog was darn right to kick our butts into gear. We would will our creaking, middle-aged bodies to exert the final push and see the leaders. "Following the Pulse of the Masters" became our rallying cry!

We swiftly swept across the 15th fairway, past the 18th tee and landed with the other patrons at the right of the 10th green. This was one of my favourite spots and the battles were heating up. Shots from Freddie, K.J., Tiger, Phil, and Lee were seen coming in. Only K.J. birdied while Freddie and Phil scrambled remarkably to make pars. Westwood left himself a 4-foot tickler after a less than stellar lag putt before finishing off with a face-saving par.

I could see the stress being ratcheted up as the "pulse" headed into their final nine with green jacket dreams dancing in their heads. Who was going to have the mental game plan to keep it together? Was there going to be a meltdown like past years? Would there be an historic charge from a complete unknown or a wily veteran? It was great to be an engaged participant in the unfolding drama of the 2010 chapter to witness the answers to these scintillating questions.

The time we spent by this green also highlighted the differences between the rock star heroes like Freddie, Phil, and Tiger and a lesser light like Hunter Mahan. Thunderous applause and chanting of names went to the former group of players while Hunter (can I give him a one-name moniker like the others or is that sacrilege?) received almost nothing—even though he was right there in the hunt for the championship with them! Here is a guy who excelled in some recent international team competitions (I know he flubbed that chip at the 2010 Ryder Cup but he has a pretty good record) and has won PGA events but he obviously did not have the pedigree to warm the hearts of most of the patrons. Instead, he would have to be satisfied knowing that he would gather tens of thousands of dollars at this prestigious shindig. Perhaps he too could become a future Mick Jagger rather than an indie-labelled artist and native of Orange County, California. In order to gain such a promotion into the stratosphere of golf superstars, he would need to win majors and somehow create a persona to which fans want to attach themselves. This is a hard thing to accomplish and only a select few make the grade.

It would be a futile effort for us to follow these groups into Amen Corner. The three of us did not want to waste our time and get trapped in this massive gridlock. I know the Augusta people would hate me for using the term "zoo" with respect to the Masters. Remember the term of "mob" being uttered to describe patrons and "bikini wax" to define the lightning fast pace of the greens? Jack Whitaker and Gary McCord of CBS respectively dug their own graves using these words and phrases. To Masters head honchos they were flagrant breaches of protocol and, from their perspective, shone a negative light on their tournament. These unfortunate and untimely word choices in separate years prompted the Chairman of Augusta National to tell CBS that the two commentators were no longer welcome at their event. They wield so much power in controlling this tournament that CBS did not flinch one iota when removing these popular announcers. Please Mr. Chairman don't hold a grudge against me if I mistakenly use a word that you disapprove of in this hole on my course. I would love to have another opportunity to attend your fantastically marvellous, brilliant, well-managed Masters! The patrons and greens are most wonderful, Sir Payne.

Back to the nearby 14th green we hiked and fortunately found our popular spot. It was as though this place had our names painted there to welcome us back. The Sunday roars were starting to reverberate around the course and it was exciting to be a part of it. This spot would enable us to see all the main players hitting their approaches and putts after they completed tricky Amen Corner. We could then walk a couple of yards behind us and watch the leaders drive past us from No.15 tee. The 15th green to the finishing hole would be packed in with humanoids. At least we had an open view at this position on the course.

One by one we saw the final groups approach the green. It was cool to see them venture out from beyond the trees that were hindering our sightlines after they had hit their second shots. Easygoing Freddie Couples, in what appeared to be comfortable topsider-like shoes (to help his bad back), rugged Ricky Barnes (and son of an ex-NFL punter) sporting that unorthodox hat, cocky and exuberant Anthony Kim, the colourfully dressed and spiky-haired Ian Poulter, stoic Woods in his red-and-black power colours, serious-minded K.J. Choi, calm and collected Lee Westwood, and ever-smiling Phil Mickelson giving us his patented thumbs-up sign. Americans, Englishmen, and a South Korean. Tension was escalating. Who would hang on for the victory?

The three of us chatted amiably with a small but excited group of South Korean American fans who were cheering on Choi. Too bad Choi's shaky putter was letting him down on the crucial inward nine. South Koreans have much to be proud of, as their countrywomen now dominate the women's professional tour. Seven of these players have contributed to winning 11 major championships on the women's tour. Anthony Kim is of South Korean heritage and he was making a tremendous late charge Sunday, including birdie at this hole (then eagle on 15 and birdie on 16). Also Y.E. Yang's impressive winning encounter with Tiger at the 2009 PGA Championship held at Hazeltine proved to be compelling competition. He did to Tiger what Mr. Woods usually does to devastate his pursuers—chipped in for eagle and made a clutch long second shot into the difficult 18th green for birdie. You can only count on one hand when someone goes toe-to-toe with Tiger in the same group to win a tournament, especially a major. The win was well-deserved. Who can forget that wide grin of Yang's when he hoisted his humongous golf bag over his head like a steroid-fuelled Bulgarian weightlifter? And amazingly enough, he is a former weightlifter so he did it with relative ease. A little adrenaline pumped into his system also helped, don't you think?

One of my most significant career choices to date had to be made—I needed to go to the bathroom badly at this most critical juncture. What was I going to miss? This decision would separate me from my mates and I would have a very difficult time to find my seat by the 16th green. Something had to give (I hoped it was not going to be my bladder) and I made a choice. Knowing there was going to be a line-up at the washroom and that it would take me away from the Pulse, I bided my time impatiently before the rope was dropped to allow me to cross the 15th fairway and access the restrooms. Once it slipped out of the Masters official's grip, I was like Secretariat out of the gates. I quickly sauntered across because a gallant charging run would have been highly inappropriate and I did not want to be escorted brusquely from the premises. The wait was minimal. A humorous washroom attendant was cracking jokes inside the facility for those unfortunate to be standing in line and wanting to get back to the golfing action. They were moving patrons in and out very effectively. Only at the Masters would you have such a colourful and professional experience near bathroom stalls!

By the time I returned from speaking with the cordial attendants I caught up to Mickelson. This spine-tingling feeling of being right there, live, and part of the final round at the Masters is irreplaceable. Viewing it on a big HDTV from a Barcalounger with a cold beverage may offer you Verne Lundquist's calming voice and a good television angle but what can replace this stony silence and the ability to feel the shot along with Phil? That is why you come in person to Augusta.

Phil was coolly preparing to hit his second shot in to the short par-5 No.15. Was he going to lay up short of the water with the lead? I stood parallel with him on the left side inside the second cut with a few others. A tree's cascading branches partially blocked my view of the trajectory of his shot. I did not know it at the time but Scugog later told me he was standing beside Mickelson's swing coach (and once Tiger's) Butch Harmon at this same moment. He must have been extremely close to my position. The guru was giving some inside code. Scugog had a quick exchange with Harmon and the coach was beaming when he saw that his student chose to launch a fabulous six iron into the green rather than taking a more prudent approach and laying it up short for a delicate pitch.

This was a great shot under pressure and the coach seemed to approve of his pupil's pick.

In past years, perhaps the product of Arizona State University may have chunked his Calloway into the water fronting this slanting green. The debate continues to rage on and off the air about his sometimes-dubious decision making on this and other golf courses. But not this time. He two-putted beautifully for birdie and looked confidently poised to earn his third green jacket.

Legendary shot-making down the stretch enhances a player's reputation—especially in the majors. Lefty was certainly erratic earlier in the round when he hit shots in the woods on Nos. 9, 10, and 11 (received a Yoda Force be with you bounce off his drive when his ball clunked a patron and came back into play) and yet he scrambled masterfully. His birdie on No.12, his famous pine needle shot from the trees on No.13 (the best of them all), and now No.15 are shots made by champions. Mickelson, I believe, now has the mental fortitude to take on Tiger mano-a-mano as long as health problems do not interfere. Is the prey now the predator (especially with all the things that have caused adversity in both of their lives over the past year)? Do these two relatively elderly gentlemen in today's PGA world have many years left in the limelight before they are shunted aside by the young gunslingers?

I fast-walked along the left-hand side of the 15th and then slipped behind the left of the grandstand that was guarding this green. As I examined the par-3 16th from near the tee, I quickly realized that I was in a whole heap of trouble. When I left this locale earlier in the day I had a good idea of where my chair was planted. There were three rows behind the rope at the time. Now there were at least seven filled rows of chairs and I was disoriented. I am sure some guy from Tuscaloosa was sitting in my chair. I craned and fidgeted my neck looking for any scant sign of Bags and Scugog. No success. My heart sunk. I was alone to watch the exciting finish.

Regrettably, I was not allowed to stand in the main thoroughfare while I searched for my spot. The Yellow Shirt Masters official ushered me along to the other side with alacrity and let me know with a subtle warning that I could not linger in this area. I shuffled discreetly to the other side and tried once again to find my place (I am a salesman after all and persistence is necessary), but I was forced back closer to the green where patrons filled the area. I was penned in.

Luckily I was able to see Mickelson's shot, even though I was 12 men deep. Just being part of the applause was worth being situated at this vantage point. Lefty would later admit that the pin position tucked in the front-left corner of the 16th green does not set up well for his usual ball flight. It requires a cut shot and he was quite satisfied with earning a par after hitting his shot to the top-left tier of the green.

Since I failed to find the lads, I had to scurry back down 16 and 15, across the back of No. 17 green and then down the right-hand side of No.18 (have you lost me yet?). I was running out of time and breath and had heart palpitations. Would I be able to get to my seat by the 18th green to see the final groups? My insides continued to churn and somehow I knew I would not be able to find my chair. Grrrrrrrr . . .

A weird kind of panic set in as I stood exploring the 18th green. The situation was even more dire than the 16th. Seeking my chair was a lost cause since the whole area was absolutely filled with patrons. You'd have to have a zero-IQ to be surprised by this turn of events. I fought the claustrophobic fear and calmed myself to just enjoy the moment. It became painfully apparent that it would be impossible for me to gain a prime spot in which to stand but I certainly could control my own level of enjoyment. I was attending the final green, on the final day of the Masters. What in heck's name would I rather be doing? Two great shots from Mickelson and Westwood prompted a familiar roar.

I needed circus-height stilts and I still could not see the final putt drop. Mickelson drained the birdie after a dramatic last iron shot from in front of the fairway sand trap. The boisterous patron reaction told me what I needed to know. This tournament seemed destined to be won by Mickelson. Westwood tried with all his English lion heart to capture his first major for his supporters. He had been in the major championship hunt over the last couple of years after falling way down the ladder in world ranking. It was good to see this tenacious battler has made a comeback as he is well respected by his peers. He comes across as a good bloke and I hope he closes the deal in the near future.

The eagle-eagle-birdie (from 13th to the 15th holes) tear on Saturday, to which I was witness along with the second eagle on the 14th, contributed greatly to Phil's newest green jacket. Are they all the same jacket sizes? And who can forget his second shot from the pine straw in the trees on the 13th hole on Sunday that ended up settling only 10 feet away from the cup! We heard the gigantic roar in response to this magnificent recovery shot. I don't know if he should have risked so much on such a difficult line to the pin and others would have been rolling their eyes. But his reputation is a "damn the torpedoes full speed ahead" and he executed the shot with remarkable precision. After missing his short eagle putt he had a longer one coming back to knock in for birdie and he did. He certainly contributed to Stress Level 10 factor when he ran it by this much. Who am I, a man from Woodstock, Ontario, with 0 green jackets (let alone any argyle ones from past Chewie Open-type local tournaments) to tell a Masters champion not to hit the shot? 3-0 now for Phil in green jackets versus this Woodstonian.

Amy Mickelson and their kids were waiting excitedly to receive him by the 18th green. It was the only day during the week that she was able to be at the course for her husband because of her health issues. This scenario of loving and loyal family was quite the numbing contrast to Tiger's lonely reception preceding Phil's group. Elin and their kids were far away and many doubts remained whether Tiger Version 2 would be a kinder and gentler one. At the time people wondered whether family could become priority number one. A little humility in Tiger's final interview and a genuinely congratulatory handshake with Phil may have helped repair the extensive damage to his reputation. I didn't see the harm in offering these olive branches, not only to Phil but to the patrons, fans of golf and Tiger. He is proud and fiercely competitive by nature and it may be difficult for his stripes to change now. I think Tiger's book will have many interesting chapters to follow.

Unbelievably, Tiger had several chances to win this tournament. I watched him three-jerk a short 5-footer for birdie on 14 in the final round with a nonchalant and sloppy come-backer effort that spun out of the hole. A distinct gasp came from onlookers and I too was a bit stunned. I thought he would not be so flippant in his stroke, especially from a man who prided himself on excellence. This brain cramp bogey put him six back and he knew the joke was over. In spite of this deflating turn of events, he promptly eagled No.15. Does he have a secret place within his being to switch to another gear? It was as though he had a conversation with himself and wanted to test his inner being by saying, "Darn it, Eldrick, you dummy, eagle the next one to prove to yourself and these patrons that you can get it done. See if you can give that one last enormous push for the jacket!"

His game was off this week; certainly he did not bring his A game, but I found myself in awe that he could have had such a lengthy layoff and still create his magic. He had four eagles in the week to tie a course record. This also during the time when swirling problems had enveloped him. The media attention would take a massive psychological toll on anyone.

Merely a year ago before this 2010 tournament, people believed it was inevitable that Tiger would match and surpass Jack Nicklaus' record of professional major championships. Now I am not so sure. Family issues, brash youngsters with few nerves like 18-year-old Ryo Ishikawa, 20-year-old Rory McIlroy, 24-year-old Anthony Kim, and 16-year-old Matteo Manassero and now less-intimidated veterans will challenge the once impenetrable aura of the best golfer. He is vulnerable. Just like Nicklaus found foils in Watson and Trevino, Tiger will see a re-energized Mickelson gunning for him and others will want a piece of him. But then Tiger has proven critics wrong when they thought he was a carcass ready to be picked. He may instead rise again from the dead but it will take time . . .

Fortunately I hung around the right area and tracked down my colleagues through sheer luck. What could I have done to hook up with them without cell phones and other devices? The three of us sat in our chairs along the 10th fairway to analyze the day. Wow! We could discuss the thrilling shots (Woods' monstrous draw on his drive by the bunker on No. 8, Moore's hole-in-one, Choi's shot into No.10 green), gaffes that we saw (Tiger's three-putt on No. 14 and Karlsson's shank on No. 7) and overall excitement with the thundering roars (Nos. 14 and 18 greens). The green jacket presentation was to take place in 10-15 minutes and this was a fantastic pause for us to come together and recap.

The first true blight and disorganization, albeit an uncontrollable one, presented itself at Augusta following the round while we sat in an atmosphere of great peace. Funny how this event is so perfect overall that such a sight shocks you. Paper cups and discarded chairs lay strewn all over the ground by the finishing hole. It was too bad I couldn't take a picture of this concentrated mess as it clashed awkwardly with the flawless way the tournament is run. Already, cleanup crews in white coveralls were readying themselves to tackle this unruly mess as though it were an infestation of rats. I am sure they were under strict orders not to allow television crews to display this carnage. Jobs could be lost as a result.

I was emphatic that, when we planned the trip, we were not going to miss this wonderful ceremony. Tradition is integral to my golfing soul. The last thing I wanted to tell others at home was that there was a playoff at the Masters and I had missed this thrilling conclusion along with the green jacket presentation because I wanted to rush to the Charlotte airport and fly back to Mississauga and have a nice sleepy-bye. No way was that going to happen on this trip, right Bags?

Every year, television viewers watch the smooth changing of the guard in Butler Cabin when Billy Payne (the Chairman of Augusta National), Jim Nantz (CBS), the past Masters champion, and the new winner congregate for compliments, quick speeches, and the handing over of the green jacket from past champion to the present one. I obviously would not see the 2010 version this year in Butler Cabin but I would catch the live version that follows in the glory of the sun setting at Augusta. The presentation takes place by the 18th green and is witnessed by a large group of patrons outside the ropes and Green Jackets within.

Mickelson's head and distinct gait made their appearance as he ambled through a phalanx of patrons extending from Butler Cabin. Phil's smile was pronounced and his longer, unruly hair was slicked. Amy and his kids joined him in chairs on the grass as they listened to Billy Payne's words of thanks and appreciation. Phil was not sure his family would be able to join him but it was a fitting reward for his superlative play.

Mr. Payne looked to be in his element as he held forth with the microphone. He congratulated the 16-year-old low amateur winner Matteo Manassero and then handed the instrument over for Phil's heartfelt thoughts. It was interesting to see the Chairman pointedly added extra time to his presentation so he could read off an impressive list of all the worldwide golf associations that contributed to the Masters success. This roll call seemed to be endless and I could sense a sort of restlessness from others for him to conclude his portion of this Masters ritual. Hearing Serbia, Bulgaria, and other non-traditional hotbeds mentioned was certainly an eye-opener for me, symbolizing how golf is now truly a worldwide sport.

Lefty followed with a good and succinct speech, thanking the proper people, including his family. It was an emotional and difficult time for the Mickelson family as his wife Amy and Phil's mother have both suffered from breast cancer in the last year. Overcoming Tiger's sometimes distracting return and charge for the lead, Westwood's relentless quest to wrest his first green jacket, and the emotional roller coaster of family issues made Phil a worthy king of the course that day. It was a special win for him in more ways than in the past.

The three of us lingered around the presentation area to see if there would be any further happenings. There were some excited young girls checking out the charismatic and good-looking Matteo. In a jubilant manner, the teenager skipped by us and went for a short run while the girls fawned. The young Italian may have been the only person I saw run on Augusta's property over the 2 days. He'd earned some leeway on this breach of protocol. This ebullient behaviour just showed to me that he was still acting like a normal giddy kid, albeit one with a bright golfing future!

After taking one last tranquil look at Augusta along No. 1 as the sun set, we visited the gift shop for final purchases of Masters mementoes. I picked up a bright green custom gym bag with a logo to parade around my gym facilities, a white long-sleever with Masters emblazoned on it, the popular yellow Masters flag, ball markers and a couple of hats. However, memories of the weekend would be more cherished than these souvenirs. I have to say that this was the highlight of my life in sporting events.

We cleverly mailed our Masters chairs to Bags' house in Oakville through an expediting service provided at a small building sitting by the souvenir shop. I thought these great keepsakes would look more impressive huddled in my home's man cave with my lead soldiers, treasured books and 1970s hockey and baseball card collection rather than rudely discarded onto Augusta grounds. In fact, a person approached us while we were sitting on No. 1 wondering if we had one of his chairs since our group had two each in our possession. He was probably thinking he would like this prize to show his buddies when he got home to Ohio. Ummm . . . no chance. I think, sir, your chair may be somewhere stacked up with all those other items back by the 18th green or being hoisted by that elated man from the Hoosier state over there!

A nice tidbit to hear while making our final stroll to the gates was a young boy explaining to his father that he'd obtained Tiger's autograph a mere five minutes ago at the practice green. There was Tiger working diligently on his game post-Masters to prepare for his next step towards winning another major. At least this little fellow would have a special story to tell his family and friends about his encounter with this beleaguered public figure. Nice, classy touch, Tiger. Sometimes people neglect to think of the good you have done for the game especially during these uncomfortable and embarrassing days . . . . Too bad we hadn't even entertained the notion of visiting the practice green.

We investigated bright lights emanating from a small building to our right and then noticed a television telecast wrapping up their analysis of the tournament. A friendly and concluding "Thank you for coming" came from a few security personnel before we ventured back into the real world from a magic kingdom. Yes, the customer appreciation at this tournament is unrivalled. What a powerful statement to leave in one's mind especially in this growing impersonal and often rude world we now find ourselves.

We had to stickhandle through residential streets to get to the rented house and drop off the pass that Scugog received earlier in the day. Bags entered the building with him and certainly found this to be a fly-by-night outfit. The multiple televisions lined up in an almost empty house may have given him a clue that this was no ordinary home with a family, two rug rats, and a dog named Boris. But the well co-ordinated setup worked and now there was conclusive evidence that if you wanted to pay top dollar to see the Masters there was a way. A healthy $750 later . . .

A severe backup of cars delayed us from returning to the main highway but who cared. This lull allowed us to each chat on the cell phone with the Chief back home so we could thank him profusely for the honour and opportunity to attend this major golf championship.

Our final goal was to end up with a celebratory steak dinner at the same place as the previous night but unfortunately we missed the cut-off time for meals by fifteen minutes. So Pizza Hut was the fallback position on a Sunday night. No booze was served in South Carolina on this day. Sunday and the Bible Belt restrictions, you see . . . I thought the lacklustre combination of pizza and Dr. Pepper were ironic food choices after being absolutely spoiled with succulent steaks and the riches of Augusta. Oh well, back to the life of reality and a smile with Dr. Pepper rather than Dr. Barley.

So, the obvious question that one might ask at this point of the story: Did the weekend at the Masters exceed my expectations? In all my conversations prior to attending the tournament, people told me how you could not believe the greenness and immaculate conditions of Augusta. Some perceived the course as being a heart-stopping Picasso painting of a real thing because it looked so unreal. Justice cannot be done by television coverage to show the opulence of the grounds and buildings along with the nuances, slopes, and undulations of the greens and fairways. Also, the customer service on the course, in concession stands, and of all places, restrooms, is incredible. Simply superb.

After finishing Day 1, I thought my experience only met expectations, although they were lofty coming into the tournament. I left Georgia and South Carolina with my expectations not only being met, but trounced. From the perspective of a sporting event this is unrivalled. The contributors to this feeling range from the unbelievably inexpensive $1.50 pimento and cheese sandwiches, to the much-appreciated thank yous from Masters personnel, to the free pictures taken while peering down beautiful Magnolia Lane. The Masters experience leaves you believing that a classy event of this scale cannot be duplicated.

The amount of detailed planning and care taken is mind-numbing. Co-founder and Grand Slam winner Bobby Jones created a golf course and golf tournament that epitomizes excellence and the royal treatment of people, their patrons. You could argue that he perfected the model because I just can't see anyone duplicating such an experience. Yes, racism exists in Georgia and no women members are allowed. I do not want to trivialize these issues. I just think these issues are separate from what I have presented and described. Tackling these issues would be a different road to travel and I don't want to go down this contentious path at this juncture. I want simply to judge the Masters as a sporting event rather than deconstructing it from a political or societal perspective.

If you have an opportunity to attend the Masters do not hesitate to say "yes." Of course, watching this tournament on television is easier and offers viewers with the tingly CBS music, highlights of the day's best shots and coverage of many of the holes. But television cannot do justice to being a participant, a part of tradition, a patron. Divorces may be threatened and other noses may be put out of joint for cancelling plans at the last minute, but for gull-darn sakes, attend a weekend at the Masters. Now, if my wife will only forgive me for cancelling that Mexico trip we were going to take . . .

Hole No. 2, Par 3. When did the golf bug first rattle your bones?

I was most fortunate in that my father loved the game. Everyone who plays golf must have had that light bulb moment when the worlds align and you knew—you just *knew*—that this game would be special. Terry Morden planted the seeds of passion in me that grew and flourished into a lifelong quest to enjoy golf. The self-proclaimed Best Putter in Oxford County needed to corrupt another golfing soul.

My father was a road warrior, selling steel tubing in American cities like Sandusky and Painesville, Ohio even though he was based in Woodstock, Ontario. These were foreign and unknown cities with unfamiliar names, not like New York or Boston. To me, the mere mention of them indicated "the boonies." Endearingly, however, these city names are the ones that remain etched in my mind when I remember him. Terry needed to pound the pavement to earn the income for our family of six. Hockey sticks and golf clubs were necessary purchases for him to keep his Number 1 and only son content.

He wore a substantial moustache in tribute to the great British army regimental sergeant majors. Not waxed, but certainly an ambitious one. This getup would often be complemented with a peaked cap and his hands would be folded behind his back as he sauntered down the main drag in our hometown, as if he were strolling down the Mall (pronounced in a pseudo-English accent that sounded like Ma-a-ll) in London, England. This was a thinking man's gait. Terry liked to toss out his wise sayings to the unsuspecting to catch them off guard and thus elicit a reaction. These axioms made me laugh and inspired me, but often left me confused (just like the other 95.6% of individuals who attempted to interpret his witticisms).

As a father, he dutifully came to my football, baseball and hockey games. And he somehow found time to be one of the only spectators to come to the finals of the university golf tournament that was held at

Guelph's Cutten Club. It also turned out to be near the end of his lifetime. I still remember seeing this lone ranger come wandering over the hill with his headgear and folded arms behind his back. We were putting on a green and I froze when I saw this figure. My emotional reaction told me I didn't want him there because his presence would make me nervous.

My recollection was that I felt conflicted—cocky but unsure how to impress him under his wistful eye. However, as persistent salespeople do, he proceeded to introduce himself to the rest of our foursome and to make sure they were okay with him watching the competition. They of course, had no choice but to say "yes" and, at the time, I didn't think I wanted him there to see me play. But now, years later, I recall also feeling how great it was that he wanted to spend his time with me and not be off selling steel pipe to some purchasing agent in Ohio. I am thankful for his efforts and support in helping me along the golden road of golf.

My father has been gone now for half of my life after he passed away at the too-young age of 57 in November 1986. I feel ripped off that I was not given the opportunity to play golf with him through my later years. My plan was to take him to Scotland and play the Old Course at St Andrews after my inaugural job in sales. This would have been my thank you and reward to him for being such a great father and mentor to me. Regrettably, my timing was off by a year and it was especially disheartening for me, since I had earned a healthy bonus to pay for this long-anticipated trip. He died and our dream trip died with him.

Terry would have imparted great wisdom to help me, not only in my golfing life but in the new sales profession that I had embarked on, a mere 3 months before his death. I miss him and the great father-son relationship we had while I was growing up in Woodstock. But his legend lives on both in spirit and in my memory. I constantly find myself using his many mottos, both on and off the course, including: "Headgear off in the mess hall," "Call a man by his name if you know it," and "Never leave a putt short." People saw Terry as a true character and he was. But he also taught me to be a person of character, linking golf with how you should live your life—a life with the hallmarks of respect, politeness, morality and integrity.

Was I a third-generation golfer? My recollection unfortunately, does not allow me to remember whether his father, my grandfather Fred, liked golf. I, unmindfully, never asked Terry because you always think you have more time to spend with your father and discuss such momentous things. This will remain a disappointing mystery. But since Fred fought in the U.S. Navy during the Spanish-American War in 1913, for the Canadian Army in World War I and volunteered to be part of the international contingent that fought in the 1918-19 Russian Civil War, he understandably may have had more pressing issues to consider upon his premature arrival to adulthood. Experiencing horrendous trench warfare and freezing conditions in the vast lands of Russia as a 20-year-old can certainly leave an indelible impression and alter one's views on what is truly important in life.

Fred, too, died at 57 so I am keenly aware of destiny's hand trying to snatch the last of the Morden male line. Is it coincidental or an omen that they both died at 57 with heart problems? Maybe that is a subconscious driving force for me to thoroughly enjoy golfing with my closest friends at my low profile private course of Craigowan just outside of Woodstock (worth it to drive an hour and 20 minutes with my 1980s New Wave tunes blaring) and to also indulge in playing the finest golf courses the world has to offer. Carpe Diem. My father did not have a chance to play the Old Course and Pebble Beach, so I have seized such days on behalf of us both. I don't want Father Time to run out on me before I have settled my own score. Less than 10 years until I reach 57 . . .

After witnessing his first two daughters evolve into very healthy kids with nicknames of Nickels and Knuckles (and two years after my birth, Bunky, my youngest sister), Terry badly wanted a son, or at least, convinced himself that he wanted a capable heir. And my father got one—but not necessarily the big, strapping lad that he was expecting. Terry fretted and wondered if his skinny little son would amount to anything. I know he couldn't call me "the human javelin" or "skin and bones" because such labels would reflect badly on his own genes—so he decided to play it cool. My dutiful mother Doris likely convinced her husband to be patient and went to bat for me by offering "Wee Wayney Horton" as an endearing nickname. As time passes, I don't know how to take that moniker, but then again, aren't nicknames given to people you like?

Ever so slowly I developed into a specimen of his liking. A plastic golf club was passed to me as a rite of passage when I was around 5 years of age as though it were a weapon of pride. The ceremony was short but, the event was significant. "Please, young son," Terry begged, "be a good golfer so I can live vicariously through you and watch your progression throughout your teens and adulthood." In my father's opinion, hockey was a fine sport for the winter; however, golf was essential to fill the vacuum of summer.

He patted me kindly on the head, shuffled me outside and I licked my chops, as I had the world to conquer with my orange plastic club. I was unsure whether my dad really believed that I would be the next Jack or whether this was an opportune way for him to dispose of a buzzing pest so that he could enjoy a Labatt's Blue or two. Let's just say he brilliantly killed two birds with one stone. "Good staff work" (another favourite saying of Terry's to describe a job well done).

What I can remember over 42 years ago was that my swing was an all-out lash at the croquet-sized plastic white ball. I whiffed the ball during my first attempt and probably fell hard on my keester. But I was tenacious. I got right back up in the saddle to ride this golf beast. Over and over, day after day, I lunged at the ball much to my great delight. Soon my tiny hands would have calluses, showing the wear and tear of constant practice.

Moe Norman, the famous Canadian golfer known for his magnificent and precise ball striking and practice work ethic, would have been mighty proud to see my dedication to the game. The great Moe would hit hundreds of balls daily (I later witnessed an exhibition he performed at Craigowan and was fascinated by his magical shots from divots, other lousy lies, long tees, and bottles). I was certainly not in his category of dedication but I was still determined to hone my craft. I practiced so much that only hunger and thirst would cause me to temporarily break from my mission so that I could refuel. Soon, I got the hang of it and was finally able to trickle the ball a few feet. Then some yards. My fragile psyche strengthened on every shot. "Hmmmmm," I thought, "one day in the future I will achieve elevation on my golf shots and treasure its flight." But at this early stage, lift-off didn't distract me from the exhilaration of playing this game. Progress was going in the right direction. Then came a momentous occasion when I skirted the ball a total of eight yards along the dewy grass. To me, this had the explosive effect of a real breakthrough and I was hooked. My bones were rattled!

To this day, I have a very fast, over-the-top, going-beyond-vertical golf swing. The sight of this John Daly-esque lashing like a centrifugal force can make people cringe. The startled onlookers are usually quite certain that I am maiming myself. Certainly Johnny Miller would have a field day using one of those demonstrative telestrators to chalk out all the breakdowns in my swing and show audiences the many reasons WHY YOU SHOULD NOT SWING THIS WAY. Nevertheless, thousands of practice shots with this flawed swing works for me. And all because I started golf shortly after I was out of my Pampers.

Everyone has a tipping point and a person or event that precipitates one's love for this game. For me, it was when my father handed little tyke Wayne T. the big-assed orange plastic club. For some of you, it could have been when your mother demanded that you find a game so you were not a pain in the butt during the summer. For others, it could have been when your good buddy suggested that you watch the Masters on his 50" big screen HDTV. It just doesn't matter. What matters is that you have been tapped on the shoulder by the golfing gods and welcomed into a special club. Enjoy each round you play and catalogue vivid memories—the feel of the match, the sight of an immaculate green and the satisfying sensation of a long birdie sunk. I am thinking of you, Dad, and I thank you very much.

Cart Girl Visit #1 with Trivia Refreshments on Outward Half of Golf Course

1. What is the connection between professional golfers Chip Beck, Annika Sorenstam and David Duval?

    Treat yourself to a healthy granola bar.

2. What do Bob Tway, Larry Mize, Robert Gamez, and David Frost all have in common, which pertains to another famous golfer?

    Enjoy a steaming hot coffee.

Hole No. 3, Par 3. Shoulda, Coulda, Woulda . . . ?

The glassy-eyed expression of boredom on my face was not caused by my wife's lengthy discussion on the brand and colour she wanted the shutters to be in our living room. No, it was prompted by something even more sinister and taxing to my attention span. The golfer who just entered the 19th hole at my home club insisted on telling me about the minutiae of his golf game. I heard the dreaded words of "shoulda, coulda" and "woulda" as he droned on and, as a result, my system shut down. Listening skills dropped to almost a zero factor. These red-flagged words and all the boring filler surrounding them converted his voice into garbled static.

Once I recovered from this self-induced haze, I instinctually thrust my defensive mechanism in order to counter this unwarranted onslaught of drivel. "Ahh, ahh!" I said this in a tone increasing in volume to catch this person's attention. My weapon of choice following these utterances is The Hand.

Yes, the symbolic Hand. It is rigidly held in a vertical position with palm facing outward. My gesture is not like Arnold in the original *Terminator* when he mimics a gay character to "Talk to the Hand." The Hand's position means the exact opposite. Don't yammer. The Hand explicitly means to stop and please stop immediately. Scratching your nails across a chalkboard could not be any worse. You have broken the code. Do not talk endlessly about your own game. No one cares.

Words like "shoulda, coulda, woulda," and "if only" are words of hope. Hope does enable golfers to return to the excruciating scene of the triple bogey from last week when Ezekiel exacted his revenge and caused the wheels to fall off. Today could be different and a well-earned par may result. We hope that one day we can hit the shot like Jack can. Golf provides us with eternal optimism that we too can have the perfect shot or the career 68. Can another game or sport allow a blue collar worker or a highly paid executive to duplicate a professional's quality shot like golf? Not really . . .

Nothing against hope, but golf is measured on what you actually did. Sure, you can chat about "almost" getting a birdie like Tiger. The argument is stale and unproductive. Did you execute and close the deal? Jan Van de Velde could exclaim: "If only I did not clunk the grandstand handrail on the final hole at Carnoustie and bounce into the Barry Burn, I could have been crowned the next Emperor alongside Napoleon" (I might like to add: Why the heck this numbskull Frenchman hit driver with a 3-stroke lead? Mon Dieu!). Or, Scott Hoch could lament that "I shoulda sunk that 2-footer on the 10th hole at Augusta in the playoff so I could wear the green jacket in Butler Cabin instead of Sir Nick Faldo."

Amateur and professional road kill victims are numerous, but it is the heroes who won pressure-packed tournaments that people want to remember and emulate. We all shoulda or coulda or woulda done better in our golf game, so why is your story any different or more compelling? And why should I really, really care?

My lack of interest or concern with respect to listening to golfers talk about their games may be attributed to my salesman training. I pride myself in being curious, I ask lots of questions, and I listen pretty well. Good salespeople need to have these tools to be successful and our profession comprehends that people like to talk about themselves and/ or their businesses. There are objectives for following these guidelines that include relationship-building, making money, and sometimes pure interest. But since active listening can be exhausting, the last thing I want to do is hear about someone else's dreary story about scoring 92 instead of that 87 if he just had a few breaks. Perhaps I just want to shut down this skill set and escape into the therapeutic golf world of chirping birds, the crisp sound of clubs striking a Titleist, and balls clattering lazily into the cup. Now, these sounds are true music to my ears!

Golf, no doubt, is a very personal game to each player and it is easy to want to one-up others when discussing your prowess on the course. You may even think other people are interested in hearing about the intricacies of your game. They may inwardly tolerate it a tiny bit, but not as much as you think.

Men are all about ego and pride and will be compelled to express their worth to others. Alpha Male Syndrome and the beating of chests will make their inevitable appearances. However, true golf and comradeship in your foursome should not be about you. Yes, you yearn for the satisfaction of sinking a 10-foot birdie putt or driving a ball 275 yards over water and making your own self-congratulatory comment and tidy analysis. And you will love to hear the grand accolades from your colleagues. But complimenting others in your group when they hit the crucial shot to make them feel good or sharing in the wonders of a beautiful golf landscape is more important and impressive. Let others do the talking for your score and shots. Keep your comments about yourself to "a dull roar," as my father liked to say.

To my critical mind, a player has a couple of minutes to rationalize his or her day's round when meeting for drinks and food following the match. Feel free to discuss great shots about other members in your foursome but minimize conversation about your own. Banter, trash talk and laughter all contribute to making this game great. Then briskly move on to other interesting topics of conversation like funny movies, tightly contested football games, and why the world is going through economic turmoil. Anything but the bits and bytes of listening to "I hit a three-wood into No. 5 and it shoulda kicked on but then I got a wedge . . ."

There was this older man with an infamous reputation—let's call him "The Bore"—who would show up in the nineteenth hole of my home course to extrapolate on every shot of his round. I mean every darn one! When he passed through the glass door, people nervously started shuffling away to the side walls so they would not be the target of this man's onslaught of gabbing. The scene was like Chuck Heston playing Moses in *The Ten Commandments* when the Red Sea parted. "Let my people go," Chuck announced. Maybe this pronouncement was also a fitting reference to the unfortunate golfers who were caught in the bull's eye of this approaching storm.

All those in attendance at the time should have implemented the Hand in unison. Unfortunately, no one felt inclined to do so. This hesitation was costly. A poor unsuspecting soul got caught in this man's line of vision. He was an inexperienced deer caught in the approaching headlights. On and on The Bore pounded away at his victim. "I hit driver with a bit of a heel shot, then I hit five iron a bit chubby. I should have hit a hard six and then blah, blah, blah." I later saw the flattened victim wavering with a quadruple Scotch gripped firmly in his mitt. The poor soul possessed a fantastically dazed and haggard look about him. All his energy had been sapped. He would need ample time to recuperate.

Words to the wise: When other golfers inquire about how you played, keep the answer simple. They may be asking out of courtesy but it was respectful of them to ask you. They don't ask how, they just want to know how many! So respect them in return because their attention span, like yours, will be short.

Think of a simple sentence or a short paragraph for an answer rather than a book that would rival Tolstoy's *War and Peace*. Askers will appreciate the brevity in your response and might even pick you to play in their foursome the following week because you didn't break the code. Golf talk should be enjoyed and is part of what makes the game special. It should not be like having a cavity filled minus the anaesthetic and without your permission!

Hole No. 4, Par 4. Do you belong to the practice tribe?

I love golf. I hate the practice range. The prospect of beating balls in the penetrating heat or chilly weather sends me scurrying for deep cover. I personally don't get it. The Scottish don't either, evidently, since there are few practice ranges over there in links heaven. Old Angus and young Seamus take simple practice swings and then hammer the ball down the fairway. After plucking their tees briskly off the ground they are both off, aiming to finish their round in 3 to 3 ½ hours so they can have a room-temperature pint or two and tastebud-tingling haggis. I share the sentiments of the non-practicing tribe. To what tribe do you belong?

When I was young and not quite world-weary, I enjoyed hitting high cuts, low line drivers and assorted iron shots while on the driving range at the local Turn and Bank facility. The reason for "practicing" these shots was not really Machiavellian in nature. My intentions were not so brilliantly pragmatic; that is, to hit balls as a means to an end to lower the scores at my home club. It was, frankly and simply, because I sought pleasure in trying to hit the aluminum maintenance shed about 260 yards in the distance.

I got charged when I heard the distinctive clang of this metal. If I succeeded in making this structure clatter, then that sound, along with my lusty guffaw, was the ultimate prize. It was not the awe-inspiring realization that my swing was grooved for a better round at Oxford Golf and Country Club. I am sure all of you have fond memories of playing at similar places in your youth like I did at Turn and Bank.

My other points of reference (or self-appointed targets) at this driving range were canary-yellow Harvard trainer aircraft and white Cessnas lazily coming in to land at an unimposing airfield. Luckily for me, this airfield was located to my right so I could imaginatively smash my patented high power fades like a Technician over the protruding cornfield in the hope that I could strike these planes. Perhaps this form of practicing is why I still

54

possess a grooved left-to-right ball flight some 30 years later. Consistency and cherished memories, you see.

I must have failed miserably in my attempts to hit the approaching planes because first, they were probably beyond my range of success (high tech Nike Sasquatch drivers were not invented yet, only small-headed persimmon ones); and second, there were no dazzling balls of fire or contorted airplane remnants found that were brought down by tired greyish range balls getting wedged in their propellers. Somehow the evidence would have been overwhelmingly stacked against me in the court of law in the case of such a senseless catastrophe.

After exhausting my attempts at damaging sheds and planes, my day was not yet done. I could then play the miniature golf course on those worn, green-matted, concreted putting surfaces with windmills and tired-looking, peeling-painted clowns that resided on the same grounds. I was progressing up golf and life's hierarchical chain from practice to mini-putt to finally acquiring what I wanted all day long—a candy bar and cream soda.

Throughout my formative golf years, practice ranges were pretty generic and straightforward. There were no lush sand traps to aim at or blast out of and there were not always clearly defined distance markers. If you were lucky you could see a bright red bull's eye target resting 175 yards in the distance. Golfers, and there were not a lot of us like there are in today's world, would hit shots at oak trees or distant bird feeders.

Farmers' fields could also be used as backdrops for simple practice ranges. Smacking balls and watching them swish through the corn stalks was a point of pride. Back then 250 yards was a H-U-U-U-G-E drive and such solid contacts were often aided dramatically by brown hard-pan turf that whipped the ball along an extra 40.2 yards thanks to the non-watered fairways. The balls travelled like they were on the airport runway at Turn and Bank. I waited impatiently for tumbleweed to follow as brown dust shot up from the surface.

We would often use our own range balls and store them in what we endearingly called "shag bags." This ball receptacle could be an unsophisticated plastic grocery bag. They could be simple, small leather bags that you flicked balls in with your club or when you tried chipping them in with your wedge. Or, you may have owned one of those handy contraptions that allow you to punch down on balls. The steel/aluminum collector would automatically store your balls vertically in a tube and a long pouch acted like those dust collectors found on vacuum cleaners. Sometimes it was way cooler to plunge this thing into the ground to scoop up balls than to actually beat the balls on the range and generate perspiration. Such are the simple things in life.

Unfortunately, you can no longer pick up your own balls or you will get nailed in the pumpkin from those numerous addictive types who are on their second bucket of balls. This may be the way strangers felt when I sometimes used the local park to hit wedge shots when I was a teenager. They had likely wondered where these missiles were coming from (I was hidden by the trees and the baseball diamond). In the past, there was a respect for practice types to retrieve their own balls. Sometimes you gobbled up new ones from those suckers who were not observant enough to check the long grass over by the low bushes. No need for helmets then to protect the cranium from errant shots. Don't even think about venturing out there now to collect balls. Leave that to the characters wearing iPods and driving those lawn-mowing machines with chicken wire and screened-in protection contraptions. Ping! I also kind of liked hitting those mobile units for fun. And I know other practicing golfers have that guilty pleasure, too!

Nowadays, practice ranges are very popular and big business. Black mats, green Astroturf concrete and artificial grass mats, soft mats, two-tiered structures, cornfields, country club facilities, academy resorts, mesh nets and natural grass. Yellow balls, white balls with black or red stripes, mid-grade balls, hard balls with deep gouges, coin-operated balls, and Pro V1s. I have tried and used all of the above.

My mindset is: "Okay, I will hit some shots." 'Some' is the operative word, not 'lots.' Usually I do it because I am with others on a trip or I find myself at an occasional out-of-town game with people who like to practice . . . so I am a gamer. It doesn't mean I care for it. I am just taking one for the team.

One area in which I do see a benefit for practice ranges is when golf club manufacturers set up temporary shop at local private or public clubs to allow interested parties to hit their latest equipment. This industry has so much selection now for individual golfers that trying before buying is a prudent strategy. The outlay of cash necessary to purchase today's gear is well worth this sampling and it may not need a lot of cajoling or testing to determine that this equipment will help your future rounds. Now get out there and play on the course!

Let's first tackle the mats for those members in the practice tribe. The word mats rolls off my tongue with great difficulty and disdain. 'M-a-a-tt-ssss.' If these dastardly mats are the only things you can use, then go ahead and utilize them. But I have to tell you that hitting off those surfaces is not natural. Exploding sparks flying from your driver, especially from the green mat variety, should not be an everyday occurrence at all. No way. This form of ball striking is cruel to your wrists. Think 'golf wrist' in the same way as tennis elbow. Lingering pain and potential long-term damage. And ricocheting clubs off hard cement as though it is a slingshot gives an ugly and false sense of playing golf.

You have no such concrete teeing area on your regular golf rounds. None. Also, those little rubber doohickey tees found on these practice surfaces are not flexible to alter heights. They exclaim, "So there you go, and you have to play it where I tell you to." What happens if you like teeing the ball up higher during your regular rounds? Tough cookies! How will this practice of forced teeing heights help you and will it throw your rhythm off during a real game of golf on the course?

I have also had the distinct pleasure of hitting balls directly from green mats in an indoor university facility and watched in horror as my Haig Ultra five iron hosel snagged wickedly in a seam, causing it to bend back like a twisted pretzel. So much for me having that club available for my important match that was being played 3 days later. Now, how did you think I felt after watching this performance on these blasted mats? Not good indeed, thank you very much. My wrists ached and my pride was shattered as I cursed "What the heck #@#%$! was that schmegeele? I pondered whether I should call my lawyer to see if I had a personal injury suit on my hands. Hmmmm . . . Peter, my friend, I think I have found you a new legal niche to pursue.

I am deeply perplexed as to why practice tribe members use these mats even though there is often an ample grass section offered at the same practice facilities. What gives here? If you'll permit me, I would like to use a tennis analogy.

Utilizing the mats rather than the grass is like practicing on hard courts or clay courts for Wimbledon competition when natural grass courts are available to use. To me this is the greatest mystery of all time. Your sensitive wrists will appreciate the softer blows if you use natural grass rather than the Astroturf, and, more importantly (and obviously), grass is the surface you play on golf courses! There is a glaring disconnect with this scenario.

Don't be lulled into a false sense of security by using mats only. Avoid them if you can—for your own personal health and safety. This decision may help your golf game.

So, those who like to practice pounding balls have many reasons for doing it. They range from: the love of the outdoors, escaping control freak wives or husbands and screeching kids, the notion that practice lowers scores, the peacefulness and solitude of this action, parents see it as a good venue for bonding with their keen kids, experimental and other possible shots can be executed, practice tribe members actually like the process and see it as an entity unto itself, and finally, they get to stare at their left arm to see that it is straight. These are legitimate and fair reasons.

For me, I look at my time in life from an opportunity-cost perspective. Practicing, to me, is boring. Stifling boredom. Simply put, I prefer to do something else with my time rather than practice and when golf is slotted into my weekly schedule I want to play on the course. The game could be for score, enjoyment of playing 18 holes on a sunny day, or the excitement of the match against individuals and teams in stroke and match play formats. That is my element.

A pseudo-practice tribe has also been created, more out of necessity rather than the simple pleasure of hitting balls. Those slotted in this category can be the ailing or aging. These players need the 15-minute warm-up to get their arms, muscles, back, and other body parts functioning properly. This helpful stretching and hitting balls for the shorter duration will allow these groups to enjoy a more satisfying round of golf.

Who needs to be carted off the course in a heap because of stubbornness and pride? In most cases, those who fall in this group don't necessarily like practicing but know it is necessary to play injury-free. My age will become a factor sometime in the future and I may have to bend to this practicality. I know there will be paparazzi hanging around to take a picture of Wayne T. hitting balls! My pal Flanagan would especially laugh at this bizarre scene because he hates practicing even more than I do. This sight of me practicing would be kind of like Luke hearing that Mr. Vader is his father. No!!! That can't be . . .

I play the game as a "feel" player. Sometimes I just feel the wind and feel my mood and select the club before launching my shot. Perhaps if I were a process—or technical-type golfer who always needed to do everything I learned on the range or that my feet needed to be 100% aligned to a faraway target, then I would gain this passion for practice. However, my internal wiring cannot be changed and I am proud of who I am.

Converting what is learned on the practice range into the real round is integral to practice tribe members. This class probably also has higher expectations when they play. They may wonder why the ball doesn't fly the same trajectory as the 50 balls they hit 30 minutes ago. Playing for something like score or against your friends changes the dynamics; so therefore what you do on the range does not necessarily translate into the game you play later in the day. Don't be surprised by these differences. Golf is unpredictable and that is one of its addictions. Non-practice tribe members relish the thought of defeating their practice tribe competitors with a stronger mental game plan and natural ability. Yes sir, there is nothing better than taking them down on natural skill after all the intense labour they have invested in their games. It will cheese them off!

My experience also taught me that I play pretty well without the need to practice. I am content and possess inner peace regarding this position. In addition, it has helped that I have played a lot of rounds throughout my lifetime. Should I say "playing makes perfect" rather "than practice makes perfect"? Hitting a few chips and putts are not in the same category as hitting balls on the range. Certainly I invest in my short game, but it is quick and painless and sometimes a time killer before I tee off for my round. At least I have tailored my expectations based on the time that I have invested in practicing and I believe others should have similar expectations.

I respect the practice tribe. They can be happy fellows who feel they have found the secret to transform their 15 handicap to 10, but they can also be a miserable lot who complain: "Why can't I just hit them solidly like I did earlier on the range?" Actually, I don't want to hear about your issues. Some still love the euphoric feeling of hitting the perfect shot on the range, while knowing full well that this may not happen on the course when the stakes are high. As a proponent of the non-practicing tribe I would much prefer to spend my time watching the Masters, sharing a question with Cart Girl on the course while enjoying a round, or just reading a book about World War II. Golf time to me should be staring contentedly at the contouring of a course's design for my upcoming shot or laughing with compatriots rather than studying the precise positioning of my elbow before launching another range ball at a distant silo. Where do you sit in this thought-provoking debate?

HOLE NO. 5, PAR 3. WAS THAT A YODA OR VADER?

"Gimme me a Yoda! Gimme me a Yoda! Ahhh . . . dash it all (or substitute your favourite swearword) . . . a Vader." The species known as golfer loves to express colourful pet sayings, maxims, and other worldly insight when describing good and bad shots. Befuddled non-golfers and for that matter, other golfers who are not versed in our idiosyncratic terms, madly scramble to reach for their dictionaries and thesauruses so they can intelligently translate what the heck we are describing. To them we might as well be speaking Gaelic.

I happen to use *Star Wars* characters and furry creatures in my golf lingo repertoire to describe my golf shots and their results. You may have your own set of creative sayings and aphorisms. Congratulations, I say to you, for joining our esteemed group of demented souls.

There is a logical method to my madness when coming up with these pearls of wisdom. Okay, no need to find and scan those valuable Oxford or Webster resources, the translation of my opening sentence is: "Gimme a good break because the Force is with me. Gimme a good break because the Force is with me. Ahhh, #%@#!!! . . . a bad break and the Force is against me. Darn you, James Earl Jones, with your spine-tingling lectures and black-helmeted evil." See, that translation is easy to understand isn't it?

I certainly do not stand alone in creating inventive phrases. It's fun for players to utilize verbal venting to comfort themselves and cushion the many disappointing breaks they will invariably encounter on golf courses. Pl-l-e-e-e-a-s-e don't go there my cherished Balata! Stop, stop, stop, you cookie! Get up, get up, get up, you dastardly fiend! Self-pleadings for golfers are as vital as oxygen. They believe unquestionably that the ball will surely listen to them and hence it will go where they want it to go. Too bad many of these shots are like father-son relationships: Joe Sr. can tell Joe Jr. what the right thing to do is but the latter does not always listen to his sage advice.

I am not exactly sure why I chose *Star Wars* characters to describe my golf shots. Like many other youngsters at the time, the three groundbreaking sci-fi pictures made an indelible impression on me. Amazing light sabres, big battle scenes and beeping robots were quite appealing to a teenager. Now let me be clear, I am talking about the first three (i.e., original) *Star Wars* movies. They are really the final three films in the series if you understand that the last trilogy of movies comprise prequels to the originals (I have run out of breath). Never mind, let me help you . . . think of the cynical and sarcastic Han Solo as the hero-man, not the whiny Jar Jar Binks and his irritating drivel. Specifically, my *Star Wars* lingo came from the late 1970s/early 80s feature films with their corny (but for their time period, revolutionary) special effects. Chewie, Obi Wan Kenobi, Yoda, Vader, Jabba the Hutt, and Ewoks are my go-to guys.

Now I will provide you with my proper dictionary/thesaurus of *Star Wars* terms so that you too can use them during your next golf game. These brilliant descriptive words will add colour to your round. I still smile at people who call me Chewie or when I hear a person I play with who uses "Yoda" on a ball that spanks off a tree and ends up in the middle of the fairway. Amazingly, I may not even know this person who pleads for help from the little green fellow. Can my phrases be that well-spread throughout society and can I make it stick worldwide? There is a possibility that I can leave an indelible mark and a legacy well beyond my death in a galaxy far, far away in the year 2090 . . .

Chew, Chewie, or Chewbacca—He was Han Solo's big, furry Wookiee accomplice with the ear-splitting roar. I use this term for the deep woods or deep, deep rough or big trouble or big hairy stuff. Golfers know what dangerous terrain I am talking about . . . . Golfers shiver when they hear "I think you are in the Chew!" A thousand-yard shell-shocked stare ensues.

Ewok or the E or Papa Ewok or Papa E—They were the short furry creatures. Oh, so cuddly except when you use the name as a golf term. Ewok is the short rough. "Fella, your slice went in to the Ewok. You may have a nasty lie." Papa Ewok is a thicker or longer rough compared to his son's version. Much better than Chew, the bigger, hairier creature. But beware of your club's hosel getting caught in this stuff when you hit your shot because it can then hook it into the Chew. I also suggest that players offer valuable presents and money to these creatures before the round so they can just happen to gain good lies when balls trickle into their lairs.

Jabba the Hutt—He was an ugly, slimy, fat slug type of a creature with a huge mouth and a monstrous appetite (Princess Leia looked mighty fine in that skimpy outfit while sitting shackled to this big guy as a slave, but that is a whole separate matter). Similar to Jabba, big mouthed sand traps have an insatiable need to be fed. They thrive on swallowing misplayed ProV1s and other balls like Jabba gobbles squids and other unpleasant prey. "You are in Jabba, my friend." This seething player will slump his shoulders and he will immediately become grumpy. The grip tightens on the club that performed this dastardly deed before being harshly slammed back into the bag.

Obi Wan Kenobi—The great thespian Sir Alec Guinness is a Jedi knight in the movie but for golf course sayings, you must focus on "Obi," as in OB, as in Out of Bounds, as in you are supremely out of play. "Hey, you are Obi Wan. I saw it fly over the white stake by that gaudy mansion with the fantastic swimming pool." Hit a provisional ball and count stroke and distance after you hit an Obi Wan Kenobi. Master Luke, you need another light sabre to replace that red one . . . This phrase is the most devastating to golfers because you know you are taking a double bogey at the very least. Grrrr . . . your career low score has just gone down the tubes.

Vader—The Force is not with you and he is the Dark Side. Enter the ominous sound of Vader's breathing apparatus. This term should be attached to a bad bounce or a bad break. "Oh, you got a Vader on that shot off the sprinkler head. It now rests against that shrub." Breathe in . . . (bubbling asthmatic rasp) . . . Breathe out . . . (more bubbling, asthmatic rasp) . . . . Luke, I am your father (whoops, I hope you have watched this whole series or I have made a terrible faux pas and ruined this surprise). A bad break Vader can range from a trivial bad lie to an outright major problem. Not good.

Yoda—Vader's nemesis and the Force is with you. A good break. The little green man with droopy, sideways-leaning, crinkled ears is a good omen. "Hey, you got an amazing Yoda off that hill and it rolled onto the green." "A Yoda it is." Smile if you get one so you can bury all the unfortunate evil Vader, Obi and Ewok shot memories during your round. Yodas are amazing gifts that keep a good round going. Thank the Jedi Master throughout your round so he can supply you with such helpful advice and positive results in future golf excursions.

I have many other terms for golf shots like Skylab (for a sky ball), Dan Blocker (a block or push of the shot into the Chew or Ewok) and Karl Marx (you have nothing to lose but your chains, so go for it). You will notice that these three examples range from space technology to a TV show (*Bonanza*) to that famous German Communist. Aren't I proving to you that I am a Renaissance man? These are worthy additions to my vast lingo library. Speaking of Marx, "All Workers Unite (or Golfers in this case) and I ask each of you to spread these *Star Wars* terms across the universe.

Golfers need their sayings like Linus needs his blanket. Build your own unique lexicon of fun terms and slogans and integrate mine. Joy of the game is paramount and your sayings will allow you to forget about the terrible swings and big slices. These comments create laughter and generate great dialogue among players. So go ahead and talk to your ball. People will not think you are too weird. May the Force be with you and keep it out of the Chew!

Glossary of Waynerisms and other lingo to use on (and off) the golf course

Bad staff work—a phrase to indicate that planning was not done very well.

Good staff work being the opposite. Feel free to use both phrases on the course, at home and in your business world.

Chubbed—to hit a ball fat or thick. It usually involves taking a divot or a big pelt of turf. The result is inevitably less than satisfactory.

Cookie—another term for buddy or fella.

Corn lurks—in reference to the corn that lurks menacingly to the right on Craigowan's long par-3 No. 14. During competitive situations you could plant the seed of doubt with the psychological warfare phrase of, "The wind is howling and the corn lurks . . ." Amazingly, balls would then sail into Big Jim McBob's cornfield! You can use this term for other situations to get the other player thinking about the big push into the crap.

Dr. Depresso—a down-in-the-dumps or negative person. Slumped shoulders, muttering, and shaking of the head are signs of this syndrome.

Dan Blocker—to block or push your shot into the crap. Yes, *Bonanza* and *Ponderosa*. Did you know Lorne Greene (Pa Cartwright) was also a Queen's graduate! Amazing what I know, don't you think?

Danny Guidester—trying to guide or wave at the ball when you swing like a pretty fella. Hit it, you wimp.

Danny Slicesters—golf term for a slice into the crap or woods.

Dunkle—small, insignificant.

Ezekiel—invoking a favourite Biblical character. Do you remember Ezekiel and the wheel? Well, in golf the wheels can fall off. So . . . . If the wheels are falling off, then exclaim to everyone that Ezekiel has grabbed you. People will understand.

Finklenuts—dummy. See **Squid**. Interchange these terms.

Grundies—from the old *Archie* comics for old people or slowpokes. Remember Mrs. Grundy?

High Step—running to a place quickly with much enthusiasm.

Jig Step Boogie—engaging in fast talking to get out of an uncomfortable situation of your own making, doing the quick step to explain and pray that it works. A new pair of shoes may be needed following the fast tap dance.

Jimmy Snipester—a duck hook of a shot. Ugly.

Joke's Over—it is done, time to move on. Thanks, Dad.

Karl Marx shot—you have nothing to lose but your chains, so go for it. Thanks for the insight, you German pinko.

Limp Noodle—usually refers to a weak-assed putt that falls short. Embarrassment and heckling from the crowd. A comment about your sister or mother may be involved.

Meister—another multipurpose term to add to words (like topmeister, skullmeister, pushmeister, shankmeister) to add pizzazz to your statement.

Power Tripper—bouncers, parking attendant cookies, ornery course marshal, officious security personnel, AMS constables at Queen's (you all know these campus dweebs), and others who carry badges and attitudes that are beyond their true power.

Pseudos—fakes, people who think they are what they are not.

Price is right—free. When someone offers you something for free then shut up and say "thank you" even if it is a light beer and you want that better tasting, higher octane stuff. Or a sleeve of those rubbery Ebco balls from 1970 . . .

Rake—self-gimme of a putt. You can also utter rrr-a-a-a-a-ke! To rake the putt away from the hole with your putter.

Rocco—to slam a putt by the hole with too much authority.

Roll the wrist—you can plant the seed of doubt through this psychological ploy by making your competitor think that he is going to snap-hook his shot. Wristy . . .

Schmegeeled—finangled, manipulated.

Schmozzle—mess, a mix-up, chaos.

Sergeant Ryker—a power tripper, someone who holds authority over you and something you want to get.

Skip Bittman—a prepster, coiffed individual (borrowed from a *Second City Television* comic character). Or, a drive that skips off the teeing area and flies down the fairway. A nice multipurpose word to use.

Skylab—a sky ball or a pop up usually involving a drive. Lunar module height.

Slumped Shoulders—a beaten man. Think of a golfer who just took quad and watch him as he lumbers with shoulders down to the next tee, muttering incoherently.

Squid—fool, idiot.

Stress level 10—maximum stressful situation. How about a three-footer to win the match?

Sturgeons (or Gurgling Sturgeons) and Lizards—creek, lake, or water where fish and other creatures like to swallow your golf ball.

Sweatmeister—perspire profusely, sweat like a pig.

Technician—a golfer who knows how to masterfully hit a shot or manipulates its flight path to gain positive results.

Temple of Doom—originally termed for hitting your ball to the back tier of Craigowan's 18th green when the pin is on the front. You will be doomed to try and get your putt down in 2 from that area. Feel free to use the term when your ball finishes at the back of any green when the hole is parked at the front. Undulations and big breaks are usually part of the equation you have to face.

Thangers—multipurpose word to describe items you can't always remember what their names are at the time or small morsels of food when you have the munchies. "Give me those thangers over there (people know what you are talking about).

Verma-pressed—to put pressure on. This is based on a person who kept hitting golf balls into me while I was playing on my home course. "Hey, who is putting the Verma or who is Verma-pressing me!"

Whammy gee ho—putting a hex on someone or purposely casting a shadow on your opponent as he is about to putt.

Cart Girl Visit #2 with Trivia Refreshments on Outward Half of Golf Course.

1. What golfer started the tradition of the Champions Dinner held on Tuesday night of The Masters?
    Have a break with a Snickers bar.

2. Who made the following comment during one of the most memorable final round mano-a-mano matches: "This is what it's all about, isn't it Jack?" To which Jack responded "You bet it is."
    Prevent dehydration with bottled water.

Hole No. 6, Par 5. What are the Old Course, Auld Grey Toon, and Chariots of Verma like?

Hitting your heart-fluttering drive over Herb's hotel on the Road Hole and standing captivated at the sight of the illustrious R &A is unparalleled in this golfer's experience. The Old Course at St Andrews or simply named the Old stands at the pinnacle. Golf was first played here six hundred years ago. Repeat this statement to yourself and ponder the significance. Until a golfer plays these historical links, he or she does not truly have a reference point to judge what golf should mean. That is why it was my mission in life to play at St Andrews at least once during my time on this earth.

I yearned for this experience since I was a young man and this higher calling in the school of golf would not release its grip on me until I made this trip happen. Pebble Beach is absolutely spectacular and I was fortunate to play in Monterey a year after my St Andrews voyage in 2008. But to understand Pebble, nearby Spyglass, Pinehurst, or any other golf course in the world you have to visit the birthplace of golf itself, St Andrews, and specifically, the Old Course. This course was not manufactured. There was no precedent. The views are mesmerizing and the golf quite extraordinary and peculiar. What are you waiting for?

When speaking of St Andrews one needs to digest many things. The Old Course is one thing—a very important one—but there is an aura and history of surrounding attractions or amazing distractions, if you like, demanding your attention. Interested individuals need to think of the lovely town, the Royal and Ancient (R & A) where the first published national rules of golf were created in 1899, the well-known University with the town's namesake, the centuries-old stone structures, the opening sequence of *Chariots of Fire* that was filmed on the West Sands beach, tasty Scottish pints, and a charming hotel called the Rusacks. The sum of these parts of St Andrews adds up to an even greater whole.

But before describing my grand entrance into famous St Andrews for the first time, I wanted to describe my impressions from earlier that same day . . . . Playing helmet golf on Balcomie Links at Crail Golfing Society was a brilliant starting point for our Scottish excursion. Twelve of us colleagues travelled across the Atlantic to spend eight days in Scotland to golf, soak in its powerful history, and examine many of its brilliant sights. Crail was our initial stop for the twelve Verma Cup competitors before we trekked across a paradise of varying links courses. We could feel it in our bones that this was going to be exceptional.

The Verma Cup was named after a young man who continually hit into me during one round early in my golfing career at Oxford Golf and Country Club (Craigowan). As you can figure, I was none too thrilled with this tactic. I thought a trophy named after him would be a tribute to this lasting memory from my home course of over 30 years and because I like coining golf terminology. The Verma Press became a long-lasting, illustrious and illustrative term of mine for pressuring (see it listed in my Waynerisms). I have a great following of friends and fans who utilize the term with great enthusiasm.

All of the participants in this group had attended Queen's University in Kingston, Ontario, Canada except for one intruder. This poor University of Western Ontario individual had to patiently endure our droning on about past Golden Gael stories and embellishments (but it was a small price for him to pay to be in such esteemed company). The strong bonds of friendship we'd formed in classes, at house parties, and in local drinking establishments enabled us to carry on our tight-knit university relationships into our 40s. To have everyone drop their normal lives and resurrect the past of being young lads again was very important to all of us. It didn't matter if you were a doctor, a lawyer, a CEO, or a salesman—we were all the same. Inner dummy behaviour and childish antics would often surface for all to see. We were carefree for a week in our lives. A Scottish golf junket was the perfect linchpin and a fitting excuse to make things happen for the worthy cause of comradeship. And vying for the prestigious Verma Cup was the icing on the cake.

As for Crail, this notable club promptly demonstrated to our players some of its dangers by the second hole. The criss-crossing of some of its shared fairways made you wonder if your head was going to be shattered by a screaming Top-Flite. What a way to die! The visible stretches of water on the majority of holes and beautiful scenery at this seventh oldest club awed everyone. These sights acted as great antidotes for any errant shots that may have come our way from vacationing Yanks or serious-minded Scots who couldn't care less. The guys loved the contrast of playing such a links course to ones that they were used to playing. Animated conversations over finger foods and libations in the clubhouse followed the round. They had never seen anything like it. In this mythical land, thoughts of North America were far, far away.

1786. Say that again, and you think, "Hey, golf at Crail commenced only 10 years after the American War of Independence and 3 years before the Storming of the Bastille!" Canada was only a country of hewers of wood and drawers of water during this era. At least, as a fervent history buff, I would draw these conclusions. Perhaps you would just settle for saying that Crail is an ancient club. But I like to use reference points and transport myself back in time. What kinds of golf clothing did they wear back then? How did they enjoy playing with leather golf balls filled with chicken or goose feathers? Did the large pints, probably costing mere cents, taste as good in the 19th hole clubhouse following a windy and rainy round of golf late in the 18th century as they did for us in the early 2000s?

Some of us were fortunate to stay behind in the clubhouse following our exhilarating round so we could listen to a distinguished gentleman. The Scotsman was attempting in his own charismatic way to sell potential members on the benefits of joining this venerable club. One piece of the presentation that grabbed our attention was his pointed mention that liners surrounding the inside of hole cups were invented at Crail. My friend Bags and I were enthralled with his weaving storyline. His delivery of such insight was outstanding.

Golf history and traditions are very important to me and I was witness to an inside scoop on my first day. "Walking into luck," as I like to say. These are the great extra tidbits you learn that turn very good trips in to remarkable ones. The Verma Cup tribe members had to yank on our sleeves with some insistence to get us to exit the clubhouse as the bus was leaving. "Hey Wayne, remember that we are now going to St Andrews." Oh . . . okay. Cue Wayne's glowing grin.

Rain started pattering on the bus window just after we stepped up to take our seats. This sign may have been a gentle nudge from the gods above to remind us that we were clearly now in Scotland and not in Scottsdale, Arizona. Our group would have to abide by the unpredictable local weather patterns. As it turned out, our 8-day trip would be free of any precipitation during our golf rounds. Hah! Take that, Mr. Weatherman and your colleagues in the heavens!

The anticipation of arriving at the game's birthplace after playing this delightful course was all-consuming for me. The boys were chatting busily about their round on the 30-minute bus ride from Crail but I blocked out this buzzing racket. Enveloped in the passing scenery and counting the minutes, I sat absorbed on this magical tour. I was in Scotland. I was arriving at THE St Andrews. Not St. Andrew's College in Aurora, Ontario, Canada from which my friend Petey graduated, or St. Andrew's Golf Club in America, the first U.S. golf club. Yes, this was the course and town whose name did not possess (or require) an apostrophe. Superlatives would abound at this destination and its impact on me as a golfer and historian were immense. I felt I belonged here, and sensed a spiritual DNA connection to the place. Mom, the McLay and the McGill genes I inherited from you are playing the bagpipes!

Our bus arrived at the Rusacks Hotel where all of us would reside for three nights. When I went to check in, I had a message waiting for me from Gordon Murray. I was to call him to coordinate a meeting the following day. Who is Gordon? He is a local legend and I connected with this esteemed fellow through Mr. George Peper, the well-known golf writer and past editor-in-chief of *Golf Magazine* for 25 years. Gordon had a whole chapter written about him in Mr. Peper's great read, *St Andrews Sojourn*. I had contacted George, hoping he would be in St Andrews during our visit so I could treat him to a nice pint or Scotch but unfortunately he was going to be in the U.S. at that time. George kindly connected me with Gordon instead so I could experience the royal treatment at St Andrews. He passed with flying grades.

St Andrews Sojourn is a book discussing George's experience living and playing at St Andrews. This was one of the required books that all participants had to read (I didn't issue a pop quiz but many appreciated what they learned from it). The second book was *In Search of Burningbush* by David Konik. This author described his impressions upon playing many golf courses that we would be touring around this week. Crail was one such treasure.

The book has a good storyline between David and his friend Don Naifeh. Burningbush is a legendary golf club described in Michael Murphy's best-selling book, *Golf in the Kingdom*. Many believe Crail

71

is the setting for this fictional story involving Shivas Irons and Seamus MacDuff because of the similarities of the par-3s described and the cave found between them. Don also felt it was important to launch a ball with a loved one's name on it into the sea from Crail's No. 13 tee. This symbolic gesture was his form of "connection" to the selected person. I liked this idea, so I was committed to repeating this action once I reached that part of the course. After a quick thought about my father and a quick holler that Don would approve of, I launched a ball 240 yards into the thrashing water as a sort of handshake with him. I then saluted him with my greatest respect by doing it the Canadian or British army way with the palm held outwardly and quivering (watch one of those great British war movies like *The Bridge on the River Kwai* and you will understand). Sorry you were not able to be here in the flesh, Terry. Your spirit will just have to suffice!

I thought it was important for the group to read these books so they could understand the significance of the places, especially St Andrews, that they we were visiting. The Old Montreal Forum, Old Yankee Stadium, Lambeau Field, St Andrews. These are, or were, all sporting shrines but St Andrews won by hundreds of years if one calculated significance based on age and its rich history. Don't you view a longer aged Scotch or bottle of wine as possessing more value?

Many in our group were not what I call avid golfers but they all arrived with a better appreciation and respect for the game and its history. They also had a more developed grasp of the rules of golf and the match play format along with more intimate knowledge of the town. I am not saying I put the fear of God in them; well, maybe I did scare them a little bit . . . . Gordon would invite all of us to the private St Andrews Golf Club the very next day. This was going to be a treat to see the 18th green of the Old Course from the inner sanctum of such a storied club. What would the experience be like?

I highly recommend that you pay the premium and stay at the Rusacks. Give up that extra cardigan jacket and knick-knacks you intended to purchase and see if this is possible for you and your group. This rustic hotel rests along the 18th hole and provides you with the most incredible sightline to the course and beyond. Ride the claustrophobic 3-foot-wide elevator that lurches up three stories to your accommodations or take the winding staircase. The rooms are not huge but quite comfortable. The dining hall and sitting rooms on the first floor are fantastic places to enjoy a pint or two and offer you first-class views onto the Old Course's opening and finishing holes. This is the ideal way to judge the true impact of St Andrews on your golfer soul.

Upon my appearance to our third-floor room, my friend and roommate Scugog impatiently and insistently waved at me from the balcony. He told me to get out here immediately. I had to twist and schmegeele my back in order to successfully slither through the window (even though a strategically positioned sign said not to open the window) so I could join him on the balcony to take a boo. We both stood in amazement while the overcast skies settled.

There it was. Spread out before us was the spine-tingling panoramic view of the 18th hole, the 1st hole, the Road Hole to our left, the Royal and Ancient building to the right and the North Sea dotted with seagulls directly in front. Silence overcame us and there was no need to speak. A minute or two of serenity allowed us to absorb the significance of this moment so we could place it in our special memory compartments. The history and birthplace of golf winked at me.

I don't think I can ever re-create the exhilarating first experience of seeing the Old Course. A religious experience . . . not exactly. For me it was more spiritual, a connection to those who had wandered the grounds for centuries before me. My stomach, no doubt, felt the significance as my neural impulses relayed excited thoughts to it. This was the best scene you can imagine as a loyal golf servant. Hel-l-l-o-o-o-o, Old Tom Morris!

This fine accommodation set the tone for our stay in St Andrews. The Rusacks Hotel prominently displays its sign on the corner of the building and can be seen when you tee off on the final and very memorable hole. This is the same glorious building you see on television, from which spectators pour out of windows and over balconies so they can see Arnie, Jack, Seve, Tom and Tiger as they march over the Swilcan Bridge towards the fabled Valley of Sin fronting the green. I leaned over my balcony joyously to envision myself as one of the lucky few who have witnessed the final round of the Open Championship passing by me. Priceless stuff indeed . . .

For our rounds at the New Course tomorrow and the Old Course on the following day, we simply picked up our clubs that were stored in the basement of the hotel and then ambled to the respective tees. On the day we played the Old Course, I hoofed the clubs over my shoulder and turned right, walked along the eighteenth hole, by the Royal and Ancient behind the first tee and reported to the starter's hut in mere minutes. How cool is that!

Dinnertime was approaching so our group wandered around the beautiful town of St Andrews. We struggled to find a suitable restaurant to satisfy our hunger pains because it was getting late. The fall-back position was a dunkle fish and chips restaurant 15 minutes away from our hotel. After indulging in this potent combination of fried foods, I examined an advertisement for a dessert on the back wall that I had always heard about—a deep-fried Mars bars. A specialty of Scottish cuisine.

My curiosity insisted that I indulge and have one, even though my insides screamed obscenities, knowing what was to follow. Bags struggled to choke half of one down because it was way too rich for his internal organs. His greenish face signalled, "I give up!" so I gallantly rescued him and ate his. I, on the other hand, conquered this challenge and digested all of my Scottish delicacy. If the fish and chips didn't clog my arteries and raise my cholesterol to orbital levels then, by God, the deep-fried Mars bar would. My punished teeth still seem to have caramel remnants stuck in them. Obviously, my dentist, Dr. Al, warned me of a possible cavity that could be caused by this decadent morsel. However, he is a devoted golfer and certainly understood the price you pay for foolhardiness in Scotland.

Our timing to arrive at St Andrews was impeccable. After dinner and some drinks, midnight encroached and that would mean Sunday. Golfers should know that you cannot play the Old Course on Sundays (outside of the Open Championship when it is held at this site after gaining special provision). Weird, but true. St Andrews is owned by the people of the town and not by some rich stuffed shirt and a bunch of cronies. If you live within the confines of St Andrews you have access to all its courses for about 100 pounds a season. Incredible. It makes me want to move to the town right now for just this benefit and I would be willing to lose my teeth and health over it!

Anyone can walk the Old Course on the seventh day and this include families who want to picnic, couples who want to walk the family dog and delivery vehicles, which can drive across the paved road that thrusts across the 1st and 18th fairways. It is a bit disorienting and bizarre to see the intrusive road and people wandering on the course. Certainly my experience at Augusta National and its stringent security practices was the exact opposite approach. The common man (along with his loyal dog) has his day.

We took advantage of this Sunday situation and wandered down the 18th hole in darkness starting from the green and working our way back to the tee. The feeling was both eerie and pleasurable for us to first walk this course at night. Glancing light reflected from buildings along this hole. My friend Pete and I chatted animatedly about how great it was to be here, when suddenly I heard two of my colleagues start laughing and I heard a thumping of bodies. What the heck was that? They were wrestling on the hallowed grounds of St Andrews!

Peter, in his pronounced lawyerly cadence, had to calm me down. I groaned at this disrespect shown by two men who I thought knew better than to give the Commish a heart attack. I doubled over at my knees, took a couple of deep breaths and offered my sincere apologies to The Almighty, the people of St Andrews, and the R & A members who may have been watching from the windows while drinking three-fingered single malt Scotches. My dad would be rolling his eyes at such boorish behaviour. But then again, he was a bit of a rascal too, so there might have been a twinkle of laughter in his eyes at viewing this sight from above. Soon my friends would be hungrily swallowed up by the Swilcan Burn like a pair of misplayed golf balls if they were not careful with their tomfoolery. I would then get the last chuckle at their expense.

After admonishing the boys for their theatrics, much to their amusement, time was now ripe to hit the sack and sleep before enjoying a day on the New Course in the morning. It was smart to have planned our first exposure to St Andrews at this well-regarded sister course before turning to its main superstar.

The New Course was fun to play but I must admit it does not leave a lasting impression. This may, of course, have been the result of our great anticipation to play the Old Course the next day or comparing it unfairly to Crail. Crail was our first exposure to links golf and the abundance of water views was terrific. But the day following our round at the New Course progressed into a more than ample night of fun.

The twelve of us should have settled for a relaxing dinner, gentle chitchat and engaging dialogue before settling in for an early night to prepare for the round of our life. No, this did not happen, at least not for a few of us. I shake my head and wonder how things can spiral out of control and change so dramatically.

After post-round beers at the comfortable New Course's pub and my dealing with possible rule infractions from the opening Verma Cup matches, we headed back for a quick shower so we could get properly attired in our jackets. As mentioned earlier, Gordon Murray had invited the group to join him at the St Andrews Golf Club located near the 18th green and we had to be on our best behaviour. This was a tremendous honour for us to be asked to such an exclusive institution. It is one of several golf clubs, including the R&A, which makes its home at St Andrews.

Our energized group met Gordon outside the gated entrance to his club. This Scottish gentleman meticulously signed in each of us, as did two other members he'd lined up for us (a member can sign in only 4 guests). This formal procedure for admission gave us a sense that we were entering a private enclave, a special place. Our Canadian contingent had now contributed to St Andrews Club folklore and tradition by adding its own distinct mark. We were mightily tickled to be included with others who had come before us.

Aged golf clubs were, fittingly, positioned on the walls by each historical stairwell. Black and white photographs of club champions dating from the 1800s and past Open Championship winners adorned mahogany walls of the front foyer. Towel service was politely offered in the loo.

Next, we ventured into the cozy drinking room to sit down in comfortable chairs and sofas. The room was full to capacity with members and some outsiders. Scarce tables and chairs were sourced and we were scattered throughout the confines. This forced us to break up into smaller groups, in animated but controlled conversations. This was not a conducive environment to bellow old Queen's Golden Gael fighting songs or holler the occasional obscenity. We ordered fine Scotches and temperature-perfect pints and I chatted with some locals including the bartender. Staring out the large plate glass window onto the fairway was pure pleasure. Taking pictures of this setting was highly frowned upon by members and, while we all respected this rule, a couple of shots were discreetly taken.

I look at the photos once in a while as a cherished reminder of being a welcomed guest into the inner circle of St Andrews and Scottish golf. Like listening to the history lesson in Crail's clubhouse, this wonderful addition to our agenda made it even more memorable. Thank you to Mr. Peper and Mr. Murray for contributing to our enlightening golf education.

After expressing our sincere gratitude to Gordon for the wonderful experience, the twelve of us walked a short jaunt to the quaint Dunvegan Hotel. This fine establishment sits about 112 yards distant or, what its logo says, "Only a 9-iron away from the Old Course (depending on the wind)." I would suggest that you visit this place during your stay at St Andrews. The pub food was good and the copious amounts of beer, wine and Scotch contributed greatly to the droning on of stories that inevitably turned into slightly slurred versions. So much for a calm night . . .

My friend Ian even had the opportunity to meet James MacArthur (sadly he passed away later in 2010). You would know him better as playing the character Danny Williams as in "Book 'em Danno" from *Hawaii Five-O*. Jack Lord, better known as Steve McGarrett and his slick hair, was not in sight but John Glenn, John Havlicek and Bobby Knight were joining him in the private dining room. I took a shot by pseudo-staggering into this room to see if I could find these famous basketball personalities and astronaut. My mission was unsuccessful (Houston, I have a problem). Only blank faces from the room's clientele met my searching eyes. Who the heck are you anyways, fella! We are famous, you are not (yet, I would like to counter). I was denied and I smartly beat a hasty retreat, believing that one day I may have a more positive brush with fame.

I was geared up for our next stop. Shouldn't I go to sleep? Yes, but when does logic ever enter the picture when good friends get together with copious amounts of booze at a place like this!

Some of us then strolled to the five-star Old Course Hotel sitting close to the Road Hole. This night was more suited to checking out the facilities than anxiously wondering whether we were going to clunk our drives off the maintenance shed part of this newer hotel on No. 17. It was very nice inside. The traditional pub called the Jigger Inn sits on these grounds. This is where, I was told, that caddies congregated for pints and chatter post-rounds. I had to make my presence known.

Indeed, the Jigger Inn is extremely old (dates back to the 1850s) and tiny. Few people can squeeze into it and the establishment was quiet when we got there, well in the bag. Too bad there were no grizzled caddie veterans for us to extract war stories about their dealings with the Dan Quayle-type politicians, narcissistic celebrities and egotistical hackers who schmegeele their artificial scores with 4-foot gimme putts. It was late by Scottish standards on this Sunday night and no one else was there to offer their disparate opinions on life, golf, and world affairs.

Since no outside influences or feisty characters were available, my friends Hugh, Billy, Peter, Chief, and I got into some good discussions. I was ready to offer brilliant analysis in my inebriated state. Many memories of that night have dissipated but I do remember one. Brother Billy and I went toe-to-toe on our respective views of stroke play versus match play. Bill is a strong advocate of stroke play and I was trying to convince him of the merits of match play. Hugh just sleepily nodded his head and the others wondered if this debate was going to achieve anything.

As usual, booze can spark a trivial argument into one of monumental importance. We agreed to disagree. The Verma Cup tournament was strictly match play format including 4-balls, foursomes, and individual matches (although the Old Course match was going to have a special aggregate 4-ball match because the majority of players wanted their score to count for a future keepsake, and discussion point with curious friends and families). I thought it was imperative that we play like the Scots do. No 5 ½-hour rounds with the tedious fiddling on the greens. Or, at least that was the plan. Many of the participants had not played match play in the past.

Well, as the last to leave this great little drinking place, we lumbered back to the Rusacks. The time had come for us in our inebriated state to reflect about playing the Old Course tomorrow. I was elated to know that I was not teeing off with the morning group. The wind would be chilly and the head would have pounded relentlessly from an ill-timed hangover.

This was not how I envisioned teeing off on the first hole of the Old Course at St Andrews. Five minutes earlier, one of the individuals in the foursome teeing off ahead of us arrived precipitously close to his afternoon's tee-off time. The Royal and Ancient building guarding the tee roared its disapproval of this grand faux pas. The culprit had taken the shuttle to the practice area near the 17th hole and found out only too late that his return ride would not get him back on time. He had to hike quite a way and here he stood with a nonplussed demeanour, wondering what all the kerfuffle was. I stood in shock.

Perhaps it was my fault, as the de facto Commish and spiritual leader, for failing to set parameters or babysitting rules to get the boys to the tee on time. Were we not mature adults (I thought)? Should I really fall on the sword and be hard on myself? For anybody who knows me well, they understand my contempt for those who are tardy for tee-off times. I can't fight the feeling that it irks me and I rank it near the top of the ladder of golf transgressions. No excuses for disrespecting the time of others. I thought that being late for the Old Course's tee time would rank as the most serious offense in golfing annals. Second only to yelling during the backswing of a famous player on the final hole of the final round in the Open Championship, maybe . . .

A separate item on their homework list that I absolutely pounded relentlessly into the skulls of all players for 6 months was to make sure they had properly signed handicap/index cards and they needed to be at a 24-or-less index. You see, golfers need to be at this number or below or you simply do not qualify to play the Old Course. I didn't care whether the strategies invoked were to be through bribery, a subtle threat of broken legs to loved ones or professional shop personnel, or just simply being a member at a golf club with a legitimate handicap. Just obtain this gull-darn vital piece of paperwork at all costs! Get it done, they must (sounds like Yoda, kind of). Golfers coming to St Andrews should never come without such documentation. I beg that you do not make this mistake or evil eyes, uniform folded arms, and mean-spirited curses will be launched as daggers to your heart.

One offending member of our prestigious group pooh-poohed my repeated emphasis on what he thought was trivial and almost paid heavily for this costly mistake. The nameless man had approached the youngster occupying the position of power and authority in the tiny starter's hut sitting to the right of the first tee. How can something so small be so significant? When asked for his index card, the Verma Cupper hesitated and did the Jig Step Boogie. The look of horror on his pallid face said it all when he failed to provide the necessary card to allow him to hit away on the first hole. He quickly high-tailed it by me and scampered to his hotel room. That look could only mean one thing from my perspective. I would never say "I told you so," because that would not be proper, would it? The frightened-out-of-his-wits one successfully retrieved the cherished index card a few minutes before tee-off. Stress had been reduced from the Level 10 stratosphere but a lesson was learned, I hope. Listen to those that know. I assumed it was a given that the Old Course demanded the respect it deserved. This is, after all, several hundred years old and is the birthplace of golf!

Thankfully, I liked both of these characters or they would have been quickly dumped over the retaining wall into the North Sea just to the right of the tee. The dour Scots would have been entertained by the North American-accented cry: "I will never beeeeeeee lllaaaaaattteee agaaaaaain and IIIIII wiiiillll alwwwwwaaaayyysss listennnnnnnn toooo youuuu frrrooooommmm noooooowwww oooonnn Coooommmmmmmissssshhhhhh . . .

Mad scrambling then ensued because our foursome of Bags, Scugog, Chief and yours truly would now have to switch places (our third group had gone out earlier in the day). We were up on the blocks. Bags was rattled the most by this abrupt change in agenda. The corporate pharmaceutical executive was ill-prepared for this impromptu thrust into his mental state and it caused him considerable anguish. No time was set aside for an executive assistant to change his plans and calm him down before an important presentation on the biggest stage of his golfing life. He was on his own. It was his first time at St Andrews and he wanted the experience to be awe-inspiring.

A tee had been tossed in the air to determine first off and he was the chosen one. "How fortunate," he must have grumbled to himself. The sky was overcast like only Scotland can deliver and there was some inevitable wind. Bags, dressed in three layers of expensive clothing, rifled the driver out of his bag but this thought process was quickly neutralized by his trusted caddie. An iron was thrust into his hand while the driver was simultaneously yanked from his grasp and thrown back in the bag. He was flummoxed for a moment. An incredulous look appeared on Bags' face but it was time to step up and be a man.

No. 1 at the Old Course might be the widest fairway in the universe (100+ yards) and it is intimidating. You stand alone. The fairway is so wide that you have difficulty in focusing on the shot and I found it a challenge to gain perspective. Usually you have a definite feel on a hole and direction but this was quite different. The historic buildings on the left hand side, the R & A to the rear and the sea to the right all affect your senses significantly with a somewhat disorienting effect. That public road with the clever name of Granny Clark's Wynd crosses the hole about an eight or seven iron away from the tee. The Swilcan Burn that winds itself across No. 1 and No. 18 fairways seems distant but it definitely can come into play on long or wayward shots. Right is no good as out of bound comes into play but there is much room to safely miss your shot left, including into the 18th fairway. The unsettling feeling that engulfed me made my strategy one of conservatism. I was just thinking that somehow I wanted a drive positioned nicely for shot number two and have the amateur watchers nod their heads in approval. Length was not an overwhelming concern. Survival of the opening jitters was.

Many locals and other golfers hover by the tee blocks to heighten your awareness that all eyes are on you to perform. The spectators lean on the gate and act as professors grading the material of an innocent student. What kind of substance and character are you made of, laddie, to tackle this St Andrews universe? Pressure builds and breathing gets out of whack.

Remarkably under the circumstances, Bags, with quivering hands, rifled his four-iron shot that bounded down the vast fairway and came to rest around 185 yards from the tee. Relief and great satisfaction pulsed through his veins. He quickly exited the area, elated at a job well done. My colleague admitted later that this was the toughest shot he has ever taken. The term 'relief' is an understatement, after completing such a monumental drive. I have heard many rumours that even ruthless CEOs who eat people for lunch struggle to hit this shot. Grade Bags an A!

My five-iron was struck well to the centre of the fairway. I passed the test with flying colours but I did not dare show my nervousness to the rest of the people parked around the tee. 'Business as usual' was the perception I sought to present to the patrons. Now the Swilcan Burn lurked for my second shot. And there was the Swilcan Bridge resting on my left where all those famous photographs are taken. I paused for a few seconds to reflect on its presence. It is small in stature but huge in historical significance. I would definitely stride across this structure on my final hole just like all those golfing greats have done for centuries . . .

Jimmy, my caddie, suggested I use a nine-iron to get the ball to the back left part of the green. I stubbornly chose wedge because, well, I thought I was a big man, and as the ball sailed, he pleaded for the ball to get up. Any golfer who hears these warning words will surely know the familiar sinking feeling it gives to the pit of your stomach. Hope and a prayer swill in your brain—and 'hope' should not be a strategy. The Pro V1 plunked a mere yard over the dangerous Swilcan Burn, almost ruining my start. Thank you, my spiritual one!

The net result from this brush with the famous hazard was that it left me an intricate, long, uphill putt. I contemplated my line with my caddie's guidance and symbolically proceeded to three-jerk on the green. The bogey was ample and deserved punishment for my lack of competent listening skills. Jimmy's furrowed brow and piercing stare at the admonished one indicated, and not too subtly, "I told you so." Yes, Jimmy, I will now listen intently to your advice moving forward. You have been caddying at the

Old Course for over two decades so you might know a thing or two about its nuances and surprises. Listen and learn, Mr. Morden. Grrrrr . . . I was grinding a little already but I needed to remain steadfast. This was the last time I doubted my amigo's prescient advice.

The obviously visible backdrop of the yellow Old Course Hotel behind the 17th hole seemed out of place when compared it to the rest of the surroundings. The building looked vaguely familiar to me from last night's hazy visit. Although it is an immaculate hotel, the freshness of this establishment clashes awkwardly with the history of St Andrews and especially the impressive architecture lining the 18th fairway. I know Herb Kohler (the man who brought us magnificent Whistling Straits in Kohler, Wisconsin) is recognized as a great owner of this property but the sight takes away some of the richness of the Old Course's history. Not an eyesore necessarily but a noticeable blemish on an otherwise picturesque setting steeped in tradition.

I finished the first hole and suppressed these trivial thoughts regarding this hotel's presence before sauntering to the second tee that rested only a few yards from the first green. Would it be my day with this inauspicious start?

After improbably sinking a long, undulating putt on No. 2 to save par following an aggressive second shot, I felt like I was given a supreme confidence boost from the legends of the game. These whispers from allied spirits told me that they knew how significant and important this day was for me. As a reward, these friends thought they would aid me in my pursuit. Golfers across the world know there are certain ego-boosting shots that kick-start an ordinary round and transform it into an extraordinary one. For me it was this niftily sunk putt. For other players it may be the skulled chip shot that clangs the pin and drops in, or another that takes an unlikely bounce off a greenside hill and finishes 2 feet from the pin. A friendly Yoda. Or it was destiny, helping this Woodstonian experience a once-in-a-lifetime thrill.

The ship had been righted, steadied. It could have gone the other way but it didn't. The fine line between success and failure was determined by the size of the cup. My round would providentially not go the way of the *Titanic* via a nasty encounter with a massive iceberg. Athletes and other hardened sports warriors know that they need to grasp this offered hand with relish. Just think of how my psyche (or any other person's) would have been affected if the ball spun out of the hole after the arduous beginning on the first green. Ezekiel's shadow followed by Slumped Shoulders lurked. A negative result would have been interpreted as a clear message that it was not to be my day. But in fact it would be my day and this was my turning point. Just dandy!

My ball striking became masterful in a way I had not felt in some time as I progressed through the round. A new energy had been harnessed. There was really no rational reason for me to play so well. I had struggled when playing earlier in the week, so hopes were not high. Sometimes your grooved golf swing and superior scoring touch just unexpectedly arrive as a welcome tag team. At St Andrews it was like an autopilot was turned on inside my nervous system. Intimidation of the course did not seep into my thought process and that actually surprised me. I was hitting greens in regulation after driving the ball to proper spots over knolls, bunkers, and fescue areas thanks to my caddie's brilliant guidance.

I also fondly remember spending a special moment on No. 4 when the four of us purposely let our caddies wander ahead while we strolled together. Smiles creased our faces, as we knew that this moment should be etched in time. Make sure you find time to pause and glance around the radiant confines of the Old Course. It is truly a marvel to examine and appreciate nature's rendition of golf.

A couple of the guys who played in the morning round followed us to take pictures, feel the drama of our match, and take advantage of seeing this majestic place once again. Could you ever get enough of this place?

My eagle attempt at the par-5 5th missed after two perfectly executed shots but I secured a birdie. Six and 7 fell in line with a par and a bogey. I marched on towards No. 8, the first par-3 of the outward nine. How many courses do you know of that wait a full seven holes before giving you a par-3 opportunity? Very few.

We noticed that there were about 20 tees concentrated in a small part of the teeing area. What an odd sight! None of us knew the significance of these tees or the way they were placed. Were the wooden symbols requesting, "Step up like those golfing brethren before you and hit this glorious shot?" Was it a Wallace clan symbol from centuries ago?

The hole demands a blind shot over a hill and I almost aced it with the ball resting only 2 feet behind the hole. I settled for my second birdie in four holes. Those tees acted as fanatical fans to egg on my success. Wouldn't that have been something to get my first hole-in-one of my life at St Andrews! I would have gladly paid the bar tab in the 19th hole for this timely result but since there is no 19th hole at the Old Course I would have settled for the R & A. Fat chance that would happen . . .

I avoided the bunker that protruded in the middle of the 9th fairway. A basic short chip remained. My mind whirled as I knew another par would make me shoot even par for the front. Usually such niggly and futuristic thoughts for golfers at these crucial times spell trouble. This is one of those nines you want to lock down in your memory as a grand achievement. A tentative and less-than-satisfactory chip left me short of the green. More stress . . . . A short pitch rolled the ball to my death zone and a 3 ½-foot nerve-jangler remained. My heart was racing and I was now in the comfortable home of Wayne's yips. Shaky hands proceeded to jab the ball and it missed. I felt like Doug Sanders when he missed his 2-foot putt on the 18th hole at St Andrews that would have won him the 1970 Open Championship. Well, maybe I was a tad less disconsolate than Mr. Sanders losing the major championship to Nicklaus. A groan of disappointment went through me because of this once-in-a-lifetime missed opportunity. But truthfully, how can one really, really be dejected when shooting 37 on the front nine of St Andrews? Suck it up, Morden, and proceed to the inward nine.

After a sandwich and a coffee at the mobile refreshment stand, I followed with a par on the almost drivable par-4 10th thanks to the wind's helping hand. This result was a strong beginning for the back nine. The way I played this hole epitomized the differences in the play of links golf. I smashed a good drive and ended just short of the green. Wind plays a constant role and courses like St Andrews can offer drivable par-4s under certain positive conditions. Jimmy handed me my putter and I poked a 40-yard, low-to-the-ground putt that danced around ridges to within 20 feet. Neato to play such creative golf on the Home of Golf!

I am a firm believer of hitting inventive shots like these testers, unlike many North Americans who want tried and true. Technician-style low pitch shots struck to deliberately catch contours and long putts from the fairways over undulations like I'd just performed, are skill sets that resourceful links players will execute. You can feel like a youthful golfer again improvising shots visualized only in your mind rather than acting on shots based on advice from a sophisticated gadget carried on your golf bag. It was not going to be the last time I would be imaginative over this terrific round.

Next, I stood on the scenic par-3 11th. The soothing Eden Estuary languished in the distance. Golfers have to watch and respect those players coming up the 7th fairway since tee shots are smashed over their heads (a quirky set-up that you have to admire and a quick reminder of what we experienced during our day at Crail). My shot exploded off the seven-iron sweet spot and landed a few feet from bouncing towards the hole. Instead it fell just short and stalled like an antiquated 1982 Lada. The cursed "matter of inches" was uttered. At least the shot did not filter in to the menacing and difficult Hill or Strath bunkers straddling the front of the green. That result would not have been convenient. My chip was lukewarm in quality and I settled for a bogey. "Hang tough," I said to myself. Two over going to the 12th . . .

Being instructed to hit a six iron purposely into the right rough on the 12th hole boggles the noggin. What? Of course I would not challenge Jimmy's thinking and thankfully, I internalized this disorienting thought. The plan was masterful. I then proceeded to hit a perfect nine-iron to the small knoll of the green near the back where the pin was delicately placed. The weight of the shot coming in at No. 12 green was well-calculated and precise.

A better attack angle turned out to be the reasoning for Jimmy's choice of iron off the tee. Angles . . . this was an important word to absorb since it was repeated and must be considered when playing the course and especially the greens on the Old Course. Why would you want to flirt with the hidden Stroke bunker lingering in the middle of the fairway? Exactly. That is when a caddy is most cherished. He is able to dissect and demystify the course for his player. And you absolutely know that you are not playing anywhere in North America when you see the brownness of the terrain, bunkers that are over your head, and blind shots that confound your brain!

My second shot into the 12th hole was one of the highlighted shots of my round. Alas, my short putt missed, but after looking at this green I was amazed at how fortunate it was for my ball to remain on this plateau. It could have easily rolled 20 feet down the slope. Par was very good with this devious pin positioning.

It was a difficult task to simultaneously enjoy the moment, take in the wonderful sights, play well, and engage in conversations with my fellow competitors and best of friends. We were all ensconced in our own individual golfing worlds trying valiantly to play the best possible round without de-emphasizing the adventure and ride of the Old Course. This balance was precarious and I was holding on for dear life.

To stand 2 over par after 12 holes at St Andrews was beyond my expectations—and playing this well forces you to contemplate the what-ifs. This is a dangerous psychological path to take. If I started thinking too much, then negative vibes of the wheels coming off my game might grab hold of me. Golfers throughout the universe know that these challenging feelings play a role when shooting those special rounds. Keeping it together for 18 holes is a marathon of clutch shots and character putts. If I had a solid back nine then I would forever possess bragging rights that I cracked the 80 barrier on my first attempt. I needed mental strength and intestinal fortitude to hoist me through the last six holes with the Road Hole and wicked bunkers being my last major physical hurdles to win the battle. Please avoid these dastardly things like Tiger accomplished in one of his Open Championship triumphs here. Was that a subtle prayer?

Holes 13, 14, and 15 were played in a blur. Bogey, par, bogey. One memory is of Chief having to hit backwards to escape from the notoriously large and deep Hell Bunker on No. 14. Welcome to Scotland, Mr. Stanton! My second shot into the 16th green was coming from an awkward, downhill lie in the left deep fescue. I hit one of the best shots I could imagine. The ball came off the clubface as though a hand guided it towards the green. It almost made it to the green and left me with a short chip. This would have been too much to ask for such a difficult recovery shot. But what was important was that I hit the shot I visualized. My chip shot was wobbly and I was starting to feel the pressure in my finishing holes. I was leaking some oil (not yet of *Exxon Valdez* quantity) and posted another bogey. Doubtful thoughts were bubbling to the surface. This was no time for uncertainty as the Road Hole beckoned.

Ahhh . . . the 17th hole at the Old Course. Like the 17th hole with the island green at TPC Sawgrass, Florida, the thought of tackling the Road Hole makes golfers quake. These are the kinds of holes that put hair on men's chests (not sure what the equivalent saying is for females). How would you play perhaps the toughest par-4 in the world?

Unorthodox, idiosyncratic and difficult are only a few words I could choose to describe this famous penultimate hole. It is this and much more. Why should blindly hitting over a storage shed of the Old Course Hotel that was formerly a railway shed be different than any other hole you have played? You have to see it to believe it. Television attempts to do justice to this hole but it falls pathetically short of a live experience.

My colleague Scugog, who was also leaking his own version of oil (maybe Shell?) down the stretch with his faulty chip shots and shaky misses, absolutely gunned a shot between the A and the N letters prominently displayed on the shed. The flight pattern was perfect and he broke into a wide grin. We all gladly commended him on a perfect shot—a true character-builder and conversation-starter for his golfing career. He grew some hair. I, on the other hand, voluntarily wimped out. If Bobby Jones could take this route during his British Amateur Championship win in his 1930 Grand Slam year, then I could too. The law of averages spoke to me. I could not shake its rational presence.

Standing on the tee at 4 over par, I thought of my options to salvage a fantastic round without falling prey to the Road Hole's nefarious charms. I conferred strategically with my caddie and asked if there was a bailout position left. Jimmy said there was such a route to take but I did not sense a keen optimism from him for me to play this shot. Hesitation and a doubtful countenance were more like it. After hitting my shot left to avoid the hotel I found out why—gnarly grass snatched my ball, pounded down on it for good measure and said, "Take that, Mr. Bailout!" My next shot was going to have to be one for the ages to advance the ball anywhere near the green. Such a sliver of hope ended abruptly . . .

For one of the first times all day I thrashed at the ball and it did not go where I projected. My crafty shot-making had wavered and my head bowed after the mighty blow. It was a flailed, low-trajectory, worm-burning shot that only travelled a short distance into more deadly fescue. Uh, oh. My utopian dreams were shattered. Golfers sometimes think that when they are in the zone, like I was, they can conquer all obstacles thrown in their paths. But pleasant dreams can turn quickly into dreaded nightmares.

I would not say that panic set in, but I wondered how this hole was going to end for me. Could Jimmy salve my wounded ego? Was I going to be scarred for life if I counted a monstrous number on the Road Hole? Horrible memories of Jean Van de Velde collapsing on the 18th hole at Carnoustie forced themselves into my doubting mind. I began deep breathing exercises as though hyperventilating under a cold shower. "Keep to the mental game plan," I inwardly preached. Talking to oneself is what golfers do in times of stress. Kind of like those irritating blowhards with

Bluetooth earpieces who walk around talking to the wind. What are they really saying to impress you? I only had to impress myself—and quickly!

Jimmy got straight to the point, "Do not go anywhere near that Road Hole bunker, do not. Play the wedge to the 18th fairway to give you a better angle. Then chip back to the pin and see if you can get a one-putt bogey." This was the firm direction and second voice I needed and the guidance was deeply appreciated. Bogey would not be a bad score to post at all. I believe he repeated this to me but I got the picture. The pin was a sucker's pin resting demonically behind this notorious bunker. I consumed and retained his command and, like a computer fed its instructions, I obeyed.

I chipped the ball fairly close to the hole on my fourth shot and barely curled in a ticklish downhill slider for 6 after my initial putt was left wanting. The small muscles in my hands were twitching as I poked it in the side door of the cup. Double bogey on the Road Hole is not an uncommon feat (and not the disaster you might think) so I joined the ranks of thousands of others with slumped shoulders exiting this hole, but with a new appreciation that it could have been higher. Some people would take multiple shots out of the Road Hole bunker and come out shell-shocked after completing this monstrous hole. There was no butchering to the extent of the grand Frenchman Van de Velde's clumsy triple finish (and only after he sank a healthy 10-footer to save the nasty finish from turning into a quad)!

To add further insult to the scrambling double, Chief and I lost the match to the other two after completing this hole. All four of us had played very well today, almost as though it was predetermined. I shook my head, trying to comprehend losing this competition when I'd played over my head. Those shifty sandbaggers.

Too bad I did not get a better glimpse of the road and the wall since I had played my shots on the opposite side of them. I have regrets for not taking the time to examine the signature aspect of the hole. My focus on finishing strongly placed me in a bubble. Bags later told me of his close-up encounter, as he had to hit his fourth shot with a lob wedge by the cart path lining the road. Clunk! The road, of course, is in play if your ball comes to rest on the surface. No free drops, my friends. Your regular rules are thrown out the window at St Andrews. Many players have to invent shots including ricochets. Entertain yourself with this YouTube video clip of Jimenez's shot at the 17th hole during the 2010 Open Championship: http://www.youtube.com/watch?v=pwDVw-EVOkY.

One of the morning players found himself in this awkward predicament and proceeded to scuff one of his brand new Callaway irons while making a seven-iron pitch shot off the pavement. Ping and ouch! I don't know if he saved par or bogey but the Road Hole had provided a permanent nick for his troubles. Stories in the watering hole could be embellished about this badge of courage and perhaps there'd be a shattered wrist to show for his efforts!

As an aside, I later found out that another player in the morning group had what he termed "Two Triumphs at the Road Hole" or what he endearingly nicknamed "The Par and Puke." This sounded interesting and noteworthy so I needed to hear the complete story. The nattily attired participant told me that he bravely drove over the hotel and eventually sank an 8-footer for par. This is a very impressive feat in itself. He famously made it a double victory later in the day when he vomited while running by the 17th hole in his dutiful training for a future marathon. Yes, there is access to do your fitness routine along the confines of this course and no, he did not intend to litter the hallowed grounds of St Andrews with remnants from his fish and chip dinner and copious amounts of Scotch. I am sure he raises a glass of Scotch every year in tribute to this fine accomplishment at the Home of Golf!

Now back to my story after this interlude . . . . The view from the tee blocks on the 18th hole is spectacular. Hotels and other historical buildings sit on the right hand side. Hamilton Hall, the former hotel and student residence and the R&A decorate the rear of the green. This perspective is an oft-photographed shot of St Andrews. I vividly remember watching Chief grossly slice his drive off the Rusacks as though projecting Al Pacino's memorable *Scarface* character and exclaiming, "Say hello to my little friend!" The Precept ball then magically deflected back onto the immense fairway. What a stunning Yoda bounce! The Force was definitely with him. I followed with a more boring shot cranked down the middle. I liked Tom's flair for the dramatic but I wanted to finish with a conventional par.

I had an eight-iron resting in my hand to hit my final 140 yards into the wind. The famous Valley of Sin fronting the green warned me not to land short while the white stakes and the R&A building threatened at the rear. My friend Ron told me that in all the times he has played the 18th hole at the Old Course he has never parred it. The hole transfixed him and he was unable to hit a normal approach shot and two putts in regulation. I understood that feeling as I examined what was left for me.

The hole is straightforward and not very long at approximately 360 yards. It certainly does not bring to mind the difficulties of longer holes like the 18th hole at TPC Sawgrass, Carnoustie, or Pebble Beach. Surrounding history of the 18th trumps the traditional definition of this meaning. Tunnel vision and resolve is required to block out all the other major distractions and succeed with a final ending score of 4. I took one grand look, swivelled my body to soak in a 360-degree appreciation of the hole, and launched my final shot into the green at the Old Course with a crisp hip turn.

The Pro V1 plunked onto the top tier where the pin sat 25 feet away. I paused for a minute to commend myself on my accomplishment. It looked like it was now a given that I would break 80 on my first attempt at these sacred Scottish grounds. My satisfaction was expanding by the second. The march to the green with my caddie walking in front was how it should be. I was Caesar preparing to step on the golden throne.

My birdie putt fell short by only 6 inches to the right. The rapturous thought of a 77, a double hockey stick, crossed my mind while it was on its way. The short tap-in meant 78 scored on the card. Well done, old chap! Dad, I know you see me up there. I battled the mental and physical elements and came out in winning form.

There were handshakes all around with my friends and caddies. The requisite picture was then taken of me as a soloist standing with my peaked hat, cool weather gear, and the R&A building sitting in the background. Beautiful. Too bad we were Verma-pressed to get out of the way for the next group because this was a most significant moment in any golfer's life. This feeling would never be forgotten. Tops on the chart, without a doubt. The fact that I'd played very well added to this exhilaration.

I know what you are now thinking after reading about my round at the Old Course. Didn't he just break his own rule of talking about his golf game? Isn't that the most boring thing in life to have to listen to from fellow golfers? Should I give him the deserved Hand? Do I want to karate chop him in the throat? I thought it was important, in order to frame a real picture of my experience, to provide some details of the course's layout and my shots to match the feelings golfers might go through while playing on these venerable grounds. My goal was to put you in my driver's seat through descriptions and historical context. Please forgive me if you feel this was a transgression by the Commish. Penalize me but don't hold a large grudge. I hope the benefits of my story supersede this deviation from the norm and I will remain a humble servant of this glorious game. Does that work for you?

The celebratory dinner in the main dining hall of the Rusacks took place later that night. Jackets were required and it was the first time all day that the twelve of us were together. The one group that played in the morning dealt with tougher conditions. They had more time to get acquainted with the Scotch, which enabled them to expand on the day's highlights. We exchanged notes and comments regarding the impact that the Old Course had on each respective player. They would be compared with another famous Scottish course we were playing tomorrow and a challenging one at that—Carnasty or what is more commonly known as Carnoustie. Back-to-back classics.

Somehow by the end of the night our large contingent was again split into separate groups. I was feeling no pain from my diverse mixture of alcohol while wandering around St Andrews with Peter, Mike, and Chief. We then ended up in the drinking room at the Rusacks, thinking we could imbibe on draught beer. One small problem though . . . the bar was officially closed. Dash it! Why do the Scots close things down so early? But just when we thought we would have a quick chat downstairs before heading to our hotel rooms to end this memorable day, we had a stroke of luck.

A couple of older and bored Englishmen stood in the same room and they looked like they needed inspiring company. We were the serendipitous solution. One was a quiet, diminutive man (Cliff) and the other was a larger-than-life version (I think his name was Nigel). Cliff reminded me of the famously nearsighted Mr. Magoo—a great cartoon character from television in the middle of the last century. Except Cliff had glasses to see what the heck he was doing at St Andrews. I almost envisioned this 5-foot distinguished gentleman pulling out a pipe. A passing thought came to me, of finding one of those real British top hats and plonking it on his balding head so he could tip it in response. Nigel was the boisterous and extroverted one. This charismatic and larger man flapped his arms and had a lot to say. I of course, wanted to fan the flames. Liquor had obviously found a willing place in the big guy's system. They were celebrating their English public school anniversary in great form and I needed to know more about these Limeys.

Nigel became my chum and we conversed about life, public schools in England, colonialism, and most importantly, we agreed on the details of "The Wave-Off." I view it as The Hand's British cousin. The gesture is implemented when someone is nagging or bothering you (maybe also Verma-pressing?) and you really want to say buzz off or !%#@! All you do is raise your arm and hand over your head and, if you are right-handed, dismissively move your hand rapidly from left to right while muttering an incoherent and not-so-nice comment or gentle expletive. We practiced it throughout the night like only two dummies would, with Dr. Scotch, Dr. Pint, and Dr. Cabernet controlling the marionette strings. Ben Hogan would have been proud of our work ethic in perfecting our art. Another stupid thing to do but there you are!

We obviously hit it off with them and all of a sudden draught beer started flowing down our throats even though the bar was supposedly kaput. How did that happen? This liquid courage was obtained illegally and I have been advised by my lawyer to plead the Fifth if asked how this was obtained. The code is invoked. What happens if the lawyer is one and the same? A quandary to tackle, no doubt. We went late into the night with our shared stories and I had a superb time. Several other public school classmates filtered into the room to join our entourage. Luckily we were playing in the afternoon the following day or there would be hellmers to pay. Do they have Gatorade for electrolyte enhancement and chocolate milk for hangover containment at the Rusacks? I fear not.

Carnoustie (probably the toughest course that I have played) would be a 2 ½-hour drive from St Andrews. Advil would definitely be in high demand. Afternoon tee-off times were good staff work on our part because, well, hangovers need time to heal.

In the morning before we left, we budgeted time to do two important things that we could handle in such a state:

1. Shoot the *Chariots of Verma* video.
2. Play the Himalayas.

The video was an obsession for one of our participants, Hugh, who also dressed in colourful and distinguished-looking plus fours for the round at the Old Course. I liked his enthusiastic idea to enhance our experience at St Andrews. The video's thrust would clash brilliantly with the class he showed while wearing his traditional wardrobe. He thought shooting twelve underwear-clad men running in slow motion across the West Sands beach would be a hoot.

There was an objective of course, for this request. This happens to be the same stretch of beach on which the 1981 Academy Award-winning picture *Chariots of Fire* was filmed so dramatically. The beautiful sights of St Andrews are clearly presented at the beginning of this film and Hugh thought the Verma Cuppers would be worthy actors in an amateurish and updated version. Let us provide our irreplaceable rendition and Canadian tribute to our British heritage on this segment of the movie for the YouTube generation.

Timing was vital. Shooting our future Academy Award-winning short film before playing the round at the Old Course would have been dangerous and almost suicidal. What would have happened if we got banished from the premises due to indecent exposure? The British tabloids would have had a field day on this invasion of a cherished site. The *Daily Mirror* would have screamed, "Damned Colonials insult not only all Scots but also all others who wear Jockey underwear!" So, we planned accordingly and shot it the day afterwards and what a thrill it was!

After we were positioned a distance away from the course, the boys pulled off their clothes in unison to expose skin of fine quality. Right away, we encountered the tough part. Who was going to be the fortunate man (a woman somehow would not fit the bill for obvious reasons) to shoot this film since all of us wanted to be participants and potentially future actors? Squinting our eyes and peering down the beach, we picked out two lonely figures. A strapping middle-aged man was walking his friendly dog. He walked towards our group of ruffians and I am sure he was mumbling to himself, what the $#@&??!!! Multiple and confusing questions must have machine-gunned into his brain. His stride became more tentative but he was apparently a gamer since he continued his stroll toward us.

Once he encountered this kooky group, he was surrounded by twelve enthusiastic smiles as the situation was quickly explained to him. This man's best friend had an inquiring mind so he convinced his master with a wag of his tail not to beat a hasty retreat. The man didn't look elated with this proposition, however, he would do it based on the dog's recommendation. I think he was relieved to hear our Canuck accents because no sane Scot would want to desecrate St Andrews in this manner by trying something so inane and stupid. A traitor to his own people never, but to these guys, well . . .

The Scotsman grasped this weighty torch of responsibility and positioned the camera to shoot the brief commercial for ugly underwear performers. To our right, we nervously caught some individuals craning their necks at us as they ambled down the nearby bridge/walkway structure by the first hole of the Old Course. These vexed ones would have needed binoculars if they wanted a true sense of our superlative performance. But I am sure their fuzzy sightlines would have given them ample evidence to deduce that this was déclassé. We knew we had to make this happen swiftly before irritated Scottish police officers clubbed each of us, wielding those rock-hard batons. No side arms necessary, Sirs. Those clubs do a nasty job all by their lonesome.

We proudly re-enacted the slow motion run from the original movie except we kept to the dry sand. Those thrashing waves looked nasty. The white Jockey-type t-shirts from the movie were replaced with both rippling and sagging muscles of the topless lads. We went regimental in our own form. Our bright white farmer-tanned arms and legs moved in suspended time and we brilliantly executed our sophisticated plan. The star of the show, the Brad Pitt so to speak, was our friend Peter who carried himself flashily with black socks, black shoes, and longer white underwear. The contrasting colours ensured that he would become the feature character on YouTube. You braggart, you!

After we completed our mission, the group scrambled to dress ourselves and again look like normal pedestrians. Damage had been contained. We all had a great laugh and looked forward to viewing the 1 minute and 27 second final product on YouTube upon our return to Canada. Just type in *Chariots of Verma* in the search area in YouTube or click on this YouTube link and enjoy a chuckle:

http://www.youtube.com/watch?v=ZpCUr9RYJUI. And you can view this opening YouTube clip of *Chariots of Fire* to compare. Which one is the greater of the two? Note that, at the end of this one, the runners leap over the gate on to the 1st hole of the Old Course with the Royal and Ancient building in the background. Fantastic! http://www.youtube.com/watch?v=L-7Vu7cqB20&p=83A4190C0E1A5F6E&playnext=1&index=43. Thank you, Hugh, for a job well done. It was worth catching a cold for the effort.

Our next event that morning was going to be less controversial. We returned to the Rusacks Hotel to shake off the sand and gather our putters and golf balls so we could play the Himalayas. The climbing was not going to involve towering mountains but mounds of twists and turns on a unique putting green. No need for windmills or cheeky gadgets to test your putting skill.

The Himalayas is officially called the Ladies' Putting Green and it is a private one run by the St Andrews Ladies' Putting Club. There are approximately 250 lady members but it is open for public use from April to September. Pay your 1-2 pounds entrance fee and you enjoy a very cool experience unlike any others you have played.

The 18-hole fun track sits near the second tee of the Old Course. The holes have contours and they all have different winding approaches to the hole. This is not your standard putting green or mini-golf course. The greens roll quite nicely. Remember, ladies, high heels are not allowed for those who want to trundle in this manner!

This visit was a special treat and our three foursomes had some competitions for pound bets. I think I reached into my pocket early with the boys and forked over plentifully. My jab stroke was working wonderfully for my competitors. The 45-minute interval passed briskly with great fun. The Verma Cuppers honed their putting skills on this irregular course before going on to challenge Carnoustie's devious greens later in the day. Time to go, sadly.

The last day at St Andrews was a tough one for me. As you can see in our time spent at this institution of golf, many activities and sideshows were packed in to make it a special visit. The second half of our Scottish trip was going to take place but a piece of me was left here. I could not have asked for anything better. Weather had cooperated to allow us to see the key landmarks. Shooting my 78 at the Old Course satiated my golfing desire to tame this great lady. I did it with the utmost respect. The visit to the St Andrews Golf Club, sharing lively stories at the Dunvegan and Rusacks Hotels, and playing an 18-hole putting green jewel like the Himalayas completed the story of the "Auld Grey Toon."

Six hundred years old. Seven double greens. Bunkers called Hell, Spectacles, Beardies, and Coffins. An endearing couple of humps on No. 15 called Miss Grainger's bosoms. The option of launching over a hotel's shed to put the ball in play at the Road Hole. Putting from 40 yards off the greens. Slow-motion running on the beach. Saluting the venerable R&A and its rules. I could mention many more but these are all significant recollections.

You may leave the confines of this spectacular place to return to your home but the spirit of the Home of Golf will ride along with you. Repeat this mantra after me: "I have to play the Old Course at St Andrews if I truly want to comprehend the meaning and history of golf." Tradition needs to be part of your golfing DNA. Couple this history with your expensive Nike and Ping technology. There is a reason why Jack and Tiger list the Old Course at St Andrews and Pebble Beach as their favourite golf courses to play in the world. All golfing roads lead to Rome er, well, actually to St Andrews. Book your flight and then cue the bagpipes. Seamus, Angus, and the lassies (and deep-fried Mars bars) are waiting for your arrival. No excuses!

HOLE NO. 7, PAR 4. DO YOU CALM YOURSELF OR HEAVE IT?

The "whap-whap" helicopter sound of a club, rotating end over end was not an unfamiliar one while I was a teenager. But it still startled me. My keen instincts warned me to cover my noggin with my arms and search for an imaginary helmet, just in case. Lee, our group's esteemed colleague and great player, had just tossed another small-headed Wilson driver into the mammoth tree lurking just off to the left side of the 17th tee. The leaves and branches gobbled it up as though the club was a keeper. They cheerfully welcomed this addition to their brood. The wooden club would be a great complement to the cardinal's nest and the furry creatures that inhabited this home. Unfortunately for this welcoming tree, my playing partner thought otherwise.

So, imaginatively and strategically, he grabbed a club not from his bag but from the third player we had in our group. Why ruin your own club when another boy's will do? Before the startled young comrade figured out what was going on, the culprit flailed a five-iron into the tree.

The javelin pierced the air and to no avail. This desperate first heave failed. However, he was not to be put off with this limp initial effort. After a second club was chucked with more authority and precision, he succeeded in achieving his selfish goal. The driver fell to the ground with a clunk. Unhurt but smarting a little bit. Impressively, but maybe not surprisingly, the other guy's iron remained as a replacement in the tree.

The tree lovingly cuddled its newest visitor and it was not going to allow us to get off scot-free after having procured such a present. The incredulous player who found himself now held hostage to this new and unhappy situation wondered what Lee would do about it. Certainly he would apologize and thank him for the use of the weapon to free his slave!

No chance. Lee's planned action was to hurriedly scamper down the fairway so he could find his ball resting quietly in the right ewok.

He didn't care that he contributed to another man's misery. Par was his mission after a less-than-optimum drive. Wow, this scenario turned out to be a majestic performance by the selfish one replete with actions that were certainly brazen. Are you a calm person or do you like to give the club the old heave-ho like Lee?

Flaring tempers during golf games are certainly common for many players. To many, volcanic episodes are part of their DNA. In fact, Steve Pate was nicknamed Volcano because of his many eruptions while plying his trade on the PGA Tour for many years. There was also "Terrible" Tommy Bolt and Tom "Towering Inferno" Weiskopf who contributed to this folklore. But I think Tiger's ongoing swearing and club pounding theatrics keeps the issue of tempers on the golf course as a front-burner topic. He has been fined repeatedly but the PGA tour does not publicly post the amounts. Who, as a television viewer, can miss his blatant antics? Is he disrespecting the game with these negative performances? I believe Tiger is.

Some argue that it is Tiger's incredibly competitive nature that causes him to lose control of his emotions and sometimes spew vitriol. But shouldn't he be able to utilize those Buddhist ideals that he treasures from his mother's Thai influence to instil certain tranquility in his internal being? Does he have the capability to turn on different switches at will? Similar to athletes in other sports who enter their field, arena, court, etc. and create a game face and attitude, Tiger and other golfers with volatile tempers morph into alternate beings.

Perhaps this could be the case; however I am not convinced that you have to produce tirades to prove you are a competitor. Nicklaus, Player, and Watson were, or are, highly competitive and they upheld the guidelines of respect. Tom Watson and others believe Tiger needs to behave more appropriately for spectators and fans like other legends of the game have done throughout the years. In fact, Mr. Watson even sent Tiger a letter outlining his concerns. From my perspective, I feel Tiger's actions are unprofessional, immature, and unsportsmanlike.

Now, Bobby Jones and Jack Nicklaus had their own demon struggles with their fury early in their careers. The great amateur famously picked up his ball and stormed off the 11th green at the Old Course during the third round of the 1921 Open Championship when he was 19 years old. He admits this immature deed was his largest regret in his golfing life. Mr. Jones corrected his future behaviour and was soon loved by the

Scots. Jack's turning point was when his temper got the best of him after hitting a shot in the bunker. He flung his club in disgust and his father, Charlie, promptly marched up to him and told him in no uncertain terms that if he threw another club, then he would not play the game again. This reprimand from his beloved father gained his rapt attention. Jack admitted that such criticism of his distasteful antics went beyond just temper but to the bare essentials of upholding the integrity, humility and sportsmanship of the game. Like Jones, his conduct on the golf course changed dramatically and they became class acts for the duration of their respective careers.

I certainly have tossed and slammed clubs, especially when I was younger, so I am not without fault. This brutal nonsense has been pretty much curtailed. My golf perfection gene was sensitive way back when I was scoring just over par. Any mis-hit Titleist DT or Spalding Kro-Flite would send an electrical charge throughout my system and it screamed for a reaction. So I didn't disappoint. I hurled insults or I violently hammered clubs into the immaculately groomed fairways. Divots flew and club imprints proliferated. My playing partners and family members shook their heads in disgust over this dreadful display. I still experience this burning sensation or "grind," now that I'm middle-aged, but it is like I have a suppressor to filter out the pain of wayward shots.

No longer are my actions composed of beating a club into the turf with full brute force. I see golf in a different light and my new world has replaced this behaviour with subtler substitutes like "Darn, I should have been smarter in not finding that deep bunker." Score is not the main driver. I play more for fun; but I won't kid you, I still like to compete. It is just that I think of my father and what he emphasized to me—see the game as being greater than yourself and respect the members in your playing group. Don't disgrace the spirit of the game with pitiful and abhorrent behaviour. Sure I can get worked up on the course. However, I try to maintain the perspective that it is a game, a wonderful retreat from outside worldly pressures. Why create more self-induced stress when this wonderful environment should be my oasis?

What coping mechanisms do professional golfers use to prevent outbursts of temper? Many do not consider themselves at fault. Some blame the hole. Others believe particles on the green diverted the ball from its path. I have heard strong Christian beliefs and values mentioned as being cushions to a rising temper. Caddies can provide the necessary soothing words to get their lad back on track. Top pros seem to buckle down and get the job done when errant shots or missed 3-footers inevitably occur. There is a certain steely confidence that they exude as they block out the negative vibes with positive emotional and visual cues. Mental strength is integral and often sports psychologists are involved to help players. These are the weapons to counteract the devils.

Let's categorize bad behaviour and temper problems into minor, major, and game misconducts. I think using football and hockey vernacular is equally applicable to golf. These transgressions can be verbal, psychological, or physical.

We all know those things that irritate us about playing partners when they go off the rails. There are the explosions that can really bother us and, in fact, cause us not to want to play with certain players. Nothing is worse than having to cringe and roll your eyes in the company of an ill-tempered golfer. Does temper on the golf course translate to this same behaviour at home and in the office? This might be interpreted as a character flaw.

A scorecard tally could be added up at the end to determine whether the temper transgressors (I think this term has poetic resonance) should be shipped to a self-imposed penalty box or exiled to a distant tennis court. Two points for minor infractions, 5 points for major infractions, and 10 points for a game misconduct. Let's list some for you . . .

Minors

- A short flick or twirl of your club to the side.
- Stomping your foot on the green. Although if there is clear damage caused by this action, then move it to the major category.
- A quick Level 1 swearword or phrase that your group can clearly hear.
- Flailing your sand wedge or pounding your club into the sand. At least the sand can be replaced with a good rake job.
- Sulking and walking petulantly ahead of the group because you are angry.
- Whining and droning on incessantly about the problems of one's game. No one cares and no one wants to play with such a miserable finklenut.
- Sarcastic and/or mean-spirited comments that are directed at you like psychological darts because that person is playing badly.

- Slamming flags into the hole. If the culprit takes a chunk out of the perimeter of the hole then move this action up to a major.
- Silence for long periods of time because of self-pity or anger.
- Roughly firing clubs into bag.

Majors

- Screaming Level 1 profanities.
- Scooping balls out of the cup with your putter head when disgusted.
- Taking a huge pelt on your shot and angrily walking away without replacing it.
- Intentionally not raking the sand trap because you are seething.
- Smashing a club into the side of the bag—especially two-handers.
- Teeing off first after having a bad hole with total disregard for honours with your playing partners.
- Intentionally flailing at bushes or trees with your club following your shot. Don't damage the course!

Game Misconducts

- Purposely throwing clubs into a pond or lake. This may seem funny in a *Caddyshack* or YouTube kind of way but there is no place for this. Switch to tennis or another game if you actually perform this move. Leave the scuba gear at home.
- Slamming the club into a tee area so that the driver's brand name is a permanent fixture in the grass. I don't like to see indentations.
- Taking a divot out of the green after a missed putt. Hmmmmm . . . I think this ranks right up there as a criminal offense!
- Throwing club into trees. See Lee's example at the beginning of this piece.
- Entrenching a club in the ground, making it a standard-bearer for all to see.
- Destruction of golf property like yardage signs, benches, and tee markers.
- Breaking of clubs—whether over bended knee or slamming them.

- Brandishing a club and chasing after a fellow member to inflict pain because of a disparaging remark made by this person.

One of the solutions our playing group has used over the years is to allow fellow players to have a 30-second or 5-minute "grind" period, depending on the anger severity. Everyone has that duck hook, weak-assed Dan Blocker, limp 3-footer, or skullmeister shot in a round that infuriates one's golfing psyche. But instead of unleashing the fury, individuals should have some official outlet or process to have some time away and cool down. Is it the adult timeout? Perhaps it is; at any rate, the grind period works pretty well.

What is important is that once you've had this time to yourself where everyone leaves you alone and it exits your system, then you have to re-integrate into civilization and return to pleasant behaviour. Talk to the lads. Smile and redeem yourself with a great shot next time you strike the ball. Any deviance should be countered by a firm warning from group members demanding that you get back on track. Or, the penalty could be that you will be ostracized from the group moving forward. Go with the other hotheads then!

Controlling your temper and performing admirable behaviour or class goes hand-in-hand with showing respect and integrity for the game of golf. Taming these beasts on the training ground of the golf course builds character and helps you to manage these emotions at home and in the business environment.

I once had to have a quick and direct chat with a competitor before we teed off in the final group of the club championships. He had quite the unenviable reputation for launching clubs and hurling epithets so I thought I would tell him in no uncertain terms that I would not accept this behaviour. No one else had bothered to voluntarily take up the mantle so I thought I would be the bold bearer of this frank news. He seemed to be tolerable that round. To this day I feel I did the right thing and others still talk about this situation. A badge of honour . . .

So, just before you spin out of control, remember that your club should not share space in the tree with animals and birds. Be empathetic and place yourself in the shoes of your mates and legendary golfers. Ask this important question: "Would you be happy to hear the dangerous 'whap-whap' sound of the hurled $500 Calloway driver whizzing by your ear?" Of course not. Place the club back in your bag gently and get back to hitting that beautiful cut shot into the green. Initiate an animated discussion about movies or other stimulating subjects with your playing partners. Magnificent to be here at this beautiful course with all you enjoyable chaps!

Hole No. 8, Par 3. Has disrespect infected our wonderful game?

The mandatory electric or gas cart, cell phone use on the course, and the young lads wearing ball caps backwards are all signs of the apocalypse. Let's call this triumvirate of pet peeves *The Lion, the Witch and the Wardrobe* (I hope C.S. Lewis is okay with me lifting his words). A Pandora's Box of disrespect may have been opened on golf courses across North America but I hold out hope that a sort of uneasy truce can be constructed between holders of the "respect" flame and others who have breached this code.

I long for the return to the more gentle golf past and its traditions. Please do not mistake me as a Don Quixote character tilting at imaginary windmills. The enemies of reverence are very, very real. Let's tackle the sinners—the Lion, the Witch, and the Wardrobe.

Lion

This dominant animal is King of the Jungle at many public golf courses. I can pay good money to play but by gosh, if I want to walk I have to ride. Wha-a-a-t? Forcing a golfer to ride or pay for a cart is sacrilege. We live in a sophisticated world full of abundant choice and options—go to your local bookstore and experience the incredible variety of magazines and books on offer. I believe there is now a magazine title that would interest left-handed freaks who listen to Slipknot music at 11:30pm on Friday nights. I am being facetious of course, but choice is what our generation expects and demands.

The tremendous revenue generator for the pro shop and the perceived improvement in speed of play are the key drivers for this mandatory curse. Some golf course managers and architects try to convince the golfing public that their designs are too difficult to walk. However, cart path-only rules and clubs forgotten in bags can help neutralize the advantages of time savings. I also happen to think it is hogwash that certain courses cannot be walked. Talk to the older gentlemen who walk the undulating links courses in Great Britain during rainstorms and howling wind conditions and they will set you straight.

Golf should be walked if your health allows for it. Golf *needs* to be walked to fully engage all of our senses. It you have the privilege to play in Scotland, England or Ireland, you will know what I mean. In the majority of cases, no riding carts are visible to ruin the beautiful sights of golden gorse and fescue, mammoth double greens, and wandering sheep feasting on brown grass. Tranquility is essential to our cherished game and nothing shatters this scenario worse than hearing the reverse beeping of a gas cart.

Flying down the cart path while talking about last weekend's drunken festivities and then slamming on the brakes after passing the ball by 20.2 yards is not true golf. Not at least in the spirit of the way the game should be played and enjoyed. It is really pseudo-golf. When do you have time to reflect on your shot, to feel the wind direction, to soak up the sights of the present while riding in these beasts? You don't. In short, this method of golf lacks the qualities that make golf magnificent and special. Take a trolley, hire a caddie, or hoist your clubs over your shoulder if you can—and pro shops, please give us the option to walk.

Witch

Sometimes I wish I could sweep away all cell phone and other electronic devices, or strap the whole lot of them along a very lo-o-o-n-n-g witch's broomstick and launch it into outer space so I could never see or hear them on a golf course again. Yes, there are certain people who should have them on their person for minimal or emergency use, but we have gone overboard. These tools are now ubiquitous and here to stay. If they are truly needed, at least have them hidden and only use when absolutely necessary. Honestly, watching a strutting peacock of a person on the fairway chatting about nonsense or of a perceived important topic while you wait on the tee to hit is infuriating. Perhaps a sizzling 250-yard drive from your TaylorMade Burner driver right in to the yakker's pumpkin will give you the proper revenge. Unfortunately your luck would have it that he would have time to call 9-1-1 and get you arrested for obvious intent to cause bodily harm. At least your buddies would have given you enthusiastic high-fives before the Man in Blue ushered you off the 16th green . . .

Quiet escape and diversion from the world of work and family responsibilities should be key reasons for playing golf. Portable devices are bothersome tethers to these environments. All I ask is to use judgment and respect the sanctity of this game and don't use them to chat on the course unless it is necessary or an emergency. And, your compatriots will appreciate your consideration in respecting their time. You don't want to find yourself in a position that you will have to pay friends to play with you because of your cell phone syndrome!

Wardrobe

The non-tucked-in polo shirt, cargo shorts with eighteen pockets that hang to the knees, and the ever-present backward-worn University of Texas Longhorn cap or others of that ilk are golf wardrobe malfunctions. This infestation of a new golfer/duder look needs to be countered. Golf courses are not skateboarding tracks or Californian-type surfer areas. Tuck in the shirt please, purchase nice shorts, and wear that cap properly. Respect the game's dress code and it would be much appreciated if golfers take off their hats in the 19th hole or any buildings for that matter. My father would be very proud of me as I uphold this very important message: "No headgear in the mess hall or the Regimental Sergeant Major with the waxed moustache will sock you in the mouth!" If you dare do this in England, Scotland, or Ireland, you will be spoken to in a very curt manner. Evil eyes from the locals will penetrate your skull. It is just not done. Your Guinness stout may not be so tasty after the remarks you hear . . .

Golf is a class game and one where integrity is imperative. It has a reputation for residing on a higher plane than other sports and games. Players will call penalties on themselves when no one else can see these infractions. Do you think an NFL offensive lineman will admit to the referee that he deviously hooked the front of the shirt of a defensive tackle to prevent a quarterback sack? You can answer this question with a resounding "No."

Unfortunately, I believe golf's sterling reputation has slipped in the last few years. Golfers need to strive to return the game to its rightful position at the top of the pedestal. Abiding by the rules, dressing the part, and using proper etiquette should be in order. If certain dress codes and other rules are posted on club websites for golfers to follow, then enforcement of them should be obligatory. Sometimes we forget about doing things the

106

right way and for the greater good because we are grinding over a double bogey. Don't forget that the game is greater than you are!

And cheers to all of you who will now respect the game with greater intensity. Pro shops: Please provide us with a choice to ride carts or walk. Businessmen and self-important people: Please hesitate before answering that needless phone call. Young bucks and adults: Please dress the tasteful way on the course that would make your Mom proud. Golf has higher standards than other sports and games, so please help contribute to this winning tradition.

Hole No. 9, Par 4. Is Jack a better golfer than Tiger?

When they were amateurs? When they were professionals? Based on pure numbers or in combination with other intangibles? Can you compare different eras? I know, I know: many questions but I am the question man, remember? This Tiger versus Jack question will certainly be one to stir passionate thoughts and opinions from amateurs, pundits, professionals, and other elements of society. Consider also: What is the definition of "better"? With Tiger's reputation and brand now in tatters because of his highly public transgressions and poor quality of golf compared to his lofty standards, will people's opinion now be tainted in crowning him the better golfer of the two? The mid-western Mr. Nicklaus has avoided the negative glare of gossip—unlike his younger Californian heir apparent. I want to reiterate that my question revolves around the better player not who is better for the game, who is more respectful, who is a nicer person, or who is the better ambassador. This is an important distinction because I think the answer could be quite different if you linked all these components together in an analysis.

Interested parties want to put a simple tag, a metric or number as a tangible way in identifying the meaning of best or better. Is there such a formula? One only has to read the myriad blogs and other articles on this subject to see that there is a divergence of opinion on how to compare great golfers. The "Hawk" Ben Hogan, the greatest amateur Bobby Jones, and fantastic golfers like Byron Nelson, Sam Snead, Gary Player, Tom Watson, and Arnold Palmer can be considered in this category. However, they seem to be shunted aside compared to the Big 2, since winning professional major championships is the overwhelming choice as the most popular measuring stick. Is it fair to judge by looking at it from this perspective?

Tiger has always proclaimed that winning 18 professional major championships (and then surpassing this number) is his most important and desired goal in golf. This brilliant golfer repeatedly emphasizes that he schedules his year around major championships so he can win them. Second place never enters the equation for Tiger, although his post-hydrant crashing has tempered this high standard. Other tournaments wait and pray for his participation but he has been adamant about focusing on playing courses like St Andrews, Pebble Beach and Augusta National of the majors' world. Who are we to complain when Tiger sets his own bar revolving around winning majors? And Jack certainly is a proud major champion record holder and he has no interest or incentive to lessen the importance of his great achievement. An important note is that each of them admits that the other is the greatest golfer. They too, have their own way of determining what their individual definition is with regard to greatest, best, or better. Such mutual respect is admirable. I, on the other hand, have my own thoughts and they differ from these two fine gentlemen's. Winning professional major championships should be in the top 3 or 5 criteria at least, but by no means should it be the only one.

I am not convinced you can put all these criteria in a blender, crank the machine, and see it spit out a synthesized answer. But as my Grade 13 English teacher drilled into me while studying the Hegelian dialectic, "the true is the whole." Thinking about all of these criteria should help you determine your own victor of this "better or best" label.

My analysis is broken down into two distinct and different categories so we can judge. CEOs, accountants, statisticians and other number geeks will first want to examine the Facts category. Liberal Arts types, subjective seekers, and those who like to slant towards softer analysis will put more weight in the Interpretative category. Both categories must be considered to give this argument true value. There are many other ways to compare these two titans but I feel there is enough evidence in what I will present that can help readers form their own reasoned and educated opinion. I have also been fortunate to watch both of these players on television and have my own sense of their impact on fans and the golfing world.

Facts Category

Major Professional Championship Wins. Jack Nicklaus has won 18. This includes 6 Masters, 4 U.S. Opens, 3 Open Championships, and 5 PGA Championships. He won in the 1960s, 1970s, and 1980s. Tiger Woods has won 14 as of the end of 2011. This includes 4 Masters, 3 U.S.

Opens, 3 Open Championships, and 4 PGA Championships. Tiger has won in the 1990s and 2000s.

U.S. Amateur Championship Wins. Jack has won two. Tiger has won three consecutively (the only player to do so). Remember that the U.S. Amateur was once regarded as a major before professional golf became popular. Some people feel the U.S. Amateur should still be counted as a major championship. I would also like to note that Bobby Jones won five U.S. Amateur Championships, and consequently, he can be positioned in a class by himself.

U.S. Junior Amateur Championships. Tiger won this championship three consecutive times. He is the only player to win it more than once. Since you are limited by age restrictions and you compete against the best in the field, this is a very difficult and special one to win. Jack's best finish in the U.S. Junior Amateur Championship was in 1956 when he reached the semi-finals.

Grand Slams/Tiger Slams/Career Slams. Bobby Jones is the only player to have won the Grand Slam. This young 28-year-old then promptly retired at the top of his game. His phenomenal success was achieved back in the day when the Grand Slam comprised the U.S. Open, the U.S. Amateur, The Open Championship and the British Amateur. Tiger did not win the Grand Slam all in the same calendar year but he did the next best thing (some might argue that it was even more impressive, since he carried on his scintillating play into the following year) by winning what became known as the "Tiger Slam." This version of the Slam represented holding all four major championships simultaneously and I feel this absolutely ranks as one of sport's, not just golf's, greatest achievements. How to compare? This should be considered in the same vein as Joe DiMaggio's phenomenal 56-consecutive-game hitting streak. Only Tiger and Hogan have won three professional major championships in one season. Jack never won the Grand Slam. His best year was holding two majors. Both Tiger and Jack have three Career Slams by winning each of the four majors at least three times.

Runner-up finishes in Majors. Jack finished second place a very impressive 19 times. Tiger has 5 second-place finishes as of the end of 2011. Runner-up finishes can be interpreted in a negative or positive way—the player lacked closing skills to win the trophies or he was in the hunt more often to win additional majors. I believe the latter is the preferable consideration. Also, great players always thrive on being in contention on Sunday afternoon. It is a testament to Jack's dogged determination and talent that he lurked on the precipice of winning even more major championships. Competitors knew he was breathing down their necks and only excellent play would clinch a championship. Collapse was not in Jack's cards. Tiger wins his majors when he is leading after 54 holes.

Winning Margins in Professional Majors. Jack's best winning margins were by 9 strokes at the 1965 Masters and 7 strokes at the 1980 PGA Championship. Tiger's best winning margins were by 15 strokes at Pebble Beach in the 2000 U.S. Open (the largest margin of win in a major since 1862), 12 strokes at the 1997 Masters and by 8 strokes in the 2000 Open Championship at St Andrews.

The Fifth Major. The Player's Championship played at TPC Sawgrass in Ponte Vedra, Florida is unofficially seen as the fifth major. This course is a magnificent test. Nicklaus has won it three times. Woods has won it once.

PGA Victories. Jack has won 73 PGA tournaments. Tiger has won 71 and counting. Sam Snead holds the record with 82 total professional victories. You don't think Tiger will surpass this?

Special Note: So, if you wanted to combine U.S. Junior Amateur Championships, U.S. Amateur Championships and Professional Major Championships then the scoreboard would read: Tiger-20 and Jack-20.

Interpretative Category

Is it more impressive for a young buck to win the Masters as a 21-year-old like Tiger accomplished in 1997 or when Jack did it in 1986 as a 46-year-old?

In 2008, Tiger played golf for 10 months with a torn ligament in his left knee and suffered a stress fracture in the tibia on his left leg after the Masters. He then proceeded to win the 2008 U.S. Open Championship over Rocco Mediate. I don't know about you readers but I find this feat to be incredible and one for the ages. He did it on pure guts, skill and confidence along with what I am sure was plenty of pain. It was simply remarkable to see Tiger suck it up and get the job done. Tiger even had to play the extra 18-hole playoff round plus one hole on this extremely painful leg. That totals 91 holes WALKING AND PUTTING PRESSURE ON THE TORN KNEE AND BROKEN LEG WHILE HITTING his stellar shots. My, I find this one hard to push aside. Could anyone else but

Tiger Woods achieve this feat through absolute will and belief in winning a major championship? Tiger holds this win as a very special one in his (and my) memory vault.

Competition during the respective eras must also be considered. Jack's top competition included Player (9 majors), Watson (8 majors), Palmer (7 majors), Trevino (6 majors), Ballesteros (5 majors), and Floyd (4 majors). Tiger's top competition includes Mickelson (5 majors), Singh (3 majors), Harrington (3 majors), and Els (3 majors). Are there more international and overall better players giving Tiger a run? Did Jack have a tougher time winning because of the higher grade of competition at the upper tier of the tour? Look at the number of majors won by others to give you a perspective. And remember that Jack finished in second place 19 times so he was pushing these competitors to the end . . .

Do you think competitors are more intimidated by Tiger than those who played against Jack?

Are there bigger galleries and more fans now watching Tiger than there were in Jack's days? Does the popularity of Tiger or Jack play a role in your decision?

Are you impressed with how Jack was able to win majors over a long duration in the 1960s, 1970s, and 1980s (as well as subsequent majors in Senior events)? Jack is done now, but Tiger still has several years to compete in majors and other important tournaments.

Is it easier to win tournaments when you are married with children, as a single (or acting as though you are single) or divorced? Jack has five children and Tiger has two. Jack was known for having a strong family man reputation.

Would Jack have won more if he had used better equipment? Did the small-headed persimmon woods and non-square-grooved irons make it harder for him to hit accurate shots? He was a breed apart from his contemporaries in the same way that Tiger is/was when he was at the top of his game. In Jack's era, skill probably played a bigger part than technology in the winning of championships.

Does widespread Internet exposure and the cult of Tiger's personality make him seem a better golfer or could it work against him now that his personal life has been exposed in a different and negative light?

What about mental toughness? Both have gained a reputation as fierce competitors in this area. Which player would you rather have on your team to hit the clutch shot under pressure?

How about etiquette, respect and integrity for the grand old game? Do the theatrics on the course affect your judgment as to who is a better golfer? I never saw Jack slam a club or use the F-bomb on screen, but Tiger has repeatedly done this. Tom Watson has been very clear about his views on Tiger's poor behaviour on the course and how he lacks respect for the game that players before him have displayed. To me, this eight-time major champion (and almost an amazing ninth at Turnberry in 2009!) has great credibility in making these comments. Watson certainly played enough with Jack to know the class the Golden Bear showed on the course.

Money earnings and endorsements should be irrelevant. The golfers played in two different generations.

Did Jack play more for the love and respect of the game? Does Tiger play for his sponsors (although less in number now) and to win major championships so he can surpass the Golden Bear's records?

How does each of these men treat their fellow players and young amateur and professional players? Do they pass on wisdom to make them better or hoard it to themselves? In short, how has each given back to the game?

How does each player treat the media and fans? Jack seemed to respect both of these groups but Tiger has often been dismissive.

Does it influence your opinion based upon whether you like the person as a human? I think this has a natural and important effect on a person's ability to judge.

Who do important commentators and media scribes think is better?

Who do the players of both generations choose in this debate?

How much television coverage did Jack receive compared to Tiger? Television broadcasters seem to have a sometimes overindulgent love fest with Tiger and will saturate viewers with coverage of his shots at the expense of showing us other noteworthy players. But then, watchers love to see this golfing genius at work. Television ratings skyrocket when he is in contention or even if he enters a tournament.

What is their match play reputation in Ryder Cup and other international competitions? Jack possesses a very good record while Tiger's results are mediocre overall. But don't discount the remarkable match play victories by Tiger in the U.S. Junior and U.S. Amateur Championships while playing this format.

Have major swing changes cost Tiger chances to win more major championships or have they actually made it easier for him to win them in the long run?

How about the repetitive execution of making amazing shots under intense pressure to win tournaments? Chills still ripple up my spine when I think of the Golden Bear winning the 1986 Masters at the ripe old age of 46. I am 48 years old myself and find it hard to comprehend that he could have beaten Tom Kite, Greg Norman, and Seve Ballesteros in their primes, as well as other young bucks who were gunning for him. That long birdie dunk on No. 10, birdie on 11, birdie on 13, eagle on 15, then birdie on 16 and 17 were extremely impressive. What a last major it was for Nicklaus to win, with huge roars at Augusta that may never again be duplicated.

Now to counter this memory of Jack's exploits at Augusta National: I can think of two shots from Tiger that make me shake my head in bewilderment. The first is the 218-yard 6-iron shot taken from a fairway bunker on the final hole of the 2000 Bell Canadian Open played at Glen Abbey. What many people don't realize is that not only did Tiger hit out of this bunker and over a substantial pond to the fringe of the green to finish with a birdie and clinch the tournament by a stroke, but he also had to strike the shot high enough to clear a tree in his line of flight. Many golfers who play Glen Abbey still excitedly throw a ball in this same trap and try to duplicate this shot. The results are painfully the same—a splash is heard, Slumped Shoulders ensue, and great wonderment crosses the mind of the individual trying to comprehend how the heck Tiger hit this Technician shot! The second shot of interest is the famous Nike ball chip-in at the 16th hole at Augusta in 2005 during the final round, which is enshrined as being one of the best shots under pressure of all time. Also, it is a fascinating example of free brand advertisement. After Tiger purposely chipped the ball approximately 25 feet away from the hole, he agonizingly watched it trickle down the hill toward the hole. The ball hung precariously on the lip's edge before the Nike swoosh smiled and clunked to the bottom of the cup for a birdie. Tiger went on to with that year's Masters in a playoff.

<u>Conclusion</u>

I must admit that I had a bias toward Jack being the better golfer. He was my idol since I was a young lad. The media provided ample coverage of this golfing great and I found myself an ardent rooter for him to win tournaments. Jack seemed to always be in the hunt and his mental toughness proved time and time again to be stronger than the others (although Mr. Trevino and Mr. Watson could throw wrenches in Jack's plans with key wins). This reputation spanned from the Arnie Palmer/ Gary Player era to the Tom Watson/Lee Trevino era to the Greg Norman/ Seve Ballesteros era. From adolescent golfing prodigy, to university and amateur champion, to major professional championship record holder, to Senior Tour Champion, his résumé is arguably the greatest. He is now a successful globetrotting golf course designer living in his twilight years and he continues to give back to the game. From start to finish his golfing prowess is remarkable. And there is always the win at Augusta in 1986. Watch clips of this win and you will no doubt be affected by his brilliance of play.

Tiger's golfing reputation began even earlier than the Golden Bear's. Have fun watching Tiger on the Mike Douglas show when he was two years old http://www.youtube.com/watch?v=vKvbSTVSMmo. Although Earl Woods, Tiger's late father, repeatedly emphasized to the world that his son was going to be special, the Anointed One still needed to win tournaments. Victories would not be handed over to him because of his perceived pedigree. He proved his father to be prophetic and Tiger has won many tournaments throughout his amateur and professional careers.

Tiger's golf book has many chapters yet to be written. No doubt this tome will be a lengthy one. I think he will probably win more professional major championships and other tournaments but not necessarily in the near future. All the great golfers have had their slumps. The strength of his knee is a question mark and could derail his plan to reach his goals. This has become more apparent and more serious. His body is aging before our eyes. The great Bobby Orr had a shortened hockey career because of his major knee problems and I hope this does not happen to another legend. Golf swing changes and adversity in his personal life are obstacles but can be overcome. He wants to prove to the world that his legacy should be as the better golfer. Can he once again resurrect his remarkable psychological and physical golfing talents and win majors? It is important for him to achieve this mark of 18.

Some think he will never again win a major and will disagree with my assessment. I do not possess a magic crystal ball. I am merely stating my opinion. This will be an intriguing adventure to follow and will be constantly addressed in the media and in golfers' minds.

For those interested in this ongoing debate, understand your respective bias and then open your mind to the possibility that you are wrong. Once I started down this path of fact and interpretative analysis, I concluded that it is a difficult decision to determine the winner of this debate. Think beyond just the number of professional major championships won by each player.

I hope my analysis gives you a better grasp on how to compare these two superstar golfers. In the end, although there is no definitive answer, I conclude that my choice for better golfer would be Tiger.

Based on Tiger not winning in 2010 and 2011 and his continued psychological and physical swing problems moving forward, many interested individuals in this debate may swing their opinions toward Jack. Now that Tiger is divorced we shall see how he copes with the changes in his schedule. Jack last won a major championship when he was 46 and Tiger will be 36 years old at the end of December, 2011. The latter can possibly return to his glory days but golf is a fickle game. Will his game disintegrate like Ian Baker-Finch or David Duval or can he resurrect his stature and game like Lee Westwood and Steve Stricker? Time will only tell whether the collision of his car with a hydrant was the tipping point of his life and golfing mastery. This comparison of Jack and Tiger will need to be updated in the future.

Finally, I think it will be captivating to see who will step up and try to usurp the crown of the Big 2 in determining who may be the best golfer in history. Contenders often become pretenders. How about Rory, Rickie, Dustin, Martin, or Ryo? Will they be the next generation of golfers remembered by first names like Tiger, Jack, Freddie, and Phil, along with the many famous one-named female supermodels and pop star singers? What fascinating stories in the future can we talk about so we can compare them with Jack's and Tiger's heroics at storied golf courses?

I would be honoured to be your moderator in comparing the successes of such challengers in the "best golfer" category while I sipped an Arnie Palmer drink on a rocking chair in 25 years' time. On second thought, a single-malt Scotch may be the drink of choice to help me fondly recall, "I remember the days when I watched Jack in 1986 and Tiger in 2000 hit those shots and I am not sure these highly touted 'pseudos' had the same skill and drive to be named the best golfer ever to have played the game . . ."

At the Turn: 19th Hole or Refreshment Hut.

1. What is the significance of St Andrews, Hoylake, Interlachen, and Merion, and secondly, Pebble Beach, St Andrews, Valhalla, and Augusta National?

   Order a delicious corned beef sandwich on rye.

2. John Cook, Nathaniel Crosby (Bing Crosby's son), and Ricky Barnes all have this in common. What is it?

   Quaff a 16-ounce Budweiser draft beer.

3. Name the players who have (or had) the nicknames of Carnac Junior, Volcano, Slick and Popeye?

   Munch on Lay's barbecue chips.

INWARD NINE

HOLE No. 10, PAR 3. HOW CAN I CLEAR THAT JUNGLE WITH MY PLASTIC GOLF BALL?

In the early to mid-1970s while my parents stewed over the political and military ramifications of the bitter Vietnam War, I had a bigger jungle to tackle—how do I clear this flowerbed with my plastic golf ball and make par in my side yard on Vansittart Avenue? You see, I started early in my life and found golf to my extreme liking. Let me take you back to my developing years . . .

I had now graduated from training wheels to almost the real thing. No longer was I hitting the oversized and harder plastic ball in an open field as in my tyke days, but the Titleist-sized plastic ball. My arena also expanded to include my back yard, side yard, front yard, and sometimes my neighbour's yard. The ball also now became airborne, much to my incredulous satisfaction. We called it "lift" back in those days. These fertile grounds had turned into my own personal Pebble Beach.

Terry and Doris, my parents, were pleased that I'd taken up a sport which did not involve looming danger outside of being blindsided by an errant ball hit by my despicable sister Linda (I actually love her, so don't get worked up). My older sibling initially challenged me on my turf but she soon became disinterested and found a higher calling—doodling weirdo chalk figures on the walls in our stinky, dishevelled garage. Homeless cats, which used the garage as a holiday retreat from the real world and as a personal washroom, may have been fans of her drawings but I was not. I was too absorbed in my own higher calling of applicable art on the golf course; namely, pars and birdies. Hour upon hour of my youth I strived to perfect my craft. Was Pac-Man available on those clunky Atari computers around then? Who cares? I had no interest in spending precious time inside my house fiddling with such a time-wasting machine because I had found my destiny—a useful one.

Plastic balls were my prized friends. I admired the sight of balls in flight. They pinged off brick houses, sliced around my parent's ugly Plymouth

Duster with its vinyl seats, and winged over my mom's somewhat busy tulip beds. Eavestroughs gobbled up a few of my misplayed balls and these jewels probably still linger in their adopted land 35 years later. May you rest in peace, my loyal comrades.

Personally, I liked the plastic balls with no holes in them because they could fly further than the ones that did not. Wind drag didn't affect those cookies as much. The heck with being a short hitter, I wanted to be like mighty Jack and slam the shots by any competitors who dared challenge Wayne T. on his private course. But I would gladly take any available type of plastic ball just as long as I could pursue the opportunity to win my imaginary green jacket.

I would swing hard at the plastic ball and the power was awesome. It would soar an amazing 15 yards. That constituted a titanic drive. Then I'd confront a major quandary because a decision needed to be made on whether I wanted to lay up short of the tulip bed with a strategic pitch shot or smash that iron and clear the hazard by a mere 2.7 yards. If I chose the latter option, then my adrenaline surged in anticipation of having a crack at birdie. Golfers know that euphoric feeling. A lay-up notion, on the other hand, evoked a sinking feeling of cowardice and I looked over my shoulder to see if any spectators might encourage me to go for the risky shot. I didn't hesitate long when making my decision and went for it; because that is what the Golden Bear would have done if he wanted to hoist another Claret Jug.

The ball whooshed through the air and dropped precipitously close to the fern guarding the west side of the flowerbed. My heart fluttered for a moment, thinking this obstacle would lead me to ruin but it landed over and was safely positioned. I sighed with great relief. This left me with a ten-yarder.

I connected on a three-quarter swing, low punch shot, and the ball travelled splendidly. It masterfully hopped once off a grasshopper's head and rested within tap-in birdie range on this very difficult par-5 full of hazards and heaping trouble. Jack, I just won my own Open Championship. Thank you for giving me the cojones to make the desired shots of my blossoming career. Pressure was what I confronted head-on in classic, manly fashion. I left winning the duel. Isn't life grand when you're a youngster, and all you have to worry about is hitting golf shots (and watching *Hogan's Heroes* and eating grilled cheese sandwiches especially with Heinz ketchup)!

Unfortunately, like street hockey that was played back then with the ominous orange ball (I, along with all Canadian boys who played during this era still cringe when we think about this rock-hard missile heading anywhere close to our personals, eye sockets or inside thighs), I don't see plastic golf balls being played by the youth of today. They seemed to have been relegated to the dustbin of history. I don't know whether to blame those gull-darned video games that are 80 times more sophisticated than Pac-Man, the mind-boggling Internet, or the lack of imagination that kids possess today. What more incredible world could you encounter than exuberantly striding down your back stoop and hitting a plastic golf ball all within one minute! Get outside and enjoy the simple things in life.

Now, I must forewarn any of you who want to pick up my baton and resurrect this great game in your own backyard that you will face obstacles. Your control freak parents may persuade you to try out for rep hockey, soccer, or baseball before having you waste time in this pursuit. They may act diligently as helicopter parents and worry that you may develop painful blisters if you play for more than an hour. Nonsense! Even if you do get blisters it is a worthy badge of honour.

A bigger hurdle however, may be disguising the huge divots you take when hitting your Technician shots over the garden and onto your imaginary greens. My loving parents were quite tolerant of my pursuit and I don't remember them giving me a hard time over this sometimes glaringly visible damage (I hope they didn't intend to have a garden party with anyone they were trying to impress). At least I don't think they had a problem as I have no physical scars on my back from a strapping or psychological ones earned by memories of irate finger-pointing and high-pitched screams. Strapping—now there is a word from the 70s . . . .

I have some prudent advice to offer when constructing your own course. Employ the heel of your adidas shoe to create amateur and makeshift holes (conveniently don't tell your parents as you can always ask for forgiveness later). Jab a branch in it and voilà you have hole number one. Keep your opening hole basic so you can get off to a safe start on your round and build steely confidence. Then you can create a more difficult collection of holes just like the master architects of the past. Place a hole by your birdbath and have that act as the historical Swilcan Burn at St Andrews. Respect its presence but avoid it at all costs. Or place a hole by your front yard's large oak tree and think of that as the wonderful 67-foot Cypress tree guarding the right side of Pebble Beach's grandiose finishing hole. Keep your shot well left to avoid this obstacle and the strategy will give you a better angle of attack. The tulip bed can substitute as meandering Rae's Creek at Augusta with a penalty stroke being taken to retrieve wayward shots found at its bottom. Be careful of this menacing trap. Finally, the family car can symbolize the mighty rock sitting in the middle of the par-5 3rd hole fairway at beautiful Troon North's Monument Course in Arizona. If it is a lower end model like our Duster, then you might take a guilty pleasure and fire a shot off its powder blue door to hear the dinging sound like I did. Giggle, but don't let your Terry and Doris catch you!

So, what are you waiting for, youngsters? Beg and cajole your parents to take you to a local golf store. Push by the racks of Top-Flites and Dunlop Locos and seek out the plastic balls. Purchase a $5.99 six-pack and prepare your next round in your mind. Hold firm with your parents, my chums, and sell them on the view that their backyard, even with a few nasty divots, could be the breeding ground of a future Tiger or Rory.

Parents, listen to your wise child. Your kid actually wants to venture outside, away from texting and playing the latest version of Grand Theft Auto on his X-Box 360. This is a healthy new addiction for him or her and is a breakthrough of tremendous proportions. Isn't it every parent's dream to have their offspring become famous so they can buy them a mansion with four-and-a-half bathrooms? Forget the *American Idol* route to stardom and riches . . .

Support and encourage this program, Mom and Pop, because a legendary son or daughter will eliminate the need for you to fight for that last scrap of potato at the old age home. Visualize the hilarious golfing movie *Happy Gilmore* when that old woman from the rest home clambers on top of his car begging Happy to get her out of there. Instead of suffering through a similar dreadful scenario, you will be able to afford to pay trusty servants. They will then gladly serve you beluga caviar and expensive champagne in your massive home with all the opulent fixings. All because you believed in the magic and joy of your fine Billy, Janey, (or Happy) hitting plastic golf balls!

Hole No. 11, Par 5. How does Pebble stack up against the Old Course?

This stimulating question for some reason makes me think of the young Danish prince Hamlet who famously states, "To be, or not to be: That is the question." Is your "to be" The Old Course at St Andrews and your "not to be" Pebble Beach Golf Links? I knew my tedious study of Shakespeare would one day have practical use for me! Of course I am not speaking of suicide, death or dying (after all, the Danes are supposed to be the happiest people in the world) but of life and living the dream of playing one or both of these famous golf courses.

I have polled many Canadian golfers on what their preferred Top 3 to 5 courses are that they would like to play in their lifetime. Inevitably, the large majority first think south as in the United States. Augusta National and Pebble are often cited. In fact, Pebble Beach is the overwhelming favourite and I would say almost everyone mentions this Monterey jewel. Some mention St Andrews or Carnoustie and few seem to choose wonderful Canadian golf courses like Highland Links in Nova Scotia, Capilano in British Columbia or The National and Hamilton Golf and Country Club in Ontario. I presume American golfers would look east to west across their own country rather than north or across the ocean to select their beauties. They certainly have an abundance of quality courses. I wonder where St Andrews fits into the equation from their perspectives when compared to Augusta National and Pebble Beach?

If I offered the same question to Europeans, they would probably select more courses on their side of the pond. St Andrews, Turnberry, Royal Dornoch, or Muirfield would probably be their favourites. Perhaps Royal County Down and Ballybunion in Northern Ireland and Ireland respectively could be added to this mix. These offerings would seem natural and worthy recipients of this honour. Nevertheless, Pebble would be right up there in their rankings (I think) if they are big watchers of television and read the promotional press of this splendid venue, which

124

is owned jointly by Clint Eastwood, Arnold Palmer, Richard Ferris, and Peter Ueberroth.

Why does Pebble usually get the nod in North America over the Old Course? First of all, the course is an absolutely stunning place to play. Yes, it is very expensive but you can gain access because it is public (unlike the very private and exclusive courses of Augusta National, Pine Valley, and the brilliant nearby Cypress Point). I believe American television coverage and North American bias also would be the main contributors toward Pebble's great popularity.

There is the annual Pro-Am that is held early in the golfing season. Laughter abounds as you watch goofy and headgear-wearing Bill Murray hook another shot into a cavernous bunker or, when he rakes a missed 3-footer then follows it up with a nifty jig dance. Don't let him fool you though; as insiders know, he is a very good golfer as well as a great entertainer for the crowds. Bing Crosby used to host this well-advertised Clambake decades ago. I thoroughly enjoyed watching the festivities of this tournament with my father. The famous crooner/actor invited many Hollywood celebrities to his tournament so they could spice up the event. As a result of this star power, there was ample coverage of the golf course along with the golfers' theatrical play. I fondly remember Jack Lemmon repeatedly lunging and flailing at the ball, much to my chagrin. Wouldn't that have been something to be his partner? "Mr. Lemmon, how did you enjoy acting with that old curmudgeon Walter Matthau? Was he that much of a slob when he played Oscar Madison and you played Felix Ungar in the *Odd Couple?*"

Several U.S. Open Championships have, of course, been hosted at Pebble. Admired players like Jack Nicklaus, Tom Watson, and Tiger Woods have proudly had their names engraved onto this trophy. Pebble adds thicker rough during this tournament to add even more teeth and nerves will be frayed. You may have seen some of this penal ewok at work while viewing the tense 2010 edition of the U.S. Open won by the Northern Irishman Graeme McDowell.

Golfers who know that you have played this special course like to ask two inevitable questions:

1. How much does it cost?
2. What did you shoot?

For those who know me well, they understand that I will not answer these questions in a direct way. The compelling reason why I parry these thrusts is because I believe it should be irrelevant. The thrilling experience of playing this masterpiece should make these points moot. More pertinent questions that interested parties really should ask include:

1. How did your body and psyche feel while standing on the 18th tee with the wind howling and the ocean lurking?

    Answer: Outstanding and exhilarating.

2. How did you feel standing over your second shot at No. 8?

    Answer: Intimidated and disoriented once you examined the beautiful landscape and dramatic cliffs.

3. The Par 5 14th green looks dastardly on television. Is it that tough?

    Answer: I think it is one of the most wonky, devilish greens you can ever approach whether you are hitting irons, pitching, or putting.

Oh, by the way, the purposely delayed answers are: "very expensive" and "my score was much higher than I liked." So Bob's your uncle . . .

Choosing the Old Course at St Andrews over Pebble as your favourite depends on your perspective of how you enjoy golf. Do you want water to come into play? Are immaculate fairways and fast-running greens important? Can you handle rude weather conditions including rain, wind, and cold? Does tradition play a role and do you appreciate history? Do you put value on viewing centuries-old buildings surrounding the opening and closing holes? Are you an avid reader of golf magazines, books, and blogs to gain insight into these wonderful courses? And can North Americans erase or suspend their memories on what they are used to in a golf game and open their minds to a whole different way to experience it? Pampered, windy, breathtaking oceanside golf on the sunny Californian coast or historical links golf with blind shots and low-to-the-ground strokes in sometimes nasty Scottish weather. What is your choice? I will tell you mine at the end.

Let me help you with this checklist to frame Pebble against the Old Course at St Andrews. Tick off the side you would prefer to play:

Majestic beauty	Steeped history and tradition
Predominant aerial game	Low-to-the-ground assault
Good and bad weather	Unpredictable/changing weather
Immaculate greens and fairways	Slow greens, uneven fairways
Conditioned shots of length	Creative, imaginative shots
Predominantly open shots	Some unnerving blind shots
Cold beer	Cool beer (the way Scots like it)

What do your selections on this list tell about how you personally enjoy playing golf? If you had the chance to play the trio of the Old Course at St Andrews, Muirfield, and Turnberry, or Pebble Beach, Pinehurst No. 2, and TPC Sawgrass, which group of splendid courses would you choose?

Now, I would like to state that I had the privilege of playing both of these courses in consecutive years (May, 2008 and May, 2009). As a golfing purist, traditionalist, and reader of history, I was predisposed toward the Old Course and my visit was nothing short of spectacular and spiritual. Pebble Beach and the surrounding area of Carmel/Monterey certainly did not disappoint and I will tell you why.

Seventeen Mile Drive, off the I-1 begins your dream journey into one of America's most compelling, incredibly striking, and wealthiest pieces of property. Driving from San Francisco (beautiful in its own right) along I-1 with its white-knuckle driving and cliff scenery to Seventeen Mile Drive is a fantastic excursion. The distractions of more breathtaking surroundings continue relentlessly as you inch towards Pebble. Don't speed, and make sure you stop along this stretch to admire the views. Patience, my friends. Pilgrims will be rewarded. Think of an impeccably paced, seven-course meal that just gets better with every stage ending at Pebble. Your mind spins at the sensory overload and thrillingly absorbs the striking significance of this visit.

Cypress Point Golf Club, Poppy Hills Golf Course, Spyglass Hill Golf Course, The Links at Spanish Bay and Pebble Beach Golf Links can all be found resting along this area. And these golf courses are just part of the whole. The ocean parts transfix you. Once visitors reach Pebble after passing a few of its holes on their drive, they need to make sure to sample lunch overlooking the 18th green. This impressive and not overly ostentatious room sits in the main hotel building called The Lodge. It will nevertheless, be hard for you to experience anything more visually extraordinary. And this means for non-golfers too. If you want, the public can even walk the path along the 18th hole. You can view the extravagant homes of the rich and pampered. I have done this in past trips to Pebble and it is really cool to gain access to this vantage point. Remember, you do not have to play or stay at Pebble to eat lunch at this location or take such a stroll. Take advantage of this opportunity and do it!

My playing partners for this Chewie Open golf excursion were the regular rascals and my great friends Chief, Bags, and Scugog. The four of us were excited to play superlative Pebble and we wanted to truly experience what Pebble had to offer. Caddies were a must to accomplish this goal so we took a duo of two-bagger carriers. It is often hard to get your own dedicated caddies in North America based on our past trips. I recommend spending on this luxury (since you are already forking out quite a bit anyway for this trip) so you can access their sage insight on breaks in putts and positioning of shots. You will definitely need their coaching advice. Not worrying about your clubs will free up valuable minutes for you to examine the beautifully conditioned course and the surrounding water views. Walk if you can, because riding an electric cart will not give you the same feel—the rhythm of Pebble.

I found the course to possess a rather ordinary couple of starting holes. Unlike the first hole at the Old Course, where you quiver in your boots, the opening hole was quite straightforward. The par-4 1st had a tough green if you were on the wrong side of the pin but if you avoided the bunker (which I did not) then you could do well. The short par-5 2nd is hittable in two for longer strikers but boy what a small green to land the ball! Pinpoint accuracy is vital. The dunkle left sand trap grabbed my ball on my second shot after I hit six-iron. Jabba seemed to become a popular friend of mine early in the round . . .

The dogleg left par-4 No. 3 gave me a small tease of the ocean. PGA player and tremendous young talent Dustin Johnson would certainly like to have another attempt at taking on this hole in his last round of the 2010 U.S. Open. His dramatic meltdown with a pull hook on his drive (following a fluffed chip debacle on the 2nd) snowballed. Ezekiel and the wheels came off. I hooked my ball into the left Chewbacca as well but I had much less at stake than Mr. Johnson. As Johnson had a grimace because he knew what this blunder cost him, I had a wicked grin in the zone of the hairy creature.

The short par-4 4th hole finally offers golfers a better visual of the water on the right hand side after tee shots are hit. Avoid the sand trap sitting in the fairway. I started to sense why this course has such impressive credentials.

The par-3 5th hole was a good challenge. However, it is the stretch of Nos. 6 through 10 that makes these holes unbeatable in intimidation and stunning backdrops. This is arguably the best five holes in a row that you could play anywhere in the world. I would certainly give it the Yes vote on my ballot.

At No. 6 you stand tall and still on the tee and examine one of the most dazzling par-5s in golf. Bags vividly expressed these thoughts to me while we admired the area. The dogleg left hole can be tamed but you must be careful. Take an extra minute to breathe it in. Sand traps dissuade you from venturing too far left on your drive. The wind whistles through your hair with authority. The fairway meanders towards the precipitous drop over the cliff and into the ocean. I saw Tiger dribble his drive over the abyss on television during the 2010 U.S. Open and appreciated the painful grinding that must have surged through his system with this unplanned result. It gives you better perspective on holes and courses—a sort of kinship—when you have actually played them after watching others, including professionals, play them on television. Finally, your blind approach shot has to go over a steep hill in hopes that the ball catches a piece of the green (man, what a carry).

I failed to position myself properly in many places on this hole by driving it into the sand trap, pitching out and then gradually finishing with a bogey. My erratic play did not however, take away from my admiration of this hole. Some people judge a course by how well they played that day.

I do not and you should not. I appreciate the holes and courses for what they offer me and my senses.

Number 7. Yes, that short and famous par-3 hole. Every adoring golfer knows it or has heard of it. This is certainly a well-photographed hole and deservedly so. Again, take a step back and admire it even if the caddies try to push you along to the tee. Would it merely be a flip wedge or a testy mid-iron blast from a meagre 100 yards out? Wind plays havoc in this remote part of the course. We were fortunate to have the shorter version and it didn't disappoint. Seek the ocean view and the boats floating nearby. Too bad my short shot found Mr. Sandman at the rear. How many times will I fall victim to these dastardly hazards at Pebble! This was a much preferred status over staring down at my Pro V1 resting at the bottom of the cliff. Another bogey, but do you think I got worked up?

The 8th hole is truly a marvel after you have launched your drive. The first shot is to be hit to a particular spot but don't go too far or your ball will disappear over the precipice. I know Mr. Nicklaus sees this par-4, especially with the heart palpitating second shot, as the best around in the world. I would have a difficult time countering this argument from my idol. The Road Hole could be included in this category . . .

Scugog wrestled a par after a birdie attempt. An impressive result. My perfectly hit drive was all for naught. Phase 1 success was exchanged for a Phase 2 malfunction. As a result of my wobbly knees and vertigo while peering over the edge, I guided a weak-assed second shot to the right and it almost carried down into No Man's Land. I was fortunate that it hung up in the grass. Assuming my awkward stance for the delicate pitch shot over a sand trap, I made sure I did not stagger too much. Visiting the seals down below by the jagged rocks was not on my intended agenda today. This position by the green was something to remember.

Nos. 9 and 10 finished off this superb string of holes. Good drives to the left side of the sloping fairways are essential as the ball hits the ground and trickles to the right as though magnets are tugging it. My large drive on No. 9 left me only a short pitch shot after navigating and maximizing the distance using the slick slope. The green at No. 10 is very difficult to approach with sand to the left and ocean sitting precariously close to the right. Very difficult. I felt like my body was leaning toward the ocean while hitting my shot from the left rough. After finishing here you gulp for air and count the damage. Your score can be high but don't be discouraged. If you have played well through this last stretch of holes, then congratulations, you just beat the odds and have bragging rights with the chums back home.

The par-4 11th, par-3 12th, and par-4 13th are strong, not great, holes. Alas, golfers at Pebble get mightily spoiled up to this point and these three holes somehow feel a bit underwhelming.

The par-5 14th is one heck of a monster. The wind is usually in your face and you have to smash powerful shots to get close on this dogleg right hole. Your mind imagines it playing 600 yards.

Then there is the green at this hole. How do I describe it? The front right part has a sinister, steep slant that will gladly spit any weakly hit balls back to your feet. This could occur repeatedly and painfully like in the movie *Groundhog Day* with Bill Murray when each day repeats itself (hmmm . . . a connection with this actor and Pebble). Make sure you hit it hard enough to grab the back third part of the green. Please listen to this essential advice.

Professionals even fall afoul of the green's warped sense of humour. A bunker lingers in the front left to capture wayward shots and you don't want to be left to hit that shot. There is no run-up area. Only the Technician shot is available to hit the desired landing and resting area for your ball. Good luck, my brave one!

When was the last time that you heard a 6 being a good score on a par-5? Are you not supposed to eat these up? Not here. Get it to the back right of the green. Not only will the front play tricks with your ball but trouble will find you if you fall down the back of the green. The ball will settle in unwelcoming grass and a tentative chip from this area will see the slope trickle the ball down to your feet. Fido, your imaginary loyal golden retriever, is carrying back his fetched stick in the guise of a Titleist. What a disorienting and helpless feeling to watch this train wreck. PGA veteran Paul Goydos suffered such a fate when he walked off with a 9 at the 2010 Pebble Beach Pro-Am after coming into the hole with a one-stroke lead. Ball rolls up, ball rolls down. I shook my head while watching this quad result unravelling on television. Game, set, and match, Paul. Your *Groundhog Day* was an extended director's cut version! You will not be the victor this year. No. 14 won this titanic battle easily.

I have never experienced such a notorious green, and in some ways it seems unfair. But you definitely remember it after such a deadly encounter. I suggest you appreciate and respect this hole more than you previously might have.

Fifteen and 16 are good par-4s but you are already thinking ahead to the crippler finishing holes. The 16th has a tree blocking your approach shot so be aware. These are makeable pars.

The 17th and 18th holes define Pebble's majestic quality. History (and you know how important that is to me) plays an integral role in enhancing the reputation of these final two holes. Respect them.

On both of these beauties, the Pacific Ocean snatched my Titleist (actually twice on the 18th). Where a fade is my natural shot, for some odd reason I hooked the heck out of my shots into Davy Jones' Locker. Perhaps it was caused by the combination of paralyzing fear and nerves. And fabulous views that transport me into dreamy thoughts of playing these holes further exacerbated my situation. Golfers know this syndrome—think it and ye shall receive it! And, I am sure my whippy hip motion had nothing to do it . . .

I stalked the 17th green as if I were a true player in the hunt. Then I stood in the difficult, deep fringe close to where I thought Watson was positioned when he made his famous chip-in to shock Nicklaus and propel him to his win at the 1982 U.S. Open. I pulled the stick out of the hole where Nicklaus remarkably rattled a one-iron off the metal in the 1972 U.S. Open. This critical shot helped him to claim his own U.S. Open. Have you heard of a one-iron? Impossible to hit well. Lee Trevino had a funny quote: If you wanted to avoid being struck by lightning on the golf course, then hold a one-iron to the sky and even God can't hit a one-iron. Funny. What a stimulating setting!

After sitting on the wooden guardrail by the tee overlooking the picturesque ocean to get the token picture taken with my three comrades, I sized up the most famous par-5 in golf. Incredible. I thought nostalgically of Bing Crosby's song, "Straight Down the Middle" that he sang during the Clambake coverage. Sing and hum along that catchy tune with me, "Straight down the middle. It went straight down the middle. Then it started to hook just a wee, wee bit. That's when the caddie lost sight of it." I blocked out these negative vibes and wandering thoughts to hit one of those superb shots of your golfing career.

Tell me that aiming over the ocean is logical. But it must be done to hit the gutsy shot so you can prove your mettle. Length plus accuracy equals grand satisfaction. I hit the perfect tee-shot on the 18th by aiming dead straight over the ocean. Jack Nicklaus and Steve Bull, my sports psychologist English brother-in-law, would have been proud of the visual technique that I used. It soared beautifully with a little fade and landed left of the trees that mark the A-1 landing zone. Also, you can't appreciate it on television, but there is Obi Wan lurking along the right-hand side by a group of pricey houses. Golfers have to be careful if they want to wimp out with a slice or mistakenly flail a Dan Blocker on this famous hole. Many prefer this course of action than a Jimmy Snipester into the smashing surf on the opposite side. Fear can get the best of us.

The clunking of my ball off the rocks into the Pacific Ocean on my second shot made me only beam. No Slumped Shoulders were necessary. I received no Yoda-type luck like Hale Irwin did when his ball miraculously jumped back on to the fairway after ricocheting off a boulder during the 1984 Pebble Beach Pro-Am. Poor Canadian Jim Nelford (who lost to Irwin in the ensuing playoff) was never the same. My brain cramp of a hooked shot did not tarnish this fabulous round. But scoring an 8 (or was it a quadruple bogey 9?) was not something I had envisioned after booming my tee-shot perfectly over the water and crashing waves. Shooting in the 90s contrasted with my well earned 78 at the Old Course. That is the mystery of golf and its appeal to followers of the wee ball. Both rounds were memorable in their own distinctive ways.

Be sure to take one last dazzling look at the Pacific Ocean from the green after shaking hands with your colleagues. Then head inside to the clubhouse overlooking the green for a pint and a sandwich. You may be lucky and run into Dirty Harry and other famous people who frequent this American institution.

Because of the financial collapse that occurred in 2008 and lingered into 2009, Pebble was not fully booked as it usually is. To entice us, or to thank us, they upgraded our accommodation to a chalet overlooking the 18th hole, gave us a $100 gift certificate to use in the pro shop and provided us with the 2-hour privilege of driving a Lexus convertible and sedan. All of these value-adds were free of charge or that is how they positioned their proposal. Is there anything really free? No need to quibble over interpretation. Timing is everything and we took advantage.

Nevertheless, I could imagine that the cost of renting these two vehicles during normal economic times would have been significant. And we loved how this enhanced our experience at Pebble and of glorious California. For one of the few times in my life this Woodstonian could feel like he was part of the tiny inner circle or better known as the patrician class. The real world of work can be punishing, so us plebes need to be spoiled with some splendid rewards from time to time.

The four of us zipped southwards on I-1 in these luxury cars. We itched to be further awed by these gorgeous views along the coastline. We stopped our cars at one point and walked down manufactured stairs to reach the sand. The deafening roar of the surf and the swirling wind was exhilarating. Another vivid memory to lock away in my personal vault . . . . Later that day we had a couple of watered-down American beers while sitting outside on plastic chairs at our villa and enjoyed watching players hit their second shots on the 18th fairway. You can't help but admire, not only the challenges of the players placing their shots, but how a piece of land so beautiful could be created. God may not be able to hit a one-iron but He certainly painted a visual masterpiece for humans to appreciate.

Following a delicious dinner, and ample beer and wine in the clubhouse we retreated to our comfortable residence. Another beer later, Chief laid down the gauntlet. He insisted—no, demanded—that we venture out to the middle of the 18th fairway and hit wedge shots to the green. There was also one caveat: We would strike our shots in bare feet. The three of us were all incredulous but since he was relentless in his pursuit, it was better to give in to him rather than absorb the brunt of his repeated dictums. Like cowering fools we slipped off our topsiders and other highbrow shoes and proceeded to our spot chosen by the dictator.

So here I was in darkness trying to determine where the ball rested. I instinctively struck a 100-yard chubby wedge shot from the centre of the fairway into the famous 18th hole at Pebble Beach. I wondered what kind of reception my ball would receive from the unsuspecting green. You see, it is used to inviting daylight visitors, not dusk trespassers. The result of this lousy shot would remain a mystery until I got closer to our goal. Did I mention it was bloody freezing to walk on this dewy grass minus FootJoys? I am certainly a big believer in walking golf courses in comfortable shoes. But feeling the ground in exposed feet on a chilly evening was raw and intimate. Not much grip, either, as my inaccurate shot proved.

I found the ball embedded in the front-right greenside bunker. Good, I could squish my feet in the soothing sand and this spot would offer welcome relief from the damp turf. This specific hazard had not affected me earlier in the day so I could experience a different perspective of the hole without any major repercussions to my score. Just a hit to my wallet.

This was not the ideal position to win the dollar bet but there were other more immediate concerns circulating in our minds.

We all imagined that a large searchlight would lighten up the horizon to catch us devious ones. A klaxon horn would then sound and a watered-down Delta Force contingent would rush from the clubhouse. Luckily for us punks, it appeared co-owner Clint Eastwood aka Dirty Harry Callahan did not want to make our day (or night, for that matter). The swashbuckling Arnold Palmer and other co-owner would have chuckled at his loyal subjects and admired such theatrics if he had seen us perform. The King might have even hitched up his lime green pants and joined us for a shot or two and then a beer after the match. "Just like I spent roaring around early in my tour days, boys," Arnie would have uttered with a sparkle in his eyes.

You just never know about the level of security that places have in our jumpy and insecure world for anything that deviates from the norm. I doubt if they have viewed many fools challenging the status quo at this American landmark but then again maybe there were or will be others doing the exact thing we accomplished. I am sure we could have talked ourselves out of this precarious predicament with a limp excuse like "Really? I didn't know that this would be a problem to have four guys take large divots, splash sand on immaculate greens, and upset people who were enjoying a night of peace! And hey, we are staying right over there in that most expensive chalet that we paid premium for so we are important people!" Intruders we were not, immature kids maybe . . .

All of our eyes were locked anxiously at the clubhouse. Silence thickened. Crickets and other small creatures chirped. And, ladies and gentlemen, you had to know we were not the most silent of humans. Chief's booming voice alone would have given away our vulnerable position to any power-trippers who would descend. Mine is not much quieter. No bushes were available for us to evade any trackers that might be unleashed.

Perhaps Edna and Garnet sitting quietly in the opulent clubhouse dining room would wonder what the silly buggers were doing. They might even threaten to submit a grievance to unsettled staff. But they probably sluffed it off as childish antics and dug back into their lobster bisque and Californian Cabernet. They would calmly ask, "Waiter, can I have the dessert list, please, to round out this fa-a-a-b-u-lous meal? We are still hungry and want to linger here just a bit longer. I want to forget about those brash Canadian interlopers." Fortunately for the marauding Canadian misfits, the understanding Pebble folks let it pass. Nothing was done. Nada.

I gained renewed faith in society that such a prestigious golf course and club would allow us to continue our improvised game. So we did. I blasted out of the sand trap, the others laughed as they chipped onto the green and we shared the pleasure of finishing out and hearing the subtle plunk of the ball hitting the bottom of the hole. We clinked our beer bottles together (forgot to tell you that we needed to bring along some travellers for extra company) and raised a toast to friendship and Pebble. My score was much better than my earlier 9. I admired the beauty of the 18th hole in darkness and was particularly relieved that there was no intrusion of artificial light from a blazing searchlight!

A U.S. dollar bill was forked over to the winner. Was it Bags who drained the putt? I forget and I don't care. Sometimes you need an impulsive and creative person to rally the troops and attempt something that will bring the joy of golf to you in a different manner. These off-the-beaten-track events are memories you most cherish. If you have the chance, just do it to live life. Thanks Chief, it was great amusement. Hats off to Clint, Arnie, and the rest of the folks at Pebble Beach. You are class acts for letting us get away with some tomfoolery and not enforcing post 9/11 security practices. As ardent golfers you understand the deal. I just prayed that I didn't catch hypothermia or trench foot before playing tomorrow's round at Spanish Bay. If I had, then I would blame it on Pebble and its lackadaisical security protection for allowing me to be such a careless soul.

I think it is also important to include descriptions of the neighbouring area when evaluating the significance of the Pebble experience. For us, it included playing the wooded Spyglass Hill Golf Course and links style (but not true links) Spanish Bay. Spyglass is a wonderful treasure with a great starting tree-lined dogleg left par five followed by a series of open landscape holes. No. 4's green must be the tiniest in the universe. I hit a good second shot and the ball ended in the rough surrounding the green. The green at that point only seemed five paces across and the pin sat only a few feet away. Diminutive and ruthless is how I might describe it. From No. 6 to the finish, the course weaved itself through trees with well-defined fairways. What a stimulating golf course that rewarded accurate shots. A highlight was watching a deer come out of the woods while playing a hole on the back nine. It felt like I was in the Canadian wilderness . . .

Our final round was set for the Links at Spanish Bay. This is an enjoyable course that I had played 20 years ago. It gives players more of a Scottish feel with some holes resting along the water. Tight shots are needed and many lost balls were gobbled up by thick ewok and other long-haired cousins. A piper appears at dusk to shrill his instrument and add class to those enjoying a glass of wine in the nice lodge situated on the premises. Ahhh . . . the Scottish tradition is upheld here in California for a bunch of Queen's graduates! It was fitting to have such a connection. Chief shook hands with Scugog after just nudging him out for the prestigious Chewie Open tournament. I have a grand photograph of this momentous ending to a fabulous trip. I was only a spectator watching this dynamic duo battling to the very end because I was so far out of it (the 9 on 18 at Pebble Beach did not help).

We also enjoyed some time in Carmel and stayed at nearby Quail Lodge for a couple of nights and two rounds of golf. Carmel is an extravagant and wealthy enclave just down the road from Pebble. Our delectable steak dinner combined with seriously good Cabernet stirred up animated discussions and contentious arguments. Thrusts and counter-punches were fired by all participants in this free-for-all. The restaurant was empty outside of a table or two. The shaky financial straits of the U.S. were quite evident even here in the heartland of serious money and beautiful surroundings. It was our pleasure as Canadians and avid golfers to take advantage of these benefits. Having the Canadian loonie hovering closer to par was an added bonus and lessened the dent in our Visa bills.

I have to admit that Pebble Beach possesses the most scenic holes on one course of all the ones that I have ever played. Nos. 6, 7, 8, 9, 10, 17, and 18. Water views are key contributors for my decision when coming to this conclusion. There is just something calming and impressive about playing in this treasured environment. Pacific Dunes, Bandon Dunes, and Whistling Straits are outstanding too but Pebble has the edge. Please tell me of a course that can surpass this in beauty. Pebble is definitely as good as advertised.

It is now time that I discuss Pebble in comparison to the Old Course. The great amateur Bobby Jones once said that a professional golfer's life is not completed without a win at the Old Course. Is a devoted amateur's golfing life unfulfilled if he or she does not play St Andrews at least once? Jones hated playing it the first time and actually walked in after playing No. 11 during the third round of the 1921 Open Championship. But later he came to respect and like the course and what it represented. He won the Open Championship later in his career at this very same place. Jack has won twice (1970, 1978) at St Andrews. Tiger has too (2000, 2005). Is it coincidental that the three greats of golf all won at the Home of Golf?

As for Pebble Beach, I have more affection for this course after traversing it. Before I played there I had two separate lunch visits to the property and sensed it was unique (and I don't want to use this word lightly). It is not until you actually play Pebble (with a caddie so you can walk) that you understand its significance and popularity for golfers. Playing Spyglass and Spanish Bay on this same trip augmented my positive experience for this magnificent area.

As mentioned earlier, Jack and Tiger have won U.S. Opens at Pebble. It was probably significant and important for them to win here just like it was to win at St Andrews. The Golden Bear won his second amateur at Pebble and has even admitted that if he had one more round to play in his life he would choose this exquisite location. The Old Course at St Andrews and Pebble Beach are favourite courses in the world for both of them to play. I now know why after exploring these vastly different courses in back-to-back years. The experience was a real education for me and playing them so close together was a privilege. These courses, one that is hundreds of years old and the other less than one hundred years old, are the crown jewels of Scotland and the United States respectively.

So how does Pebble stack up against the Old Course now that I have described my great Californian experience? Hmmmmm . . . . This is the most beautiful course to play. Course conditions were immaculate. The final hole is great even though two of my balls have probably been digested by unknown sturgeons or other monstrous fish. Pacific Dunes in Bandon, Oregon is close but . . . this is Pebble. History. Celebrities. Money. Quality. Check, check, check, check. Water sightlines are unsurpassed. Having lunch overlooking the 18th hole. Simply fantastic! Customer service at all the facilities was excellent and we did not sense any arrogance from staff when they handled our requirements. Cypress Point and Poppy Hills are other golf courses to see. Carmel. Access to San Francisco is a couple of hours away (get to this incredible city). You feel that I am waffling here don't you? Don't worry. I am not.

The Old Course at St Andrews is my winning selection. The opening drive and the final shot combined make this unsurpassable. I could mention the Road Hole and other things too. It is not the quality or difficulty of these holes but the feeling you have while playing it. Intimidating at times, spiritual, disconcerting at times, and special.

The first hole at Pebble doesn't have it, although the final hole does in spades. The birthplace of golf at St Andrews with the Royal and Ancient sitting and watching. The Rusacks Hotel. Scotsmen leaning on fences and a tiny hut starting you on your way. No pro shop like Pebble's. In fact, no pro shop at all. You feel like you are part of history with Old Tom Morris and the many other worldwide travellers who have set foot on the original golf course in the world. This is the shrine of golf.

Speaking of sporting shrines . . . I would now like to provide comparative lists so you can examine and evaluate from your own perspective. This list provides good symmetry with the one I provided near the beginning that outlines the differences in playing links and non-links golf courses (even though Pebble has Links in its official title it is designated as a cliffside course not links). So what do you see? Is there a pattern? I wanted to thank my golfing comrades Ron and Jim for discussing and helping me to compile this interesting group of stadiums, arenas, courts, and golfing venues with me while sipping on an after-round drink at Craigowan:

Old Yankee Stadium	Wrigley Field
Lambeau Field	Old Soldier Field
Boston Garden	Madison Square Garden
Montreal Forum	Maple Leaf Gardens
Notre Dame Stadium	The Rose Bowl, Pasadena
The Old Course at St Andrews	Pebble (Public), Augusta (Private)

I will let you think for a bit so you can analyze and calculate what I am debating . . .

The left-hand column represents the number one place that the three of us believe devoted or true sports fans and/or players need to visit for professional baseball, professional football, professional basketball, professional hockey, college football, and amateur and professional golf, respectively. The right-hand column indicates the second-place finishers in our minds. We determined that historic moments and players who passed through these sites in the left-hand column made them superior. Championships won at these sites were also important. Watching and feeling that you are part of the picture, the greater whole while attending was another piece of this puzzle. Based on these criteria, they are clearly the winners.

Babe Ruth, Vince Lombardi, Red Auerbach, Jean Beliveau, Knute Rockne, Old and Young Tom Morris. The argument then becomes how distant the No. 2 choices are. The Old Course and its hundreds of years' head start, history, and tradition defeats the beauty of Pebble. The Old Course is No. 1 and Pebble No. 2. Can you honestly believe that, as a football fan, not a Bears fan, that you would be satisfied with only attending a game at Soldier Field? No. Lambeau Field is required to enter the equation if you wanted to experience the true crown jewel. State the same for the other comparisons and, in particular, golf.

I would like to conclude my hole by stealing a comment that I heard while wandering the small pro shop at Gullane No. 1 in East Lothian, Scotland. A passionate American golfer was sadly explaining to the pro shop person that he enjoyed playing great golf at Muirfield, the New Course at St Andrews, Carnoustie, and Gullane No. 1 but he did not book a time for the Old Course. His shattering last words were, "It just doesn't seem right to come to Scotland and not play the Old Course." You are right, Sir, and I would like to add that it would not be right if you only played Pebble and not the Old Course!

In the end I suggest that you play *both* the Old Course and Pebble. This way you can then thrust yourself into Hamlet's shoes so you can decide for yourself if you are a "to be" or a "not to be"!

HOLE NO. 12, PAR 4. WHERE'S MY KATO?

I know the majority of golfers have not had the distinct pleasure of using a caddie (or caddy). There are many reasons for this fact. It may be because they feel they don't need one, or because it is too expensive, they feel they are too good, they don't think that a caddie can help lower their score, or they never thought of using one. Well, people, I think it is high time for all of you to play a round with one. Such a selection elevates your golfing experience. High and low handicappers will benefit from this tremendous way of feeling golf in a different way. There is nothing quite like playing golf at a high calibre course with a caddie in tow. Golf with a caddie at your local course can also be a tremendous treat if they are available.

Think of a caddie as that back massage or spa treatment that you crave. Yes, we know you don't need to have one but isn't decadence and spoiling yourself important to your healthy existence? Splurge on the $60-$100 to get this helper. Forget about doing an opportunity cost of spending analysis in your head. Do not envision a caddie as an expense but as a strong investment in your golfing education. By gosh, if you can afford a big-assed Nike Sasquatch driver, 15 practice lessons, a rangefinder thanger, six green fees at beautiful courses, and several pints in the 19th hole, then you can spend this money on an obliging caddie. He will appreciate your patronage. Nod your head in approval now.

The Green Hornet needs his Kato, the Lone Ranger needs his Tonto, Batman needs his Robin, and Phil needs his "Bones." I have always maintained a romantic notion of possessing such a dynamic and trusty sidekick while attacking fairways and greens. Watching your compadre striding confidently down the fairway with your bag hanging over his shoulder and irons clacking while you blissfully twirl a five-iron in your mitts is a liberating feeling. Watch stress-free Freddie Couples stroll on the golf course and you will get the idea. Alone, golfers can play courses well, but together with a caddie, they are lethal weapons that can challenge the demands of Pebble and St Andrews' nasty bites.

Speaking of St Andrews, my time spent with Jimmy on the Old Course was tops. As a veteran looper, he was a perfect fit for me. This Scottish gentleman commenced his journey as a caddie when he was a youthful 15 years old and 33 years later he was still walking these celebrated links. This profession grabbed him forcefully and never let go.

I am not a control freak so I agreed to a straightforward social contract with him—he would make decisions for me and I would execute on his counsel. A fair and noble trade, I ascertained. And Jimmy could certainly be persuasive in his judgment of how to play shots at the oldest golf course on earth. "Just play, don't worry." A nice tag line (not quite like Bobby McFerrin's 1988 hit song, "Don't Worry, Be Happy").

Caddies, especially veteran types, like to wield this power. They usually pride themselves in having their player hit good shots into proper positions and will not-so-subtly demonstrate to the golfer that the master is really the one carrying the bag. Respect for his trade, so to speak. No one wants to be told how to do his job, right? They will even have fun side bets with their caddie colleagues on how well their man plays.

The outcome of my round on these ancient grounds positively shattered my expectations. I shot 78. There is no possible way that I could have shot this tidy score on my first try at St Andrews without Jimmy's huge assists. His sage opinions were vital to my success. He looked after my club selections, helped me navigate numerous blind shots and hidden bunkers, provided vital bursts of encouragement when doubts crept into my mind, explained bump-and-run strategies while navigating the seven double greens, and emphasized the intriguing options for driving on the Road Hole—over the Old Course Hotel maintenance shed or to the left of this structure. Striding mightily up the 18th hole on the Old Course with my caddie and three of my closest friends is the best golfing memory I could have—ever. The ultimate golfing experience.

Time now to put on your fantasy caps. Imagine you are Arnie Palmer with his faithful caddie. You flick a Camel cigarette butt to the ground like he did in his early days (not politically correct but the visually dramatic) playing at St Andrews or Augusta National. Seconds later, perform a theatrical toss of a blade of grass to measure the soothing breeze. Your wise veteran caddie Festus clearly states, "A two-club wind is in your face. Your ball will need to travel a little right of the deep bunker to give yourself a birdie chance. You better hit a five-iron, King."

Wind tossing through your hair, you feel the golfing gods whisper their excitement for your upcoming shot. The chosen five-iron is ripped out of the bag with unwavering cockiness. This is a shot that will be knocked cold by the stick. It is a demand. Festus likes that his boss believes in him and has taken his expert advice. Trust has bonded them. He nods his head in approval and stutter-steps the monstrous bag a clear five yards away so he is not in the line of sight. He has provided the arrow of wisdom and it is now your turn to unleash the bow on target.

After one methodical practice swing and a brief respite, the club knifes through the air with a crisp-sounding whoosh. The ball glides off your iron and sails clear of the bunker by 5 feet, rolls smartly up the first tier of the green and settles a mere 6 feet from the pin. You then brightly add, "I was thinking six-iron, so I owe you a double shot of Lagavulin following the round!" Festus gingerly places the small divot back in it original position and looks up to his master's beaming smile. He wasn't thirsty 5 minutes ago but it is amazing how a well-earned compliment and mention of a top grade Scotch could change a mood so dramatically. Both of you share a special moment and then high-five each other. Together you march into the sparkling sunshine towards the penultimate green, knowing that one without the other would not have contributed to this glorious success today. Thank you, Kato.

The preceding paragraphs may sound like a fictional account or the events in an engaging movie but your dramatic experience with a caddie could be similar. I have already described my Old Course experience . . . but what about the first one?

My initial round with a caddie was during the final round of a long-ago club championship when I was in my 20s. I was at the top of my game, playing to about a 2 or 3 handicap and was in the last pairing of the final round. Confidence was high and the thought of having a supportive colleague would keep me in this psychologically positive condition. I wanted to believe it was my time to rise to the occasion and capture the championship in front of my peers.

Man, I did feel like Arnie as my pal Blake carted my clubs and dished out his thoughts about the task at hand on the crucial shots. He was a fellow golfer and could empathize with the thought processes that would be needed to succeed during the pressures of this final day. All I had to do was visualize the shot I wanted to hit and perform it. Life was focused and

I felt important. He cares, he really cares. I sound like Sally Fields in that now-infamous Academy Award-winning acceptance speech . . .

Did I close the deal and win the Craigowan chalice? No, I say with sad regrets. My closing 80 dashed those hopes. But the Blaker, as I called him, was not the reason for me losing this important championship. Simply, it was my frayed nerves, a balky putter and a shaky driver that contributed to my demise. I didn't have it that day. Possessing a caddie for the day was a special feeling and I wanted to do it again and again. And so I have at top courses in North America, Scotland and Ireland. Regrettably, many places do not offer them.

Caddie programs, like bald eagles, are on the endangered species list. This is a sad state of affairs. The modern scourge of electric and gas carts have shunted this horse to pasture except for select destinations. Sometimes the horse is definitely better than the car (or cart). Turning a profit and riding convenience replaces the pure pleasure of caddie golf. Fortunately there are some modern and historical courses that still offer these services and hold resolute to the traditions of this centuries-old trade. I applaud their efforts at clinging to such ideals.

The Old Course at St Andrews, Carnoustie, Kiawah Island, Pinehurst No. 2, Pebble Beach, Ballybunion, Lahinch, Old Head, Bandon Dunes, Pacific Dunes and Whistling Straits are all courses at which I have had the privilege of using a caddie. Rattle these course names off and you will no doubt recognize their excellence. Is this coincidence? They get it and know what golf should really feel like. In some cases these courses only offer the option to walk with your bag, use a pull cart or utilize a caddie. No electric cart use outside of emergencies or with written doctor permission.

Caddies can be of varying excellence and experience. They may be students paying their bills before once again hitting the books in the fall, retired older gentlemen who want a pleasant walk in the country with excited folks, or lifers whose existence depends upon the golfer who wants no part of the electric cart and welcomes the opportunity to experience golf this way. Their quality of standards may differ; however, all words of wisdom from caddies are welcomed to maximize the enjoyment of your round. They are united in wanting the paying golf public to support their way of life so they do not become extinct. They believe in the value that is provided by their efforts and wisdom. And I am sure caddies desire that golfers have a primal need to play the game in this manner.

My preference is to have a dedicated bag handler but double-baggers are more common at golf resorts and courses enabling caddies to maximize earnings. It doesn't matter. The time spent without dragging your own clubs and the benefits of local knowledge they provide can help you immensely with both score and the enjoyment quotient.

My friend Bags even turned his game around during the round at the renowned Ocean Club on Kiawah Island. His caddie gave him a couple of instrumental tips, suggesting to get his hips through the ball better, and strike it with greater authority. It magically worked and I was witness to seeing him hit two brilliant four-irons to the 17th green and the playoff hole to win yet another Chewie Open Championship. Bags still talks about the impact of this caddie's guidance that day. He is a true believer. It certainly worked for him and can certainly work for you. The gentle giant is a man of few words. I call him E.F. Hutton after the memorable John Houseman commercial. When Bags talks, people listen; so when your caddie talks, you should listen too!

Golfers marvel when watching the Masters, the Open Championship, and other popular golf championships in part because they want to see poetry in motion. Tiger's clutch pressure shots, Phil's deft flop wedges, and Boom Boom Couples' graceful, long tee-shots are all beautiful to watch and appreciate. We sometimes wish we could emulate them and their lifestyle. And guess what . . . these golfing heroes all have their loyal caddies standing by to help them win. So, if you can picture yourselves as Phil for just one shot, then why not feel like being Phil for a day and hire your own private Bones?

Your caddie may not be a tough ex-New Zealand rugby player like Steve Williams but the young American with a distinct mid-west accent or grizzled veteran with a delightful Scottish brogue will make you feel like a King for a day or an Adam Scott, if you must. Try it and you will undoubtedly love the experience. And your final count on your scorecard may reflect that pleasant surprise you have been waiting for your entire golfing life!

Cart Girl Visit #3 with Trivia Refreshments on Inward Half of Golf Course.

1. Who are/were the only three living persons to appear on a Scottish banknote?

    Drain a cold Heineken.

2. Tiger Woods won the Open Championship, The U.S. Open and The Canadian Open in the same year. Who is the only other golfer to duplicate this great feat?

    Eat some honey-roasted Planter's peanuts.

Hole No. 13, Par 3. How do you avoid folded arms?

Well, first of all, do not tell her that the golf round will only take 4 hours! If you do, folded arms from your special acquaintance, your nearly perfect, yet sadly golf-impaired girlfriend, your exasperated common-law or irate wife will spring at you like a loaded 357 Magnum upon your return to her unhappy presence in 5½ hours. Breathing Captain Morgan's dark rum will surely create even further havoc. Yes, there are females who will reverse the roles and be the golfers in the relationship. But somehow I think these boyfriends and husbands will be more than content to take this time to slump on the couch, flick on the boob tube, and watch the football game or an old war movie if they know they have 6 hours to themselves. Men who brandish folded arms just don't have the same persuasiveness. I am sure you agree. I therefore (if you don't mind) will focus on the perspective of females and their folded arms.

This symbolic and universal defensive posture (or is it an offensive stance, since she is hurtling her feelings towards you at warp speed?) has impacted most male golfers at least one time in their careers. In order for you to truly enjoy a round of golf without causing unnecessary anguish, players need to be smart in the big picture, specifically your home picture.

The sales pitch can be a difficult one to win, especially when it involves non-golfing other halves. They will not let you off easily when this request for a good day on the golf course is first posed. Snippy comments that make you feel guilty may be cast in your direction, followed by exaggerated eye-rolling, and the aforementioned folded arms posture. Disbelief, coupled with wonder, becomes her dominant state of mind as she contemplates why you would dare, really dare, to go golfing with your buddies when you could spend a day with her collecting three gnomes and a new entrenching tool for the growing hydrangeas in the English garden.

The goal of course, is for her to strike a weak nerve in your system to see if she can make you quiver and then change your mind. Hold your line, men. Do not give in. Inform her that you will be golfing. Take this worldly advice from me, your relationship consultant, and a golfer of more than four decades.

Make it up to her later in your own way through an extended romantic dinner, by listening attentively to her troubles of the day or by making that long-postponed trip abroad to reconnect your relationship. Is this bribery? Well . . . that is a fine line, isn't it?

Boys, we all have our job cut out for us when we want to slip out for the lunge on the golf course. It is vital that you manage expectations properly and clearly when providing the duration of your rounds. Set the precedent early and then be consistent in delivery of these expectations. All will then be well in the world.

Some straightforward rules from this golf relationship guru for you to avoid "folded arms":

1. Give yourself an extra half-hour cushion when determining the length of your golf game. Don't necessarily arrive home too early or she might catch on to this schmegeeling ploy and make you pay for it on a future round. And Pedro the pool boy may be involved while you are away and, well, this brings a whole new set of rules to bear with when dealing with your other half. . . . This successful timing formula needs to include a series of components: two-way travel time, a frost-delay buffer, the extra time caused by grundies who plod along in the three foursomes in front of you, a quick 19th hole break after nine holes, the inevitable after-the-round drink and/or quick food replenisher, and add 5 hours for the round.

    Eliminate the need to rush off the course after your round since the post-mortem conversation and drinks in the 19th hole with your chums is important to the overall satisfaction of your golfing day. Using my crafty analysis to determine the golfing duration will allow you to predict a better and more accurate assessment of the time needed on the course. Grin brightly on a job well done after you have made your winning calculation and yell "A-ha" as though you have satisfactorily solved the most complex puzzle. Then notify her that "I will be at least five-and-a-half hours." She may not necessarily hear the words "at least" but since you did your homework and have room to manoeuvre you will be safe.

2. Even after you follow my cleverly created formula to the letter in Point 1 and are somehow going to be later than agreed, ALWAYS MAKE THE PHONE CALL TO HER AND TELL HER YOU WILL BE LATE. Yes, you will take major heat but you can minimize the folded arms situation upon your tardy return. If you do not make the call then I can assure you that folded arms will be the least of your problems. The situation could painfully escalate to the dreaded hands on hips motion and therefore prompt a pronto rushmeister high-step to the flower store for quality flowers. Belgian chocolates might be a good addition . . . . The ice queen technique, multiple chores to do by 6pm, or changed locks may be worse punishments for you to finagle.

3. Thank your loved one for allowing you to play when you see her, following the round. Now, asking politely for a much-needed nap may be pushing it too far but this personal downtime can be accomplished if you have a proven and healthy track record. Don't overplay your hand too early, as you have to earn the right. In addition, if you are raring to go (see if you can exert some extra effort and energy) then take her to a bookstore, a movie, dinner, or a walk. If you have kids then you may want to proactively offer taking the rug rats off her hands for a healthy period. It would be my pleasure, dear! The pendulum has swung and it is now all about her. Do not talk about your golf game because that is a crippler to the mood. She won't care about your thinly hit five-iron on the 16th hole or the "should have made a par" comment about your putt on the 11th. Her mood, her smile and the enjoyment of the rest of the day is your primary focus.

Boys, we can sing the old adage that a happy wife is a happy life. This is very true. By following the simple rules that I have outlined you will smack the ball around with your comrades in peace, comfort, and pleasure. We are familiar with strategic golf course management so translate this skill set into tidy home management of expectations techniques. Score will probably be lower since you have now eliminated negative and niggly thoughts that might creep into your head.

Gentlemen of the clan, be the well-crafted and regal tall ship that coasts through calm seas towards home base. Do not be that dilapidated tugboat caught by surprise in a nasty storm, straining to avoid jagged rocks upon its return. Your homecoming viewed through your binoculars should be a welcoming sight like a friendly lighthouse blinking at you, not one fit with the peril of folded arms!

Hole No. 14, Par 5. Is the secret choice for your annual golf trip to Oregon or Wisconsin or . . . ?

"Where are you going tomorrow for your golf trip?", a curious acquaintance asked me. Anticipating a concrete answer, he instead heard, "I don't honestly know." Confused and intrigued, he wanted to know how I could possibly not know where I was going for a 5-day jaunt. I told him that we had conducted annual mystery golf trips for the last few years. "Cool, very cool," my colleague uttered in a manner lathered with green envy. I thought so too and all of those people to whom I have mentioned this strategy feel it is a great way to go on a yearly boys' golf trek. Others only wished they were part of the equation . . .

The annual Chewie Open foursome (Scugog, Bags, Chief, and I—the Commish) commenced this brilliant mystery golf trip brain wave in 2004, when I was responsible for surprising the group with a trip to the Robert Trent Jones Trail resort at Capitol Hill in Montgomery, Alabama. The individual responsible for the trip would confirm a date for the 4-to 5-day trip (usually between mid-April to early May) after gaining the blessings of the other three posse members.

Pithy but also misleading emails by the leader would be circulated with short cryptic comments. This curveball scheme was to throw off the curious queries made by the others during the run-up to this glorious event. Control freaks in our group (Chief and Scugog) might probe with questions but their thrusts were neatly side-stepped. Psychological warfare tools were utilized in these communications and such messages could state, "Bring your raingear but it could be sunny. Shorts may be used on a couple of days but you might want to bring three levels of clothing." Such advice was useless, of course, as the controller wanted to throw off the scents of the hound dogs. Game on!

The three clueless members would then arrive at the appointed time at Toronto International Airport. These flight details were revealed only late in the game so the fellas wouldn't try to schmegeele and calculate where they might be going. The code was kept in place. No leakage was allowed to those who could damage the integrity of this secret. Death was the only option if such a failure occurred. We demanded to be surprised.

Then after all four had congregated with high-fives and back slaps, the controlling sergeant would ceremoniously unfurl the packaged itinerary with our marching orders. Once the script was unrolled, the oblivious would transform into the enlightened and elated ones. More jubilation ensued and the focus was now on dreaming about what awaited us in a few hours. Remember those early days of your lives when you gathered around the Christmas tree, wondering what was in that big thanger of a package with your name on it sitting in the corner? Yes, you have warm and fuzzy memories of those glorious days. Good ones, of course.

I have been most fortunate and privileged to travel to well-known golf destinations like Pinehurst, North Carolina; Palm Desert, California; Kiawah Island, South Carolina; and Pebble Beach, California. Each of our Chewie Open boys' trips has been great—just different degrees of great, if there is such a thing. From tree-lined fairway golf to cacti-and-rattlesnake-infested desert golf to breathtaking ocean-view golf, they all possess their own distinct charming qualities. Finding those hidden golf jewels or choosing well-known destinations is an exciting proposition to surprise the group. Scugog in fact, read about Bandon Dunes on the Chewie Open flight the year before it was his turn. We are pretty diligent in reading golf magazines and sourcing different places.

So a question from the readers might be: "How can I have a similar successful mystery golf trip with my closest comrades?" Well my friends, I have some good suggestions.

Recipe for annual golfing success:

Commitment. This is probably the linchpin that will make your trip happen. Not the "let's go out for lunch sometime" kind of commitment but one that states very clearly, "We will have lunch next Wednesday at 2pm." The latter statement is a true commitment not a waffle. Your group, in our case a foursome, all need to be on the same wavelength. It must be a priority. A lockdown. We are all good friends with busy lives but the trip is important to each and every one of us.

Setting Expectations and Priorities of the trip. Very good golf experiences take precedence for us, period. Everything else aligns with this fact. If shopping in malls and sightseeing on cable cars are more important festivities, then you better discuss this up front or you will have a war of dissension on your hands during the trip. For us, tee-off times will not be missed at any cost (maybe lightning strikes, but a brutal hangover is not an excuse).

Budget including accommodations. Pricing for your trip can certainly range widely. You should discuss among your group so there are no surprises. Fun and quality trips can be done in Alabama as much as in Pebble Beach.

Numbers. Four is a very good number for us. We play together every round, eat together and have long, stimulating conversations together. The boys know what we get and this set-up has been successful every time. Once you go beyond four then there can be a lot of moving pieces to keep consistency for everyone on the trip. Chemistry of personalities must be measured. Will anybody be selfish and dominate the whole? Quickly determine this quality in the individual and if there is not a good fit for the overall group, then nix this idea of his or her inclusion.

Trophy. Purchase a trophy even if it costs $50. Our Chewie Open trophy has been through some exciting times and the beleaguered figurine has lost its wooden club. Our own version of Linus seems lonely and lost without his blanket. After the final round of each tournament, the past champion says a few words and then presents the trophy to the new champion with polite applause from the participants. The enviable winner gets to carry this chick magnet through airport security on the way home. Everyone, including the usually serious airport security power trippers, fellow male golfers, old ladies, flight attendants and inquisitive young women want to know what famous championship you won. Being a celebrity for a day gives you good incentive to win the darn thing. He has the power to embellish the hardware's significance by mentioning words like "major" or "prestigious" and enjoys many complimentary interactions with fellow humans. All four of us have triumphed multiple times so we appreciate and respect the honour bestowed upon the title holder.

The responsibility of the winner is to engrave the trip's location and the year they won it before the beginning of the next competition. These places etched on the trophy are great reminders of our destinations and strengthening friendship. The different font sizes indicate the ranging egos in our group. Chief, just remember that capital letters and 16-point Times Roman font is too big if we don't want to purchase a second trophy in 3 years!

The winner is the holder of the chalice for the year and the other three competitors cannot touch it. Superstition and respect, you see. Much pressure is put upon the champion to convince the family (especially the wife) to have the trophy displayed prominently in the main living room area. This is a prestigious ornament and should find a place next to family heirlooms or the treasured Royal Doulton china collection. The record of staying in a high profile spot is I believe, 4 weeks. Bags then sulkily found the trophy unceremoniously dumped in a faraway closet housing 1975 baseball cards in a shoebox along with multiple dust bunnies.

Steak dinner and nice wine. We are not vegetarians. The rascals are red meat types of guys. The steak dinner (if not multiple times) is a special night for indulgence and toasts with a microbrew, beautiful Cabernet or single malt scotch. This has never been missed.

Hot Tub/Cigar/Lounge chair reminiscing. Hot tubs have tended to be a must on our trips. The reason is that these facilities are not only extremely relaxing after a round of golf but also symposiums for us to freely conduct "code of silence" and other usually off-the-record kinds of discussions. This is the once-a-year time to ask tough questions and to creatively dodge uncomfortable answers. There have been cases where the blasted machine was malfunctioning or non-existent, but almost always, we are able to source a hot tub. Smoking cigars outside in comfortable chairs or while standing when utilizing practice putting greens that surround eating establishments have also been highlights of our stays.

Golf format by the rules. South Carolina was the beginning of the trend. On our initial trip in 1999 (before it was a mystery version), I had convinced the others that we should use stroke play rules. Every putt had to hit the bottom of the cup. The other three had not been accustomed to playing this formal way of the game since they were more leisurely golfers and understood the past familiar use of the "raked" 2 ½-footer. But upon completion of the tournament, the Commish gained acceptance from all, without hesitation, that this should be the way we do things all the time. Make sure group members are on the same wavelength regarding the rule format you intend to play, especially if money is being exchanged.

Friends can quickly turn in to enemies if fine points and expectations are misconstrued.

Timing. March break time with the family makes it tough, so we have seen early May (maybe mid to late April) as the time to go on our trip. Booking such a trip well in advance is a necessity to schedule the details properly and eliminate any wafflers who may bail on you early in the process. Ask for some money up front and that will help you to determine who is serious about coming on your golfing expedition. You don't want to be left holding the bag when crunch time arrives.

How much golf? Some like to play numerous rounds in a day while others do not. Get a sense of what is desirable for the foursome.

Downtime. Naps, exercise and some quiet times are essential during such a trip. You may strangle another mate if he acts too much like a Siamese twin!

Roommates. We have determined who the control freaks and easygoing guys are. One of each per room is best. That prevents two guys from either fighting over the converter or constantly arguing on what to do. Perhaps you will base it on introvert/extravert or partiers/non-partiers. Your call.

Warm up. Golfers have their own peculiar habits with respect to how they would like to prepare for each golf game. Some absolutely need a big breakfast and/or 30 minutes to lunge practice balls. Talk this over once you are at your destination to avoid grumpy players in your group.

Challenges. Selling the trip to your family, especially your wife can be an undertaking. Remember the folded arms syndrome I warned you about? I think this may be a tougher chore than taking time off from work. The first year is a tough one to sell to her. The second year may be even more difficult. Why? Because your loved one will see through your crafty attempt of setting the stage for an annual golf excursion. The dreaded lockdown, from her perspective. In short, the precedent has been set. If everyone sees this trip as a priority, then each will find their own unique way of placating home obstacles. It is tough but the job can be done. If all else fails, try embellished flattery or bribery.

So let me tell you about one of our secret boys' trip to Bandon Dunes. Oregon for golf in the month of May, you say, old chap? You betcha! (as our moose-hunting, hockey mom Sarah Palin might retaliate). This pure golf destination may be the best boys' golf trip you could possibly take in the United States. And you are likely to be one of the many who have not heard of this place. This hidden jewel (although it is getting more recognition as years progress) has only been open since 1999. Imagine some Pebble Beach sightlines and feel while playing links golf in Scotland. Be prepared for the weather if you go there in the spring but it is well worth the journey, regardless.

All four of us agree that Bandon reigns supreme of all the Chewie Open trips we have taken. Although we cherish trying new places, this is one destination that we would willingly choose to return to in a heartbeat. I think this is the ultimate tribute to Bandon especially after outlining the other top-flight golf resorts we have visited.

We flew to the Oregon boondocks in 2005 to see what all the fuss was about. Leading golf magazines were starting to rave about the relatively new Bandon Dunes and Pacific Dunes golf courses (the latter was opened in 2001). Both of them were ranked in the Top 10 list of public courses in the United States. Impressive indeed to have two courses at the same resort listed. This was even before the more recent addition of Bandon Trails that was opening later that very summer and Old Macdonald, which came on board in 2010. My images of Oregon were of lumberjacks, timber, and the Trail Blazers. But the insiders were telling me to use different kinds of woods when you set foot in this out-of-the-way place. How come so few people I have spoken to have heard of this place? Was it the Oregon location that threw people off?

I like to think we experienced Bandon Dunes before it became more cliché or popular. There is something stimulating about being part of a small, secret society, a fraternal brotherhood. Bandon gripped us with this invigorating feeling. Clint Eastwood and Bill Clinton were two well-known personalities who were rumoured to have trekked down to this special enclave on private planes to play a little golf during the early days. What the heck? If Dirty Harry and Slick Willy were customers, then we might as well join the parade!

Don't kid yourself; this trip is a long haul if you live on the east coast. One scan of the busy itinerary provided by Scugog at Terminal 1 confirmed this fact. From Toronto we flew to O'Hare and gained an hour. After a short layover and a quick latte, we transferred to a plane to go to Portland, Oregon and gained 2 more hours. At this punishing rate of a 27-hour Pacific Time day, I wondered if I would slouch over with exhaustion. My metabolism was being shaken and rattled but no whining was allowed because we would be golfing the next day. How bad can that be?

Next up on our demanding schedule was a plane flight to Bend, Oregon and then on to North Bend. I was almost delirious because of this wearying travel. Would South Bend be next? Oh no, that is not right. South Bend is the town of the renowned Fighting Irish of Notre Dame (my favourite American college football team) and it resides in Indiana. I didn't want to cycle back to the Midwest! Is there Sideways Bend? The dipsy-doodling of the puddle-jumping propeller airplane made it quite clear to me that I was entering Hicksville. Looming thoughts of the terrifying movie *Deliverance* and Ned Beatty entered my consciousness . . . . A rental van was booked for us in friendly North Bend so we could traverse the final 45-minute drive on this incredible milk run.

We found this place in the middle of nowhere—and that is exactly how golfing traditionalists want it. A welcome sign for Bandon Dunes Resort sprouted just off the highway (if you want to call it that) which we had taken. The drive into the property took a few minutes and we found ourselves enthralled by the surroundings of nature's gifts of grass, woods, and birds. And no sound but the sounds of nature. This is an unadulterated golf mecca. Forget about any jewellery shopping at Birks or other fancy retail outlets. Female shoppers hungry for Manolo Blahniks would starve to death and men looking for some greasy burger joint would be completely disheartened. On consecutive days, I would later see a nattily dressed woman in pink golf attire searching desperately for new and diverse outfits sitting on racks outside the pro shop. She stood out like a third arm as there were few females on the grounds. This was the wrong setting for a successful shopping quest and she was battling a losing cause. Bandon was undeniably a guy's enclave and catered to this golfing crowd (although dedicated women golfers would love the golf, food, spa and environment).

Fatigue had set in from the long day of travelling but there was a collective sense among the four of us that we were starting another great adventure. Anticipation of the first smack on the inaugural hole of Bandon Dunes swept away any lingering lethargy that might have been creeping into our psyches. The first day of our brief trips always gives us this splendid feeling. Do you know why? All we had left was brilliant, mesmerizing golf, unlimited chatting, joyful banter, hearty libations, and juicy steak dinners. This was quite a strong and enticing agenda . . .

We checked in and admired the pleasant main clubhouse at The Lodge. Without the least bit of hesitation, Chief and Scugog commenced peppering the poor, unprepared front desk lady with eighty questions about the facilities, restaurants, and their concerns about fickle weather. Bags and I stood silently to the side, highly amused, as these two titans took control. Scugog raised his hand dynamically to Chief to send him an ominous message and shuffled him to the side.

Essentially, CF2 (Control Freak #2) was telling CF1 (Control Freak #1) that he was in complete control and in our order of delegated hierarchical power, this was Scugog's trip. Chief knew the joke was over and he settled for being a follower to this leader of the pack. I noticed his teeth clench. His turn would come again in 3 years as per the stated points in our Chewie Open Constitution.

The two illustrious courses were situated behind this building. They had very good practice facilities a short distance away from the Lodge and golf lessons were provided for a fee. I detest practicing but Bags took advantage of this amenity and took a lesson later on in the trip. He found it very useful; so those in the practice tribe should take note to use them when they come to Bandon. His taking this lesson may have had something vaguely to do with him careening consecutive sliced drives off a shiny metal shed with a thud, and then seeing his balls finish clearly on the wrong side of the out-of-bounds markers. Notably, these lousy results were on the first hole at Bandon Dunes during Round 1 and could not have seemed to him a good omen. Perhaps his anticipatory excitement caused this system overload. Or was it the swirling wind, or the beautiful setting, or the competitive situation . . .

The resort's buildings did not overwhelm you like the opulent Sanctuary Hotel at Kiawah Island or historical Pebble Beach but the charm and warmth were evident. We later enjoyed a sumptuous dinner in The Gallery serving high-end fare and lots of great Cabernet and other choice wines. The restaurant offered an enticing view through a large window onto the golf course. One floor down, we discovered a very nice spa to relax in and we took advantage of it one day. Ahhhh . . . nice to be spoiled once in a while with such an indulgence! McKee's Pub was conveniently positioned next to the pro shop on the opposite wing. High-and low-end food choices at the resort meant we could portray ourselves both as gentlemen of distinction if need be or as primitive men when draft beer and chicken wings were preferred. I like having this range of food and drink options at such destinations to indulge different moods.

The skies were overcast and looked threatening. Coming as we did at this time of spring meant that we would have to contend with the elements. Our rounds featured a smattering of rain, coolness and wind along with bursts of sun. All kinds of weather patterns. So this is what those grizzled Scotsmen, Irishmen, and Limeys have to endure back on the British Isles! I wanted to transport myself in to their shoes and see how I would measure up in the face of Mother Nature's diverse weaponry.

If you are wimpy, fainthearted or own lousy rain gear, then this golf testing ground will not be the place for you during this part of the season. No way were we going to be classified in these undesirable categories. In all of our trips, we have never been rained out and that is an incredible run of good luck. That last day at Myrtle Beach on our inaugural trip did, however, test us to the limits. The torrential downpour was relentless and we waffled about whether we should continue. All of us persevered in the end. We passed a test of sorts to see if we were true golfers . . . real men.

We felt the percentages were in our favour to continue our providential streak in Oregon. What really is the deal breaker in deciding to walk off the course? Could it be when a bolt of lightning strikes 3 feet from you as you jangle your clubs down the fairway? Or is it when your smile disintegrates because of extreme discomfort even though you are playing on truly great golf land? Tough to gauge, isn't it?

Our two-bedroom cottage/villa rested a mere 3-minute walk away from the main clubhouse and golf courses. These pristine confines were exactly what we envisioned. The adjoining rooms were a nice touch. Great, no shuttling on buses at designated times or fiddling to get to the courses. It was extremely convenient not to have to worry about dealing with such organizing tasks on these trips. You don't want to miss your ride because missing a tee-off time through bad staff work constitutes a cardinal sin.

Next morning we giddily sauntered up to the pro shop to check in, and 2 minutes later we were on the tee, ready to lunge at Bandon Dunes. And to my pleasant surprise, no riding carts! All you enthusiastic electric cart people take note; unless you have a written doctor's note, these machines could not be utilized. Caddies, using those big black-wheeled pushcarts or walking with clubs slung on your shoulders were your choices. The exercise is well worth it. I alternated days between hiring a caddie and using the pushcart. Using caddies on a new and magnificent course is a great experience. Do it.

No wonder I had a great feeling about this place. Golf needs to affect all your senses. Walking and feeling your attachment to the course's contours keep you constantly engaged while riding carts hinder this sensation. My traditionalist tastes were satisfied. This wonderful place understood the way golf should be played.

There was an interesting quirk about the rules of engagement with the pushcarts. Bandon allowed you to drag them across the greens. Wh-a-a-at? I have never been able to commit such a grave breach of etiquette in the past because of my extensive golf training and upbringing so my brain had a hard time reconciling this odd local rule. Seeing a push cart trucked across a green is as natural as seeing a Spanish soccer player failing to dive upon contact from a Portuguese defender in the penalty box area during World Cup action.

In my first attempt to cross the green with the cart it was like I was welcomed through a force field that had been sustained throughout centuries. I reached out to see if Captain James Tiberius Kirk really was dropping his intimidating defences to allow this Klingon to play through in this alternative universe. This was a bizarre and disorienting foreign land that I was visiting. I am sure the others laughed at me; fully understanding the Commish's engrained views of these things. Such a misguided gesture would have been sacrilege—until now. Local rules trump!

Pebble Beach in Scotland. That is how I like to describe the combination of styles of play at Bandon. The Pacific Ocean raises its head on several holes as you play this course with links conditions. The land is rugged and untamed in among dunes and it is obvious that there is a Scottish or Irish feel to this special place. Different teeing areas are offered and they provide with good visuals in order to see proper landing areas.

Penal pot bunkers with great lips poke their heads out at strategic spots and will skyrocket your scores if you have the pleasure to visit Mr. Sandman—otherwise known as Jabba. They are not always the normal types of traps through which you can advance the ball but ones that are sometimes ragged in aesthetics and truly penal. Just blast short shots to extract the ball out of the pit and survive. Fescue is plentiful so avoid this gnarly stuff if you can. There are some blind shots but not too many to frustrate your efforts. Trees behind some of the greens add to this gorgeous scenery. The putting surfaces can be sizable, which I like; and sometimes tiered with humps, making 3-putts inevitable.

You know you are in pure golf heaven when you struggle to find yardage markers, don't glimpse electric carts anywhere and are alone in the world away from other golfers and civilization. As an explorer in this kind of golfing world you feel and sense your shots more acutely without such distractions. There is an obvious rawness when you play in this manner and it is far, far removed from being pampered golf. Any signs of blatant commercialism are purposely minimized at Bandon. The silence is deafening (although the wind will have its say).

No. 4 a par-4, 410-yard hole with an ocean backdrop on your approach shot stood out in my mind as a fabulous and special one. The hole commences with a sizable hill to the right of the tee. As the wind increases in tenacity and you walk to your drive in the fairway, the hill dwindles in size until it no longer exists. In its place is one of the most memorable sights in golf and the view hits you like a sledgehammer—the Pacific Ocean stands before you with what looks like a tiny green nestled in front of it. Truly captivating and incredibly photogenic.

Both times we played this hole it had a fiendish three-club wind driving into us. This incredible force felt like a hand was pushing you back as you hit your shot, which was intimidating. Chief reminded me of this as he smiled knowing this was an ultimate test and that I tend to hit my irons into Sputnik space. We were so cowed by the prospect of hitting this shot that we both knew that it would fall achingly short of the green. Mine didn't even come close. Never has failure been so terrific.

Bags found that this specific hole created a spiritual golf awakening for him the second time he played it during this trip. He had reached his tipping point with this game. My friend is an occasional golfer but his appreciation of the traditions and enjoyments of the game have increased. He now understood that golf was beyond achieving the lowest score and I have now bestowed him with the coveted title of Associate Commish. The walk, the scenery, being with good friends, and experiencing such a divine piece of Oregon turf was an honour for him.

Some other favourite holes on Bandon Dunes . . . No. 3 par-5, 543 yards with a nice all-encompassing view of the terrain and No. 5 par-4, 428 yards with split fairways that then funnel into the green. This hole has a spectacular sightline with lots of nasty fescue surrounding the fairway and green. No. 12 par-3, 199 yards with the ocean as a backdrop is a stunner. No. 16, par-4, 363 yards offers golfers split fairways to go high or low in the approach to the green. It has a great panoramic view including water on your right. Don't forget to look back at the hole once you stand on the green. Spectacular views. This is a wonderful challenge and great photographic shots can be taken.

We finished the round and found the experience to be terrific. If Pacific Dunes matched this sensation, we would be delighted. This sister course was even better.

Natural bunkers come into play on Pacific Dunes. Thick rough and fescue also lurk. The ocean views seemed more plentiful on this course. There is the beautiful stretch of these water sights to start the back nine from No. 10 to No. 13. Back-to-back par-3 holes are not usually found on courses but they were a treat to begin the back nine. The first one was a long downhiller with the water as a backdrop and heavy rough while the following par-3 is an uphill shot and the dunkle green is surrounded by gorse, long grass, and sand traps. Short and treacherous. Two holes, two completely different ways to appreciate par-3s.

Some other favourite holes on Pacific Dunes include: No. 3 par-5 of 499 yards where you have to finagle around sand and deep fescue and No. 4 par-4 of 463 yards. No. 13 is one of the best and most difficult holes to play anywhere at 444 yards with sand traps and if the pin is positioned at the back then it is even more terrifying. You can feel like you are running off the end of the earth. Take extra time on this hole to enjoy.

Like Bandon Dunes, golfers may want to use low-to-ground putting or chip shots to avoid trouble surrounding many of these greens. Creative golf. Outstanding stuff!

If you drink the Bandon Kool-aid and find it refreshing then you will become an exuberant ambassador to spread the word. I really like George Peper's term, "Bandonistas" for these Kool-aid quaffers. I am certainly proud to be included in this group and so are my three colleagues.

Since our trip to this resort, I have run into more people who are convinced that this is THE place to go for guys' golf. While having a continental breakfast in Kohler, Wisconsin during the 2010 Chewie Open trip, a Texan emphatically told me that Bandon was the best place to go. And he likes to go to nice venues. With such a groundswell of support from people all over the map, Bandon may become the de facto choice for future boys' golf trips. I have no hesitation in telling other passionate golfers that this is the one place they should absolutely go if they want a pure golf trip.

Pebble stands on its own for beauty, ocean views, tradition, and class. Perhaps if you bundled Cypress Point, Spyglass and Spanish Bay with this course, it would challenge Bandon's four diverse course offerings. But don't even dream that you will be offered the opportunity to play at Cypress Point. Like Augusta National, Cypress Point will most likely remain elusive and exclusive, and remain in its own insular world.

If you never have a chance to go to Scotland or Ireland, then Bandon may be the next best thing. In fact, filmmakers believe this. Michael Murphy's well-known *Golf in the Kingdom* was filmed at Bandon Dunes and substitutes for Scotland. The movie is based on the best-selling fictional golf book that was produced in 1972. It is about a mysterious teacher named Shivas Irons, "true gravity" of a backswing and the holy man Seamus MacDuff guarding the ravine off Burningbush's 13th fairway (remember my telling of the story about Crail's possible significance for Michael Murphy when we played at this location during the Verma Cup trip in Scotland?). This film was launched in the fall of 2011 and I have not seen it yet.

You may recognize the Shivas Irons Society that this book has fashioned. Interestingly, this society is based near Pebble Beach in Carmel. Their mission is for loyal golf servants to share the love of the game and respect for its deeper dimensions. Personally I prefer Part 1 of Murphy's book before it delves into Eastern religion in the second part. But it is a good book to read for those looking for a more spiritual connection to the game.

I look forward to my next trip to Bandon when I can compare all four wonderful tracks now available to the public. And to add even more value to a fantastic resort, Bandon will open a new 13-hole Par-3 course in May, 2012 called Bandon Preserve for those wanting a lighter way to enjoy golf on a lazy afternoon. Great becomes even better. Perhaps I will appreciate Bandon Dunes and Pacific Dunes even more on my second tour. The resort is also more commercial and less of an exclusive and secret club (not quite like the Shivas Irons Society) but that will not detract from the excellence of the golf. No electric carts, remember, and nothing but memorable golf.

I might also recommend that you place Whistling Straits in Kohler, Wisconsin next on your list if you liked your experience at Bandon. The destination is within a couple of hours drive from Milwaukee. This is a stunning golf course and brings to mind many things I liked about Bandon.

And very few people knew about this course in the home of bratwurst, beer, and Cheeseheads. The 2004 and 2010 PGA Championships have been hosted at this course so these tournaments have raised awareness of this golfing treasure.

Others may disagree about my assessment of this contentious course. And you can ask the budding PGA star Dustin Johnson what he thinks of Whistling Straits after being penalized on the last hole of the latest PGA Championship for grounding his club in the bunker. Johnson's dubious lie certainly didn't look or feel like it was a bunker but it was. Considering there are a remarkable 967 bunkers of all shapes and sizes on the course, it may have been prudent for him to ask a friendly marshal to clarify that this was not one of them. One vitally missed question. One lost major. There was ample warning to players that week about this scenario possibly rearing its ugly head. Many did not read these published instructions and Johnson paid the piper for his lack of attention to detail. It was neat to play this course earlier in 2010 so I could comprehend and appreciate his confusion surrounding such bunkers. That finishing hole is a monster—including 96 bunkers and a massive ravine before the green!

Before teeing off at Whistling Straits make sure you venture to the left of the practice putting green by the fantastic clubhouse and position yourself near the 10th tee. Take a look at the course from this perspective and it will take your breath away. Shoot a picture or two. Lake Huron rests in the distance but it is the hundreds of bunkers strewn all over the fairways and rough that gives you a memorable feeling of being on the moon. Also, this pleasurable shock to the system immediately forces you to think, "Man, is this going to be one challenging course and a beautiful one at that!"

Herb Kohler, the popular local businessman, avid golf fan and owner of the Old Course Hotel at St Andrews, commissioned the prominent golfing architect Pete Dye to have him create a magnificent gem along the coastline of Lake Huron in Kohler, Wisconsin. Having a deep affection for Scottish and Irish links golf, Mr. Kohler offered Mr. Dye 2 miles of coastline to create a masterpiece fitting for those who love this type of golf. I loved this landscape and my comfort level resulted in my playing this course well in two rounds. This positive experience made me think of my magical scoring round at the Old Course.

Some courses just feel right and it is hard to explain why some find a special place in your golfing heart. Whistling Straits is positioned in my mind as one of the Top 5 courses I have played in the U.S. The sight of sheep while walking down No. 16 and No. 18 brought a wry smile to my face and the wind raised its not-too-subtle head. What country was I in again? They got it right. No electric carts were allowed and four of us used caddies both days. What a magnificent walk in the country!

Nearby Blackwolf Run and The Irish course at Whistling Straits are also well worth playing. I just missed gaining an ace on a seven-iron shot at the Irish Course after hitting blindly to a green over a huge knoll. This blind shot prepared me well for the two I confronted on the Klondyke and Dell holes at venerable Lahinch in Ireland one year later. The first gave me a crack at eagle when a beautiful seven-iron soared over the hill obstacle. The second was a perfectly executed shot that flew a large mound and landed (and finished) to within inches short of the hole for a conceded birdie win of the hole during the final Verma Cup match in our Ireland team match play Championship. Skilful? Lucky? Intuitive? All of the above, I guess. It was exhilarating to experience these memorable events both in Wisconsin and on the Emerald Isle.

Lumberjacks and Cheeseheads. Bandon, Oregon and Kohler, Wisconsin. I will never look at the west coast black-red-and-white plaid jackets or Kohler faucets and toilets the same again. Should you venture on a boys' trip to the boondocks for fantastic golf? You betcha!

Cart Girl Visit #4 with Trivia Refreshments on Inward Half of Golf Course.

1. Fill in the blank: Steve Burdick, Casey Martin, Tiger Woods, Will Yamagisawa, _____.

   Indulge in a Monte Cristo cigar.

2. What are the three oldest golf clubs in North America?

   Sip on a beautiful 15-year-old Oban single malt Scotch.

Hole No. 15, Par 3. Is business golf a different animal?

I knew this game of business golf would be a different kind of golf. After watching my client rake a 3-foot downhill putt back to himself with his trusty putter and counting it as a gimme, he asked me to mark 7* (asterisk emphasized by the customer) even though the score was actually a 9. My eyes darted hurriedly to the skies. I had hoped the Great Divine One would offer me helpful guidance for my predicament. My wise father had passed away so that option was closed, but I imagined what Terry would say. An eerie silence ensued and I soon jumped to my own conclusion that golf with business customers should be enjoyed for its own sake. Strict use of golf rules should take a hiatus for the day.

I had always been trained to believe in the sacrosanct Royal and Ancient's Rules of Golf since childhood. But my exposure to customer golf necessitated a new way of thinking with respect to these rules. It was high time for me to create a virtual divider between what I believed in terms of rules and what this world of business golf entailed. In due course, I would adjust and enjoy my visits to this new planet. So, I would mark the number 7 with the glaring asterisk on the scorecard without a feeling of dread. A dawn of a new age was born.

The inauguration of the business golf spectre impelled me to think about two principal questions:

1. How do you look after your customer(s) respectfully and play business golf rules, etiquette, and score?
2. Does the way a person plays golf parallel his own business and social behaviour?

Before I continue, please note that, while there are many successful businesswomen who play golf, for my purposes (and to avoid awkward "his/her" and "she/he"), I have kept the singular male pronoun for businessman throughout this particular chapter.

Back when I was a young golfer, my father provided me with some great advice. Terry offered: "Number 1 Son (and the only one), I want you to continue playing this beautiful game throughout your life because there will come a time that you will be able to use it to your advantage in business. People will be impressed if you play the game well and I want you to behave yourself with class. These honourable skills will help you to conduct meaningful business transactions." Senior Morden should have expanded this message by saying, "And customers may take advantage of the score but it is still a great walk in the country."

When you carry out business golf games, forget about traditional rules of the game that you play with your buddies. I am not saying that every businessman cheats because that is a harsh word to use and it is untrue. Don't gnash your teeth when subtle foot wedges, obvious ball tampering in the rough, and ad hoc mulligans are utilized during the round. Customer golf should be enjoyed for the beast that it is.

Your goal is not to shoot an error-free 71 or 81 but to make the person enjoy a day away from damned spreadsheets and complaining employees. So what if there is cheating or loose interpretations of the rules of golf if you are trying to gain business or form a better connection and impression with that person? Learn from his behaviour and pay attention to yours. Remember the virtual partitioning of rules that I outlined earlier.

When meeting your client, please make sure you get to the golf course in plenty of time to pay for the green fees and/or cart. This is your responsibility and an important one. Upon his arrival you can ask him if he needs any tees, a golf glove, or golf balls. Set the tone early with your acquaintance that you are going to look after him for the day. He is probably watching how you behave and how you play the game. He may even be a member of a private club so he will know what to look for in your makeup as a player.

I have participated in many games of business golf throughout my long golfing career and I have adjusted to its nuances. One is riding in gas or electric carts. Unlike my personal preference of walking and feeling the game better, most customers like to ride rather than walk. I think as a rule, the lower handicap golfer prefers to walk but he may also want to be treated as King for one day. Either way, I am more than happy to go with the flow. Be the driver and act as his chauffeur. Buy the drinks and food on the course to keep him fuelled and content.

Let your customer tee off first, regardless of who has low score. This is a small but important gesture as you are putting him first in priority. After you old chap . . . remember that honours off the tee or shooting a scintillating score are not your priorities. However, you will certainly want to perform well and utilize proper etiquette on the golf course. Hold the flag stick on putts, pick up his leftover clubs from greens, and always genuinely compliment good shots.

Minimize business discussion during the round unless the customer offers it. Your goal on the course should be to connect more closely with your customer and have your image bolstered in his eyes. You represent your company's brand and it is imperative that you should exude class, etiquette, and politeness. I have often found that good business conversations take place in the relaxing 19th hole when you have a drink or dinner because there are no distractions. Don't kid yourselves—he knows your purpose for this golf game.

Your business partners may help spread the word to others that you are a good golfer and carry yourself smartly. Although many business people may not play the game as well as they would like, I have found that the majority do appreciate watching a good golfer when he uncorks a 275-yard drive. After playing a round, you now have a common theme with your customer and, as is common knowledge in the brotherhood of golfers, this bond can be very strong. It should help your case in doing business with this fellow but don't rely on or expect to receive business with your customer just because you had this game together. "Earn the right," as I like to say. He remembers the day . . .

The second question I had posed at the beginning of this hole is a little trickier one to answer and can raise an ethical quandary: Is there a parallel between how a customer conducts himself on the course and in his business life? As an analytical type myself, I can't help but observe behaviour on a golf course. Curiosity is a trait I enjoy exercising in my life. Is he a risk-taker on a shot or does he lay up short of the creek? Does he make you pay for everything or does he offer to pay for a round of drinks? Does he fudge the score? Is he pleasant to play with? Does he use strong etiquette? Does he compliment your shot? These may all be signs of how he will treat you in the business relationship. Retain the clues you have learned from the course to help you better understand how you could succeed in working with him.

When it comes to scoring, there are two distinct groups of business golfers: those who don't know the rules and play fast and loose with scores, and those who know the rules and schmegeele their scores. For the former group I do not pay much heed to their scores or rules of play. Walking across your line or dropping an extra ball down and not counting a stroke are harmless infractions. The latter group, however, is one to watch if you have important business dealings.

Be prepared for some business practices with these kinds of players that you may not agree with and some behaviour that may be quirky, dangerous, or enlightening. But (and this is vital) if you are the one trying to garner favours or gain business, be careful how you execute. This is especially true if you are playing with a good golfer who abides by stringent rules (and you know from my other articles that the Commish likes to play by the rules). He may be testing YOU to see if you are worthy of his business. Don't let the client down and ensure you play your own ball by the proper set of golf rules.

Possible Translations of Actions from those Business Golfers who Know Better

Tees off ahead of the tee-blocks=Getting the edge even though it is not really important.

Chats up the cute cart girl=Gregarious type and fun to deal with.

Lays up short of a hazard although he could clear it=Conservative and safe in dealings.

Purchases four beer for the cart=A generous type and relationship-driven.

Really wants to keep his own score=Controller who wants to make own rules.

Laughs at his awful shot=Can laugh at himself and is comfortable in his own skin.

Gives himself a tricky putt and marks lower score=Entitlement to do what he wants.

Adamant that he wants to buy a round of drinks=Willing to cooperate, trustworthy, share the business win.

Tips up the ball in the rough when you are not looking=Be aware that dealings may not be quite the way you think they are.

Talks during your backswing=Lack of respect, thinks of himself first.

Hitting several mulligans=Always looking for better terms and advantages.

There are certainly more examples but I think you get my drift. Business golf is not just another golf game. It is a different animal and should be treated as such. You cannot control others but you certainly can control your own actions and behaviour. Take notice while you are playing and enjoy the day. In the end, you are on the golf course, probably in sunshine, and you have a chance to accelerate a business relationship and/or transaction at the same time. Would you rather be staring at a computer in a cramped cubicle? No, Dilbert, I wouldn't.

HOLE NO. 16, PAR 4. WHY DON'T NORTH AMERICANS ENJOY MATCH PLAY?

"Your hole, pick that up, and let's go to the next tee." "Five and Four."

What the heck is this foreign golf language? It is too bad that these match play phrases are not more familiar in our golf course lexicon. This brilliant format is a different and strategic way to enjoy golf.

Scotsmen, Irishmen, Englishmen, and other Europeans love match play competitions. They also place a significant premium on playing golf swiftly and aim to finish in 3 1/2 hours. No dawdling. When players are out of the hole or when they have won the hole, they move on to the next tee. There is strong incentive to play in this manner since tasty pints await them in the 19th hole. And the British Isles do indeed have fantastic ales and lagers on tap!

Why don't North Americans enjoy match play? I think it really comes down to score and ego. Thriving to shoot lower scores fuels pride in golfers and provides bragging rights for the low men or women to utilize against colleagues and cohorts. Also, there is limited exposure to match play events outside of the Accenture Match Play Championship, Ryder Cup, and the President's Cup. Golfers prefer to say they shot 121 (maybe even with an asterisk). A defined score or a results-oriented philosophy is valued more than saying fuzzy words like "halved" or "dormie." Maybe it is the obsession of having a true metric like a run, a touchdown, or a basket found in other sports and games. Let's call this the North American scoring syndrome.

Our continent's fans, admirers, and sports participants are programmed to understand the easily quantifiable number of a basketball falling through the hoop, the football crossing into the end zone, or the clunk of a spike hitting home plate. They demand scoring and lots of it. Who can forget about the high-flying, offensively minded Edmonton Oilers of the 1980s, and the St. Louis Rams "Greatest Show on Turf" juggernaut led by quarterback Kurt Warner in 2000? Those were exciting times to watch hockey and football when the Oilers and Rams lit up the scoreboard.

So any time scoring decreases in major North American sports leagues, fans panic and complain vehemently. Officials in these leagues then bow to the pressure and try to address this contentious issue. I don't blame them because I like scoring too, but I do also appreciate a great defense and how these teams are meticulously constructed to stop offensive thrusts. Do you remember the year when the New England Patriots defense played so superbly to stifle the Rams offense and win in one of the bigger Super Bowl upsets in 2002? Perhaps this is a major contributor to why soccer has not been as massively popular in our culture as in other countries.

No wonder many North Americans slag soccer (or football, as the rest of the world calls the round-ball game). Who cares about David Beckham bending the ball to Kaka (or substitute another one-named Brazilian if you like), who in turns foots it to Wayne Rooney, who in turns fires it to . . . you get the idea. Instead of appreciating the artistry of skill on display as an end in itself, we hear the great North American sports masses exclaim, "But did he score?!" A nil-nil finish does not usually excite. Embellished Academy Award-winning theatrics and melodramatic acting by players as they fall to the ground because their toenail is barely clipped does not help the sport's case. Tough hockey players competing with three teeth hanging out and suffering from fractured noses would shake their heads in disgust. "Wimps," they would mutter.

Like golf match play events, there is a more limited (but growing) number of soccer games televised except for outstanding World Cup Soccer coverage offered every 4 years. Do North Americans fear what they don't know or understand? Is the rest of the world so wrong in its insatiable appetite for soccer? There should be enormous satisfaction in golf if you are winning each hole or sawing off your determined competitor with an 8-foot uphill breaker putt. Supreme fulfillment for the game doesn't just have to be about making par or marking 4 on your scorecard.

Let me convince you to forget about playing the course and aiming for the lowest possible score and just play the man, woman, or team. Yes, I know this may seem unfathomable. I am not suggesting that you stop playing stroke play altogether because it is the de facto standard, but I simply suggest that you try to appreciate the benefits of playing match play competitions. Grasp this format as though it was a fun game of Hearts versus your usual Texas Hold 'em competition. Both are entertaining card games with their distinct redeeming features that your blokes will enjoy. And your matches can be quicker to play so you can rush home to your wife and lovely kids . . .

In match play, imagine every hole as being a golf course in itself. Forget about the marathon stroke play mentality of 18 holes or a four-round tournament. Your focus is solely on winning each solitary hole man versus man (or team vs. team if you are playing a foursome or 4-ball). For example, in a singles match, if your competitor slices his shot into the woods, the situation is now to your obvious advantage. What do you do?

Decisions need to be made to win the hole and your competitor's shots will often dictate how you choose to react. The present state you find yourself in may scream emphatically that it may not be the most opportune time for you to be macho and hit the big drive. If it is stroke play, you may pound away like usual. But in match play, you may replace taking off the driver head cover and hit a three-iron instead. Shoot for position. Who cares if you win the hole with a bogey? Dispel this from your cranium that such a score is negative in connotation. You won, period. End of story. Bury your ego and place 1+ on your scorecard. And the scorecard will not be cluttered with writing, only where you sit in relation to the other(s) in your match. Halved, lost, or won. You are not playing the rest of the field like in stroke play, so focus on the job at hand.

Many years ago the U.S. Open was decided by a 36-hole Sunday match play final. Talk about a grind and Stress Level 10 finale! The mindset was completely different and this long day was seen as a legitimate way to win major championships.

I travelled to Scotland with several of my Queen's University friends and we purposely used the match play format for a two-team competition. My logic in arguing the case of match play with the rest of the Round Table decision-makers was to indulge in the game like the Scots have for centuries. "When in Rome," I preached . . . . My colleagues bought into my argument wholeheartedly. Many of the players had not ever played this format and I was curious to see their reactions.

After playing scintillating foursome (alternate shot), 4-ball (two-man teams taking the best net score) and single competitions at revered courses like St Andrews, Carnoustie, Gullane, and North Berwick throughout the week, this format transformed these Canadians into dedicated converts. Matching certain personalities for this competition intrigued the field and many stories were told over Scottish bitter at the conclusion of the rounds.

Team match play instils comradeship and provides stimulating competition. Some of the shots and behaviours that are specific for these team competitions include: teammates exchanging thoughts on where putts break, having one teammate finish a putt so the other can try to sink a longer putt for a lower score, or offering advice on club selection. Gimmes are accepted and gladly. All of these characteristics are unheard of and illegal to utilize in true stroke play competition.

One key strategy used in a foursome is to determine whether a player tees off on the odd—or even-numbered holes. Is one of these players a longer ball striker? If so, then you may have that player hit on the longer par-5s depending on where they sit on the card/course. Is there a better iron striker? Perhaps this person on your team should be chosen to tee off on the majority of par-3s (whether they are odd—or even-numbered holes). These are some intriguing storylines that can craft a compelling match. Remember to best position your team to win the match—not necessarily to shoot the lowest score.

Singles matches are simple—beat the other person. There are no partners to help you out when you have a bad hole. Individuals are alone and pressure will be ratcheted upward. This form of match play is a true character builder to see if you can come through in the crunch. 4 and 3. 2 and 1. You can pound your competitor or just sneak by in the end. Just have 1+ showing at the end of the round. Watch the last day of Ryder Cup and President's Cup and you will see enormous stress in the singles matches. Reputations are duly earned.

During the Scottish trip, there were plenty of high-fives and cheers were heard in abundance. It was a pleasant surprise for me to hear this from the participants, as I had hoped they would appreciate this way of playing golf. Higher handicap players told me that they were more comfortable knowing that they did not have to rely on every one of their shots. This made them more relaxed to perform in this team atmosphere. Pressure was minimized. But when they did contribute there was great sense of satisfaction in helping their cause. Control freaks and High Type A competitive personalities liked the grind of singles matches. Team players and strategists loved 4-ball. Foursomes were a peculiar brand of golf but the quirkiness was a welcome break from the other two more conventional types of match play.

The majority of these participants now say that this is their preference of play. It was a great hit and the popularity exceeded my expectations. Overall, they seemed to enjoy the game more.

Now I will switch gears to Tiger. How about Mr. Woods and his match play credentials? Many focus on his indifferent and maybe substandard performances in Ryder Cup and President's Cup matches. His record pales in comparison to his prolific stroke play success (at least until 2010). But don't forget about his unrivalled reputation in winning important match play events when he was a younger man. Remember his three consecutive U.S. Junior Amateur Championships and three consecutive U.S. Amateur Championships? If you don't, then please take a spare moment and think about these incredible accomplishments. No one has come close to duplicating these match play feats. In the past, he has had a fierce reputation as being the best match play competitor when he has his self-described A-game (sometimes his B-game is sufficient).

With his unyielding nerves, Tiger absolutely willed some critical shots into the hole to win his singles matches at these amateur championships. I watched some of these enthralling televised matches. Just when you thought his grave would be dug, BOOM, he drained a 40-footer and totally deflated his competitor. These were psychological daggers aimed directly to maim. Match play can reverse fortunes in a heartbeat with a chip-in or a long putt sunk into the centre of the cup. The driver's seat can turn instantly into the banishment corner. I would be hard-pressed to find anyone more devastating in making repeated clutch shots than Tiger. Jack would be in the same realm.

As a professional, Tiger has won the prestigious World Golf Championship-Accenture Match Play event three times and lost one to Darren Clarke in a final. He smoked Stewart Cink 8 and 7 in the 2008 final. Do you think he doesn't lick his chops when he has a chance to throttle opponents in match play? He bettered that record by annihilating Stephen Ames 9 and 8 in the 2006 opening round. Ames, the Canadian who came via Trinidad and Tobago, jokingly made a comment the day before his match with the No. 1 about how amazed he was to see Tiger score so well when he was spraying the ball all over the course. Tiger wasn't laughing at this perceived slight the next day. He can take these thrusts very personally and he knows how to respond appropriately.

Tiger won this match with Ames after starting with a run of six consecutive birdies. When asked by the media if he heard Ames' comment he said "Yes." When probed for his reaction he simply and succinctly stated "9 and 8." I saw the interview and loved his frank reaction. This short statement really says, "Can you say 'massacre' like General Custer's Last Stand?" Don't raise the ire of the Tiger.

For all of you who enjoy watching golf on television, you should not miss the Ryder Cup match play competition held every 2 years. Alternate years it is The President's Cup in which the Rest of the World (minus Europe) challenges the Americans. The latter matches do not seem to stoke the fires of rivalry as much (though it is also very good to watch) as Old World Europe versus the ex-British colony, the United States. In a way, it is more gentlemanly and less contentious.

Maybe not surprisingly, since I am Canadian, I cheer for the Europeans. My ties to the Queen must be stronger than I'd anticipated. Do New Zealanders cheer for the Aussies when they play the South African Springboks in rugby? Probably not, unless the Australians are helping their own All-Blacks to advance further in to the competition or standings. This argument seems logical.

The Masters, The Open Championship and the Ryder Cup are locked down on my golf-watching calendar. The President's Cup is one that interests me since Mike Weir has played in recent ones and Canada's little tiger has shown he can win. The singles win against Tiger at Royal Montreal in 2007 was a great clutch performance to go along with his 2003 Green Jacket. Augusta National's tournament, which I have attended, ushers in the spring and the beginning of golf season. This competition allows patrons and viewers to glimpse the most immaculate golf course you can ever imagine. As for the Open Championship, the traditions of this national championship and the intricacies of links courses like St Andrews, Turnberry, and Carnoustie are enough to warm your heart. They are not beautiful courses in Augusta's way but magnificent for what links golf represents—creativity, battling the weather elements, and sensing the ghosts of history. The 3-day Ryder Cup and President's Cup match play competitions start with foursomes and 4-balls over the first 2 days, and then end with gut-wrenching singles matches on the final day. Winning for King and Country, as they say!

Pressure to win for your country during this final day in match play competitions is staggering. Just ask Hale Irwin or Bernhard Langer what their experiences were like in the 1991 Ryder Cup "War on the Shore" at Kiawah Island, South Carolina. Langer, a two-time Masters Champion missed a 6-footer on the last hole that would have tied his match with Irwin. The Europeans would then have retained the Cup. Instead, the German was saddled with the loss for his side and golfing lore would suggest that he was a man who couldn't close the deal for his mates. My memory still conjures up a devastated figure bent over with his head in his hands. Irwin, a three-time U.S. Open Champion and no slouch himself, 3-putted the 17th and chunked a chip shot on the 18th, before barely hanging on to win. See what major champions can do in such match play competition? It is a very different challenge. I like this quote from Irwin: "I couldn't breathe, I couldn't swallow. The sphincter factor was high." Here is a link if you want a great read about the grand pressure of match play at Ryder Cup, 1991 http://www.golf.com/golf/special/article/0,28136,1833804,00.html

I will admit that in my view, stroke play, especially over a 4-day tournament, is the ultimate test of nerves and execution. Everything needs to drop to the bottom of the cup and your focus needs to be on all the time. There is certainly a mental drain from this marathon of golf and I know readers will continue to play stroke play as their match of choice. The great Irish amateur Joe Carr once stated that stroke play may be a better test of golf but match play is a better test of character. I like this comment.

All I ask is for golfers to grab three of your friends and think outside of the North American syndrome. Be open-minded and have fun with match play. Play a 4-ball competition and complete it in 3 1/2 hours. Pick up your Titleist when you are out of the hole. Contribute great shots and low scores for your teammate when needed. Charge those putts by the hole when you know your partner is well-positioned to win the hole. As that old television commercial for Life Brand cereal preaches, "Try it Mikey, you might like it!"

Hole No. 17, Par 4. Is Ryder Cup now a guise for war talk and dubious sportsmanship?

I think I much preferred the 1969 Summer of Love period to the painful and dismal 1991 recessionary times. What say you? The classy image of two worthy opponents by the names of Jack Nicklaus and Tony Jacklin striding off the final green with arms draped over each other's shoulders at the 1969 Ryder Cup is a memorable one. Jack had just conceded a 2-foot putt to the 1969 Open Championship winner at Royal Birkdale that halved the match and the competition. The U.S. retained the Cup with this tie. Their beaming smiles told the story. There was no need to make him putt it, at least not from Jack's eyes. American Captain Sam Snead certainly thought otherwise and gritted his teeth. But then Jack knew better. Mr. Nicklaus upholds sportsmanship like a knight protects a king. Such preservation of this ideal, to him, always trumps selfishness and other petty thoughts.

Now fast-forward to 1991 when there was an economic malaise lingering in North America. A different and more negative feeling pervaded our lives. The War on the Shore at Kiawah Island, South Carolina sprouted. Was this a new kind of war precipitated to purposely make others forget about the Vietnam War that raged in 1969 and which subsequently ended in dismal defeat for the American forces in 1975? Maybe it was this arduous 1991 economic recession that contributed to the disintegration in the gentleman's spirit for these Ryder Cup matches and the increase in war rhetoric. No doubt the recent impressive Operation Desert Storm victory in Iraq during that year was a major contributor to these combative feelings. War talk seemed more prevalent than sportsmanship. In what dangerous direction was the esteemed Ryder Cup heading?

When I played the magnificent Pete Dye-designed Ocean Course at Kiawah Island in 2007 during one of my Chewie Open tournament stops,

I found it easy to collect thoughts about the Ryder Cup when it was played at this venue. There were some compelling storylines created, especially in the final singles matches. They involved American Mark Calcavecchia's colossal collapse against the Scot, Colin Montgomerie, Hale Irwin's thickening collar on the last holes versus Bernhard Langer and, finally, the latter's famous missed short putt to lose the Ryder Cup. The German memorably lost a third war for his country in the twentieth century.

Rattling of snare drums and thunderous battle hymns seemed more likely to appear in 1991 than the honourable scenario of having someone concede a 2-foot putt for the good of the game. Desert Storm caps donned by American players helped to accentuate the war theme. Did Kiawah Island's ocean and beaches also remind the Americans of their own invasion of Normandy, France on June 6, 1944? Was the increase of military jargon their defensive response to European golfers' incursion onto their South Carolinian turf? From my perspective, the spirit of the game had taken a crippling body shot and Americans were deviating from the scripted storyline by using war as an analogy for a golf competition. I do not view golf in this way. Maybe "battling" my wits when I was attempting a 3-foot downhill putt . . .

An hour away from Kiawah Island is Charleston, South Carolina. What a majestic city to visit. It exudes Southern hospitality, charming pink, red, and blue coloured homes are on display in the downtown area and the city is steeped in history. While visiting on my golf trip, I walked down to the scenic boardwalk and peered out to see Fort Sumter standing sentinel in Charleston harbour. As a self-described history buff, I knew the significance of this coastal fortification.

The spark that set off the Civil War powder keg happened at this spot. Students from The Citadel at nearby Morris Island fired the first artillery shots of the war. It was now Southerner versus Northerner. Rebel versus Yankee. American versus American. Brother against brother. I pondered the thought that nearby Kiawah Island was the commencement of a different type of war between distant cousins. The Ryder Cup was a war of provocative words, shiny weapons (Callaway and Ping), and hostile attitudes.

I love watching the Europeans take on the Americans in Ryder Cup action. This is not just a great golfing event but also a thrilling sporting occasion that can be enjoyed by both golfers and non-golfers. Every 2 years I block off the necessary time to absorb and appreciate it. You should too.

The Ryder Cup played in the fall is purely match play. North Americans only infrequently get to see either foursomes (alternate shot), 4-balls (better ball) or singles matches (man on man). The team competition is gruelling and exciting stuff with people in many countries viewing anxiously to see if their main men can handle the pressure. Momentum changes. Holed sand shots. Winning for the side. Euphoric emotions. Victory for the country or continent. Pressure, you bet. Brilliant stuff!

Ryder Cup should be watched for the great shots, strategic management, comradeship, and the spirit of the matches. Decisions on who hits first or from what tee they choose to alternate their drives come into play on team games. Helping your teammate line up ticklish putts or monster ones is encouraged. Caddies get involved in the process as they circle the greens to read how putts will break. High-fives, fist pumps and roars from the crowds electrify viewing audiences. These should be the lasting memories. It is a game. A fun sport. Golf. Such competition should not remind us of the Battle of the Bulge waged in the Ardennes Forest or the quagmire of trench warfare fought in Flanders Fields.

I find it quite ironic that the Americans, the isolationists before World Wars I and II, have initiated a sense of waging war over golf matches. What changed for them to divert from this consistent stance of staying out of Europe's affairs and problems in order to bring on a fight with them for golfing supremacy? A banging of the drums, so to speak.

The more recent successes of the European side against traditional American dominance in Ryder Cup competitions have escalated tensions. I like and respect Americans. Heck, I even proudly possess Yankee blood from my Downington, Michigan-born grandfather who spent time in the American Navy. I understand that they like to reign supreme in their sports and wars but when others encroach on these territories, then look out! They are passionate and very patriotic about their country and will want to fight for pride and repel such threats. The result has created increased animosity between both Ryder Cup sides.

The 1999 Ryder Cup held at Brookline, Massachusetts near Boston built upon the combative-themed Kiawah Island past and created an uglier monster. Frankenstein with the neck bolts. This time the Americans wanted to offer another Boston Tea Party.

Justin Leonard's impossibly long 45-foot putt jammed hard into the cup on the 17th hole and prompted a premature celebration. Tom Lehman led the charge of other U.S. players dressed in those garish red golf shirts with old pictures on them. They poured out onto the green like East India Company's tea did into Boston harbour centuries ago. Caddies, wives, and fans also joined the swelling mass of people on the green to hug their hero and champion.

Television coverage made this pivotal moment look surreal, almost cartoonish. U.S.A.! U.S.A.! U.S.A.! The obnoxious chants reverberated. I thought it might have passed for one of those World Wrestling Entertainment Saturday night Smackdown events. Wasn't this supposed to be an affair displaying the positive lights of golfers and fans alike rather than airing a gong show that lowers the standards through boorish behaviour? Take that, King George and your bloody taxes! But wait . . . the match was not over. Pain set in. The disgust on the faces of Jose-Marie Olazabal, the European Captain Mark James, the Assistant Captain Sam Torrance, and others in the golfing world was obviously apparent. I had a blank face while watching this train wreck fall off the rails. The thousand-yard stare. Olazabal still had a chance to sink the putt to tie but the damage was done. A line had been crossed. He never had a chance to make it after this flagrant violation of sportsmanship.

On the European side in past Ryder Cup matches, the fiery Spaniard, the late Seve Ballesteros, straddled the line of good sportsmanship with rumoured coughing at inappropriate times and other not-so-subtle gestures of gamesmanship while playing and coaching. Seve was bigger than life with his swaggering style and daring shots. A zealous teammate and menacing opponent. He had a confrontation with Paul Azinger during one Ryder Cup and pointedly played psychological warfare games in his matches. Coach Seve's constant presence while roaring around on a golf cart at the 1997 Ryder Cup team agitated some Americans players.

He thrived on these matches and his élan was contagious with his fellow teammates. A leader to follow without hesitation. Seve got under the skin of Americans. Some feel he crossed the line in some of his actions. His inspirational teleconference speech to the European side at Celtic Manor in 2010 helped to spur them emotionally on to victory exactly on the number they needed to wrest the trophy away from the Americans. Seve will be missed.

And Colin Montgomerie became the famous whipping boy for American fans. He did not take the constant heckling about his weight very well and fought back with his own vigorous gestures and pointing of fingers. His sometimes-surly moods toward the media and fans often kindled the combustible situation. Shouldn't a person from the country that gave us St Andrews get more respect? Thankfully, his fantastic record over numerous Ryder Cup competitions spoke for itself. Major championships may have eluded him throughout his very good career but Ryder Cup action was definitely his forte. European fans loved Monty's great and emotional play. His win as the European Ryder Cup team captain in 2010 was icing on the cake and provided a sense of poetic justice.

What happened to the more chivalrous times? Shouldn't Ryder Cup participants perform like the early World War I airmen who tenaciously fought each other in dogfights but would also salute with deference after the engaging aerial battle? There were things you did and didn't do. You did not rake the airman with bullets when their machine guns jammed or while they lay helpless on the ground. Stay off the green until Olazabal finishes his birdie putt. Don't shoot this airman while he is vulnerable!

In the 2010 U.S. Ryder Cup, Captain Corey Pavin brought in air force fighter pilot Major Dan Rooney to motivate his "troops" in the upcoming clash. Interesting or coincidentally, Pavin was a playing participant at Kiawah Island. I have always liked this spirited and diminutive man. His perfectly struck four-wood into the final green at brutally tough Shinnecock Hills propelled him to a great win at the 1995 U.S. Open victory. Many fans fondly remember this masterful shot under the pressure cooker of a national championship. But did Pavin really need to further stir the pot at Ryder Cup? Military awareness and bonding continues to percolate. A Desert Storm reincarnate.

I much prefer the fun-loving European fan chants who gathered around the first tee at Celtic Manor in Wales before the Monday morning singles matches. They introduced European players using the tune of "Guantanamera" to make it laughable. Also, as the fog hovered and these players warmed up, they used a call and response style of "Foggy, foggy, foggy" from one side of the grandstand with a reply of "Oi, oi, oi" from the other. Good clean spirit and fun was embraced rather than war chants. The Brits have their charming way, don't they?

I may be imagining it, but European players look merrier during their play in the Ryder Cup. They come from different nations and cultures yet they all seem to genuinely like one another. English is probably the common language to link them together into a cohesive whole when they are playing on the European tour. This connection makes them more brotherly, in my mind, than the Americans. The cast of characters are guys I would feel comfortable with drinking a pint in the nineteenth hole or puffing on a Monte Cristo cigar outside on the patio. Participants like Darren Clarke, Lee Westwood, Ian Woosnam, and Miguel Jimenez would be included in this engaging group. They also seem to keep the respect for the game above all the other negative banter and sabre-rattling.

My loyalty resides with the Europeans even though the U.S. lives next door. My cheering for this side goes beyond the fact that my sister married a classy Englishman with a grand fondness for golf. I perceive Europeans mostly as underdogs trying to slay the mighty American dragon. See, there I go again. More war stuff has infiltrated my system. It is almost like an addiction that I have acquired!

Seriously, do the majority of Canadian golfing fans cheer for the Europeans over the Americans during Ryder Cup? I have met very few who want the Americans to win. Is it a natural condition for us to want them to lose due to our constant comparison with them? Is it our colonial past and the loyalty to the Queen and the British? Or, do we simply like the European blokes and relate to them better? Europeans seem to be men from humbler roots who have to claw and scratch to get to the pinnacle of their profession.

The U.S. Ryder Cup team usually does much better in singles competitions. Can this be attributed to the fact that their democracy was built on the individual's pursuit of the American dream? Is this the reason why they grasp this format with greater enthusiasm? Four-balls seem to have been their nemesis and their overall futility in playing this format has cost them several chances to win. American players may prefer the stroke play mentality and/or singles matches because they don't have to rely on others. Are American players selfish or merely desiring autonomy so they can play for themselves and keep score for their 18 holes?

Positive socialistic tendencies of European countries have permeated their societies and have translated very well into a winning formula in these Ryder Cup team formats. European players seem to have stronger bonds, better spirit, and simply look like they are enjoying the game more when they play together on the PGA and European Tour. It is apparent this belief system reigns superior over pioneers and mavericks of American society. Maybe implementing universal health care in the U.S. will alter their Ryder Cup's team fortune in future competitions. Government control can have its benefits for its people (and golfers).

Individualist versus Collectivist; Capitalism versus Socialism. Creepy . . . this is bringing back memories of my difficult second-year Political Theory course at university discussing J.S. Mill and Karl Marx and their competing trains of thought. And all of you thought that graduating with a Liberal Arts degree was dubious at best (have I proven you wrong yet?). You be the judge of why there is such a clear demarcation between American and European success.

Watch past Ryder Cup matches where the usually subdued American David Duval gets revved up by pumping his arms. Witness rookie American Jeff Overton yell out the now-famous "Boom, baby" after jugging an eagle from the middle of the fairway. Feel the pressure for Irishman Paul McGinley before he calmly sinks the 10-foot putt to win the 2002 Ryder Cup at The Belfry and take pleasure in viewing the consequent jubilation. Great shots under duress and collapses of epic proportions are both sides of this venerable competition. This is why I watch the thrilling drama of Ryder Cup. There is no need for military jargon like "doing battle" and hiring military speakers to get in the way of this classic tournament.

Ryder Cup needs to return to its time-honoured roots when the competition was an exhibition played among gentlemen. It was not about money but pride of winning for your side. I favour the positive memory of Jack Nicklaus putting his arm around Tony Jacklin rather than the sight of the Storming of the Bastille or better known as the Brookline debacle story. The Golden Bear's gesture hearkens back to the "special relationship" that the U.S. and Great Britain possessed during World War II. Roosevelt and Churchill. Nicklaus and Jacklin. Friends and allies fighting the good fight, not sniping at each other and banging war drums. Ryder Cups should be remembered for this simple fact.

No more War by the Shore shenanigans. Golf is a game of respect and sportsmanship. There is no need for talk about storming any beachheads.

Hole No. 18, Par 4. How is your sportsmanship on the course?

Respect for the game, integrity of the game and sportsmanship during the game are all interconnected, or should be, on the golf course. They are the pillars. I would like to focus primarily on the sportsmanship aspect. How you handle hitting a bad shot, losing a hole to a competitor during match play, or countering a well-pointed jibe from your good friend will tell you something about your character and how others will perceive your sportsmanship qualities. Are you content with how you perform them?

For me, the infrastructure of these redeeming golf fundamentals began at the nightly Morden dinner table. Manners were properly and relentlessly drilled into our family of six and they certainly made an indelible impression on me. Terry, my beloved father, set the tone with me for things to abide by: I could not wear a hat (or headgear as he described it), slouching was frowned upon, I had to wear a shirt; and no elbows were allowed to rest on the table. "Bad form" is how he termed not following these rules.

As an aside, it was amazing though, that he emphasized the importance that members of the Morden clan, specifically me, should stealthily slip a piece of my roast beef to our cat and my father's comrade in arms who sat strategically beside me. Perhaps the Big Boy, as my big-bellied half Persian/half tabby breed was affectionately nicknamed, felt that I was a softie with marshmallow attributes. I presume Terry convinced himself that this was a magical exception to his dinner rules or the corollary to his theorem. This was a sneaky weapon to implement, I thought.

He was an authoritative figure so I didn't dare challenge him on this blatant inconsistency. I took this fatherly advice like an innocent and impressionable young man should and obeyed. Shadrach, aka Big Boy, certainly appreciated the appetizing human food I contributed to his ample gut. These dinner table rules were my baptism before graduating to my confirmation class—the future behaviour lessons that he would instil upon me when I played on my home golf course at Craigowan.

The equivalent of my table manners on the golf course became: dress in proper golfing attire; shake hands with competitors and look them in the eye; commend them for their good shots; and always be a good sport to your fellow players, especially when you lose. Unfortunately, I must have had a thick skull early in my golfing life because I often did not heed his pithy counsel. Slamming clubs and selfish thinking were the rules of the day. I was a teenaged tornado, slashing a devastating swath through sportsmanship, disrespecting the game like it was a Kansas trailer park caught in my unpredictable path.

Players are easily tempted by golf's competitive spirit to selfishly ponder their own game before thinking of others. Playing in this bubble can suffocate golfers. As a result, the corrupted ones focus on tallying their own score, winning all the marbles, and the heck with everybody else. Enjoyment of the group game is pushed to the background, causing many aspects incorporated into the spirit of golf to suffer. As I grew up, I began to realize these actions were not right or appropriate and, for me, a new dawn broke.

There had to be far more to this great game than what I was experiencing. I slowly crept out of this enveloping fog and found welcoming sunlight. My new promise to the golfing world was that I would no longer be satisfied with being Cro-Magnon man during the move up the evolutionary chain. This mission would shift in a more positive direction. I would transform myself into an enlightened artist from the Renaissance era—a golfer with an acute awareness to gain more satisfaction in the match, appreciate the enticing walk in the country and expose my colleagues to a more enjoyable way to spend a day on the course. It would be about them, us. The big picture.

In my 20s, I competed with (and was often beaten by) a slightly older player who was an excellent golfer. He would not exactly pummel me but he was definitely in a different class, even though I won occasionally. His demeanour was humble in victory and gracious in defeat. Somehow he made me feel good when I lost to him. It was a foreign feeling for me to be beaten, since I usually found myself on the other side of the ledger. But you only raise the quality of your game by taking on this challenge of playing with superior golfers.

How could someone make me feel so pleasant when I finished on the vanquished side? What was his secret formula, other than maturity, so I could learn from it? I reflect back and wonder if this was truly my proverbial kick in the butt—the watershed time period or turning point for me to switch gears from self-indulgence and selfishness, to seeing golf in a more beneficial way for all who played in my band of brothers.

This classy player complimented me when I hit good shots. He thrived on the intense but exhilarating competition and even though he passed such welcomed accolades on to me and other competitors, these gestures amazingly did not suck oxygen away from his own game. In short, just because he gave, it did not mean something had to necessarily be taken away from this gentleman. Here's a sincere and brilliant thought: All parties benefit when things are done in this gracious manner.

So I concluded that genuine compliments enhanced the playing experience, made us all play at a higher level, and resulted in our greater enjoyment of the round. And it didn't cost us anything. Not a penny. My score would not disintegrate because others joined my golfing world. Comradeship was important to this player and it clicked for me. This was sportsmanship as my father tried to teach me and I finally got it. Terry, those table manners turned out to be transferable skills!

This ongoing education ever-so-gently forced me to see golf in a different light. Score was important but it was not the only thing. My competitors and partners should view the positive side of my being so I would compliment them on the fine shot or speak with them during the walk up the fairway rather than fussing or cursing about my own trivial inadequacies. Others would see a transparent window into my soul and character. There would be nothing fake about my behaviour and compliments. The excitement of the match, to be happy for everyone, not just for myself, should be the driver of our great time spent together on the course. The quality of time should take precedence over self-aggrandizement. Sportsmanship. No rattling of keys in a backswing or talking at address.

A second, more recent experience that furthered my appreciation of the excitement of the match and the importance of sportsmanship was when my good friend Pat and I took on my visiting English brother-in-law Steve and his English mate Nigel at my home club. We chose to play 4-ball. If you have not had the privilege to play this match play format, then I highly recommend that you do it because it is a fantastic contest.

We created our own mini-version of Ryder Cup. Substitute Yanks with Canucks and Europeans with Limeys. I love match play and this very competitive day accentuated its benefits.

To Steve, it is the thrill of the match's competition and its twists and turns that drives him to play this compelling game. Sure, he wants to win, as he possesses a battling spirit like all good golfers; but this is secondary. The English also have the added touch of practicing good manners, emphasizing appropriate etiquette, and possessing a grand reputation for sportsmanship. Pat and I could learn a few lessons from these chaps. Terry would have gladly welcomed the duo to the Morden dinner table for a four-course steak dinner.

Our 4-ball match careened back and forth all day like a sailboat thrashing in rough seas. A chip-in on No. 7 by Steve enabled us to commend him on this brilliant stroke. Good shot, old bean! Nigel hit a fantastic lob from the deep ewok on No. 11 to save the side and earn applause. Great pressure shot! Pat drained a crucial mid-length putt on 17 and Steve responded in kind. Large grins and incredulous head-shaking rippled like a wave through our group of four. All of us loved how individuals rose to the occasion under this tremendous strain of competition. I then had to sink a downhill two-foot tickler in to the left side of the cup for birdie on the lengthy Par 5 final hole to win the hole and halve the match. My nerves were tested mightily. I came through nicely in the crunch. What an adrenaline rush! Crucial shot after crucial shot was executed and all of us got swept up in the moment, gaining great satisfaction on the day's events. We enjoyed it immensely.

To others who have not yet learned the elation of the match as an end in itself, halving a match rather than winning it would have left an empty feeling or seemed a lost opportunity. The four of us did not see it that way. We agreed that the excitement of the game and the good sportsmanship conducted by all trumped the selfish need for the win. Both sides desperately wanted to win but not at the expense of demeaning the great spirit of the match. It was a real triumph. We all still believe this to be the most exciting golfing contest that we have played. Pints served in the nineteenth hole following the game were fantastic. We continue to remember this fine day with fond affection.

I have seen and heard enough examples of the antithesis of this behaviour. Jangling of change in pockets, screeching of carts in the backswing, theatrical throws of the club, and mean-spirited psychological warfare tactics can be cunningly utilized as anti-sportsmanship weapons during play. Watch the hilarious film *Caddyshack* with Rodney Dangerfield's antics and the yells of "Noonan" and "Misssss . . . . Missss . . . ." and you will understand these kinds of transgressions. Funny in the movies; not so much in a real game.

And how about those wretched people who grumble incessantly about the terrible state of their golf games? Don't dampen the mood for your foursome, cookies. I apply the 30-second "grind" rule (sometimes extended to 5 minutes) that allows people to be ornery before being reintegrated into the flock. Cleanse your system of these burdens and get back into the positive world or you will definitely be scolded. Isn't it better than being at work, Dr. Depresso?

Constant whiners and gripers are not tolerated at home dinner conversations or sporting arenas so why should you let these culprits dampen the mood on the golf course? It is each golfer's responsibility to have diplomatic chats with people who indulge in this boorish behaviour. Try to address these situations so they don't ruin your experience on the course. If you fail to do this, then these scenarios can cause awkward feeling and avoidance of eye contact and conversation. I don't want to feel like I am walking on eggshells. No, I won't accept it.

Also, there is a hearty and good-natured way to needle your comrades and have fun. Then there is the crossing of the line in proper behaviour. Take the path of the enlightened, and show character in your sportsmanship. This can be learned but not necessarily faked. How you operate on the course will spread like tentacles to other roles in your life.

Think of Jack Nicklaus when he conceded Tony Jacklin's 2-foot putt (called "The Concession") on the final hole to halve the match and tie the 1969 Ryder Cup at Royal Birkdale Golf Club. A class act from a true sportsman. How about Nick Faldo's kind gesture toward the Great White Shark at the end of the 1996 Masters? Everyone remembers the negativity of Norman's collapse but Faldo understood the importance of being human and showing empathy, which is why he consoled him with a few words of encouragement. Limit the scarring of a fellow golfer's psyche. The Englishman knew how important a green jacket would have been to the Australian. And people forget that Faldo shot a fine 67 in his own right compared to Norman's 78. Great golf with a human touch.

On the other hand, don't duplicate the performance that was better known as the Brookline Massacre. This was the 1999 Ryder Cup when

Tom Lehman prematurely led the charge with other players and wives onto the 17th green after Justin Leonard drained a very long putt. Olazabal still had a chance to tie the match for the European side and stared in disbelief as they trampled all over his line. A disgrace and a step back to caveman sportsmanship. This event is still talked about by golf fans on both sides of the Atlantic.

Shake hands with your competitor(s) before the round and wish them well. Respect the honour system of who tees off first. Doff your hat on the final shake of the hand. Be the first to congratulate the other even though you lost the match. Compliment a competitor's great shot into the green even though you just blocked your second shot OB. Don't take away the satisfaction of your competitor's win by saying you lost it. Such a comment is insulting to their fine play. These are just some of the tenets that mark the code of sportsmanship. Golf and sportsmanship should be a natural pair. This combination should be hand-in-glove.

If you struggle to find a visual representation in your mind of what it is all about, then research the famous Duel in the Sun between Nicklaus and Watson at the 1977 Open Championship played at Turnberry. After Nicklaus lost by one stroke to his younger competitor (even though he shot scintillating scores of 65-66 on the weekend compared to Watson's even better 65-65), the Golden Bear memorably wrapped a big paw around the redhead's shoulder and marched him to the scorer's tent. Great golf and great sportsmanship from two greats of the game. I wonder what their dinner table etiquette was like with their families when they were young!

Nineteenth Hole Following the Round.

1. What did Augusta National become during World War II?

    Order a pound of hot wings with lots of napkins.

2. Tiger Woods said there were only two players who "owned" their swings. Who were they?

    Drain a tequila shooter.

3. This player known now more for his new role in golf was 46 years old and retired from professional golf for 5 years when he won at Pebble Beach in the 1990s. Name him.

    Pay for two jugs of premium microbrew for the table and congratulate everyone for respecting the game and making the round enjoyable!

PLAYOFF HOLES

HOLE NO. 20, PAR 4: IS THAT A FLYSWATTER YOU'RE USING?

Not really, but that is what the appalled Kiawah Island caddie thought I was trying to master. I swatted with the club. That much was true and the movement was ugly. But it was not an irritating insect that would pay the piper on the receiving end of my weapon of choice. The unorthodox and violent stab I made with my wrists at my 3-foot putt reminded the bag-carrier of his own familiar and tedious chore when he was killing pests at his quiet parent's cottage over the past summer. Was this not supposed to be golf rather than a vacationer's mecca of solitude in the backwaters of South Carolina?

The caddie casually shook his head in disgust. He turned away from this horrific scene after my colleague Bags gave him a précis of my sad story. The local lad had just witnessed the severe affliction that has plagued me for over a decade. I had just failed to sink another one of those simple putts that have perplexed me (for me these putts are certainly not straightforward but quite painful). The Poison of the yips has infiltrated my system and lingers. It is quite content to remain in this inviting habitat. Can you enjoy playing golf if you have this major problem of missing short putts because of bad nerves and jitters?

Golf is so much a battle of the mind. Putting in particular should be the easy part. It is not, for me, especially in the knee-knocker zone. In my personal and business lives I often find my biggest disappointments come when I expect something and then it fails to come true—the theory of rising expectations. Twenty-foot putts are not usually ones I have high hopes of sinking, at least not by many golfers, so I am willing to settle for near misses. But those dastardly short putts, in my mind, should see the bottom of the cup every time. Unfortunately, the ball does not often adhere to my expectations.

For fellow players who don't know my putting prowess (or lack thereof), my flicking putting action stuns them. They scratch their heads and scrunch their eyes. These golfers wonder what fitting words of advice they can offer so they don't have to witness such egregious repeated offences. Don't even try. I see my hand rising subconsciously so I can say "Stop" to prevent such intrusion. Ahhh . . . . I know you want to soothe my soul with pertinent solutions. Shhhhhhh. Such "helpful" comments will only irk me. And others in this surprisingly large clan of yippers would agree with my assessment.

Unfortunately because of this nasty habit, I stand vulnerable to much ridicule from my friends, competitors, and the rest of the peanut gallery. There is no use in denying it. Some believe that it is open season to pummel me with a right cross of witty putdowns. I have no defensive Maginot Line to prevent this blitzkrieg incursion, so deep down I need to let it simmer. My tidy response to the heckling and snide comments is to pound a drive 40 yards by them so I can achieve some measure of the proverbial last laugh. If only I didn't have to proceed and 3-putt and hear them cackle again at my blatant incompetency.

It is bloody awful to have the yips, I must say. I know I am not alone on this lonely planet. My friend and playing compatriot whom I nicknamed Flanagan may have it even worse. When I see him miss another short putt with the flip of his wrists (he was a very good hockey player), I execute an improvised Michael Jackson moonwalk and slip back a few extra yards from the seething Irishman. My human backup response signifies that I know what is coming. The volcano is about to explode.

Flanagan reaches Stress Level 10 swiftly, steam rises from his ears, and his putter shifts gradually from a vertical position over the ball to a horizontal one straight in front of him. The contact-lensed eyes of the Irishman roam longingly to the skies as they search for an answer to his reoccurring syndrome. He absolutely knows a message will not be forthcoming but he nevertheless intently prays.

A slow-burning sensation of his internal digestive system ensues, which our group calls grinding. This is the seething and sickening feeling that golfers experience when their insides just eat away at them for the just-missed opportunity that presented itself. The emotion reverberates throughout their golfing souls.

As a Catholic, my friend does not believe He can be so cruel. Flanagan offers a soft curse, slumps his shoulders, and mutters as he lumbers towards the next tee. I know he wants me to meet his eyes but I keep them fastened to the ground as though a tractor beam locks me in this position. My own time of agonizing grinding is drawing near and I can ill afford to be reminded of my inevitable fate while playing for pars.

I feel his pain. I really do—in a genteel Bill Clintonesque, empathetic kind of way. Flanagan and I can commiserate and we exchange morbid tales of such complete ineptness. Sometimes we even laugh wholeheartedly about our pathetic state. Others cannot understand nor do we expect them to. We don't have any false expectations that fellow golfers would want to join our exclusive club. For Flanagan, the solution is now the long putter. He has waved the white flag and is now joining the growing masses of golfers willing to roll the ball on greens in this manner. My own time may be approaching.

Plug in the word "yips" on any Internet browser and a multitude of articles written about this lousy problem will appear. The psychology of the yips, the biochemistry of the yips, the physiology of the yips, and more research and theorems are bandied about, back and forth, like a frenetic game of badminton. The subject has been discussed ad nauseam for many years and there are more victims than you can imagine.

Think of this select and distinguished company that Flanagan and I have joined who have suffered through the yips some time in their careers: Tommy Armour, Ben Hogan, Bernhard Langer, Sam Snead, Johnny Miller, and Tom Watson. These are big names, serious names, and major champion names. Vijay Singh also comes to mind as a successful PGA player who constantly fiddles and fusses with different grips on long putters, regular putters, and belly putters. He may have had the yips or suffered through other flagrant putting woes but how can you doubt the success of someone who wins a green jacket and two PGA championships? What category should he fit in? Don't you have to be a pretty good putter to win such tournaments?

Why not just use a long putter or a belly putter? Take a putting lesson with a pro? Think of good-looking women in bikinis while you putt? Sorry, but those are not words that necessarily help. You won't understand until you stand in my shoes. When stricken with the yips, often nothing can be done about the busy flyswatter move even though there are supposedly many ways to cure it. Who knows where this dreaded curse came from during my golfing career? One day I was putting well and then all of a sudden I was brutal—or perhaps it was a gradual disintegration of this particular skill set and I was in deep denial . . .

Trying to shake this problem cannot necessarily be practiced and alternative science will probably fail miserably. Sports psychologists and other mind gurus can be shipped in to help. One of them, Bob Rotella, has written *Putting Out of Your Mind* that emphasizes the importance of attitude over mechanics. Perhaps this tome can help but I have my doubts about its success.

Yoda is sourced to no avail. The cuddly green man can ask all the questions in his peculiar reversing words in a sentence kind of way, but forget about it! You can stand on practice greens and hit putt after putt into the heart of the hole from 3 feet. Of course you can sink these practice putts when you have nothing riding on it. Once you add the metric or meaning to that 3-foot putt then all bets are off. Are you playing for a dollar? Are you trying to sink one for your partner? Are you trying to sink one so you can defeat your antagonistic enemy and win the Verma Cup?

Once these dreaded thoughts enter your brain, then you get nervous and the wrists flick and flinch. I have even had the pleasure of freezing over a putt from three feet. Truly petrified. How can this be when I have little concern about hitting a drive over the Pacific Ocean on the 18th hole at Pebble Beach? The mind is a very mysterious and confusing thing. Of course, I could try harder to exorcise the yip demons but I choose not to so I need to suffer the consequences. I am accountable for my actions. Is this affliction conquerable? I really can't answer that question unless I make a concerted effort to solve the riddle. Converting terrible putting rounds to tolerable ones is a worthy goal I pursue.

If fate has been so cruel as to deal you a chronic case of the yips, can you tolerate playing the game with this major problem? It is a battle that needs to be waged in your mind. This is an integral question to ask yourself and you must be harsh in your self-critique. Some cannot overcome putting problems and have quit the game in total exasperation. Others constantly threaten to leave for other pleasures like gruelling 25k road bike races involving long climbs. Here is a simple directive from me so you can come to grips with your conundrum: "Do something about your yips and stop the whining or enjoy the game for all the other beautiful aspects that it presents." Can I be blunter?

I have been able to tolerate the yips because other aspects and characteristics of this wonderful game are WAY, WAY more important to me. A 4-ball match in the dew on an early Saturday morning with my good friends is one. A business game with an important customer on a sunny afternoon is another. Or, how about the exhilaration of actually pounding a critical drive up Hogan's Alley at Carnoustie's devious par-5 after my partner just duck-hooked his shot out of bounds past a startled farmer and a group of hungry sheep! I think when you look at things from that perspective, then golf should be a welcome forum to appreciate rather than an excuse to slump your shoulders because of a feeble 3-putt from only 8 feet.

Sure, I get dejected when I miss a short putt but the feeling is not all-consuming. I don't lose sleep over it and I do sink some putts to put joy in my gut. The fine comradeship, the sparkling walk in the country, the contentment of a match well played supersedes the pain of the yips. I can also draw upon fond memories of my glory days when I was a youngster and could putt very well. This proved I once had the mental and physical skills to perform this task at least one time in my golfing life. I had no small muscle nerves on my putting touch and played for fun during the competition.

The argument can be made that young golfers have no fear. Just make the pendulum putting motion. As an adult, there is the creep of worry and the need for results that maybe a kid doesn't think of at his age. Mortgage issues, business deals, and marital strains enter the picture and affect the golfer's mindset. How many kids that you know have ever said they have the yips? They don't, they just slam the 3-footer directly into the centre of the cup with grand authority.

Flanagan and I know how our score should be much better even if we could be pitifully categorized as just bad putters. But we are terrible putters. Thirty-six putts, 38 putts, 40 putts. Man, some people look at the snake-bitten Hands of Stone Brothers (my endearing nickname and subsequently called HoS Bros.) and wonder why we have not turned to tennis. It is especially frustrating when we can hit professional quality golf shots into birdie range and walk off with rotten bogeys.

However, the HoS Bros. know that many of these same people would gladly give their third-born son to us if they could launch the occasional 300-yard drive like we can. My argument to Flanagan about this point is received well and connects us. I guess I can say I would rather have the chance to hit the ball beautifully and putt badly than the other way around. This may of course be my own justification for this ineptness around short putts (Flanagan and I are not too bad outside of this death zone). Funny to think that competitors worry more when we have a 10-footer to win the hole than a 2 ½-footer!

Now I happen to have the yips. But other golfers I know have their own afflictions. Pick your toxin:

- I can't hit the five-iron because I just can't. So what gives here?
- This hole does not set up well for my eyes. I just can never make par. What is wrong with me?
- I can't hit 80-yard wedges. I have no feel and no confidence. How do I fix it?

The yips will continue to be an issue for me unless I seriously want to address it and do something about it. I do not. Since I am unwilling to sacrifice the time for the necessary fix, I am at peace with this decision. Like my non-interest in practicing golf, I prefer the opportunity cost of doing more important things in my life. No advice is needed to pass along to me, but thank you all the same.

My passion for golf with my friends and strangers trumps this putting angst. Throughout my golfing career I have been fortunate enough to play great courses across the globe. No doubt I have taken advantage of these opportunities and not once did I have my putting problems prevent me from grasping them. Why let this negative part of my game destroy the joy of swinging the sticks? Now look out, here comes a titanic drive on this beautiful Wednesday afternoon at my home course of Craigowan!

Hole No. 21, Par 4: What is the new 250?

Is it 275, 300 or 325, perhaps? A 250-yard drive used to be a big deal.

H-u-u-u-ge. When I was younger (it seems like ancient times) I could accomplish this feat of 250. I was known as a big hitter. This was a proud label to wear and own. A puff-out-the-chest kind of feeling for a golfer. A He-Man. No longer. Modern golf equipment and technology renders the up-to-recently impressive phrase of "He hits it 250" obsolete. It is so passé to utter such a statement now even though in reality, this is an awe-inspiring distance to club the ball. Players are pushing their drives by me and they now enjoy seeing me in their rear-view mirrors. Where is technology taking us?

Driving 250 in yesteryear could be accomplished in myriad ways. No one ever used 240 or 254 as the pivotal number. A nice round number of 250 came to be the gold standard. But it was not going to be accomplished by using 90 or 100 compression Titleist balata-covered balls. You don't hear the word 'compression' as much anymore but, instead, phrases like low spin and clubhead speed. Only hard swingers that exceeded 100 mph clubhead speed could take advantage of the harder cored 100s, so I qualified. My looping, going-beyond-horizontal, masterful swing gathered a great amount of centrifugal force when it came through the ball making it scream for mercy once it was pummelled.

In the past, a definite focus was put into striking balata balls well, or your allowance money earned from cutting the grass or working in the pro shop would shrink to a mere pittance like a dime (I might still be able to buy a Snickers bar, though). You older folks know these types of balls—the expensive ones that were soft-covered and easy to gouge after only a few shots. The balatas were great for stopping softly on greens and better control but would not travel as far off the tee as the surlyn-covered, Titleist DTs or, alternatively, hard-covered and hard-wound balls usually made by Spalding. Also, any off-centre hits on the smaller headed drivers would cause these types of balls to flutter like a shuttlecock and distance would be greatly diminished. The Grip It and Rip It method would face off against the thinking golfer's game, in which better course management decisions could be made. Brawn or brain? I eventually came to the conclusion that I preferred to use the noggin.

On the off-kilter days of your striking ability (and there could be many), these valuable balatas with deep smiles carved in them would be quickly disposed into waste baskets dotting the course or heaved with frustration into the course-hugging corn stalks. Skulled fairway and sand shots were major contributors to making this an easy decision to implement. These graveyards became great welcoming committees for such luxury items and giving them up due to your incompetence meant a failure in your golfing mission.

I am poignantly transporting veteran golfers back to some glory days when acid rock, disco, punk, and New Wave music all collided. Remember the hair? These were the grand times, including the mullets, long flowing locks, and multi-coloured Flock of Seagulls 80s New Wave hair. To climb the mountain to be consistent and over the magical 250 line, one usually needed to pull out that hard-assed Spalding Top-Flite (or cheaper Kro-Flite and Canada Cup alternatives). Ebcos were those cheap, rubbery things that flew off the club like a limp noodle so they would not do. As mentioned, balatas were quite expensive and I did not have much dough (although sometimes I was able to wrestle some of these beauties out of the pond with a trusty scoop). They were a sporadic guilty pleasure. So if you were determined to strike "cannonading drives," then there was a clear choice (thank you, Danny Gallivan for your colourful phrases as commentator at the Montreal Forum). I also mistakenly de-emphasized the need to hold or "bite" my shots on greens and convinced myself that such a strategy was for artsy or cutesy types. Power was the name of the game. We accurately nicknamed these Top-Flites "rocks."

On frosty days you could feel your hands go numb when you flailed one of those babies off the heel of your wood or iron. Your appendages would quiver like a tuning fork. Ouch. You were mighty proud to tell your group members that you survived this torture from the rocks. I still cringe thinking about these memories. On the other hand, when you cleanly connected "on the screws," as we used to say, these balls flew a long way. It helped that our sandy brown fairways (before irrigated fairways were installed) possessed concrete-like qualities.

The Top-Flite would launch from our small-headed, screw-enabled, tiny-sweet-spotted persimmon heads and land firmly on this turf. The ball would explode from this hardpan surface like that memorable Super Ball ricocheted off your grade school asphalt. Ahhhhh . . . the days of youth and the exhilaration of tossing the Super Ball against stone walls and watching them bound over the schoolyard fence. Ancient Gertrude's backyard became a great collector of these prizes . . . . Anyways, I digress; the Top-Flite would bop along the ground with bounding force until it rested a close 140 yards from the pin in the middle of the fairway. My face would be creased by a contented smile, as a result of the length I achieved with this mighty blow.

So, based on my brilliant calculation, I hit the tee-shot 255 on this 395-yard length par-4. Yes, I am a big hitter. Can I now switch back to a softer ball for my approach shot? No, you can't switch, my friends. I know you thought you could pull one over on your competitors and the Commish; however, it is against the rules. Unless there is a cut in it . . . oh, wait. It is a rock—not a balata—so fat chance of that happening!

Too bad that when I hit it into the green the ball would smack hard and roll off the back of the green. No holding power. Dash it! But I hit it 250 . . .

I would conveniently not bother to tell the blokes in the 19th hole that I used a Top-Flite, Canada Cup, Kro-Flite or the other Spalding hard-as-bricks portfolio of balls. Just that I hit it over 250. This is all they needed to know in order to enhance my reputation. Let them murmur amongst themselves. Perception, you see, is a powerful ally. On the other hand, maybe they just couldn't care less as I was talking about my golf game and they wanted to enjoy their Molson Canadian in peace.

The screws in the Wilson and other drivers of that era have now been replaced with high tech materials. Gargantuan-headed drivers, high tensile steel stiff shafts, and Titleist Pro V1 four-piece quality balls that can carry for absurd lengths make golfers hitting 250 seem like weenie drivers. Balls slingshot off these clubs and the massive sweet spot makes it more difficult for players to err. My older Wilson graphite-shafted driver left me very little room to mis-hit and I cherished my skill to hit them properly the majority of times. I was also lucky enough to be playing several times a week to keep up this high-calibre play. These older clubs might as well be added to those glass-covered museum cases displaying relics of the past like hickory-shafted putters and mashies.

My mind is still trying to comprehend the idea of how length and soft feel can be combined into making a competent golf ball. It can and it has with Pro V1s, certain Callaway versions, the new TaylorMade Penta, and other high-grade balls. But when I see Top-Flite balls like Stratas that say "soft" somewhere on the cover, I shake my head, wondering if soft and Top-Flite can realistically be found in the same sentence.

This is a paradox for me when I think of this brand. The 15-year-old in me cannot dispose of the feelings I had for "rocks" in 1977. To this day I cannot play this ball because I want good control on the greens. Don't even begin selling me on the fact that certain Top-Flites can be held onto greens. Any time spent on convincing me will end in abject failure and I may utilize "The Hand" to stop your argument abruptly. My memory is crystal-clear of these balls smashing hard and bounding through the well-conditioned greens and into that nasty rear side Jabba or thick surrounding ewok. I was none too pleased to suffer that ensuing bogey. Scars from the past remain permanently.

Today there is a large variety of ball brands suitable for every kind of golfer. Many golfers drool when they see "distance" or "long" emblazoned on the cover of Pinnacles, Maxflis, and Callaways. Poll the average golfer and distance is still the most important thing for them to achieve. "Let the Big Dog Eat," "You Da Man," or other similar exhortations will be chanted. I think, however, that the great feel on and by the greens should be more important when golfers select the ball for their respective games. Invest in good balls, too. You will notice the difference. Too bad I am a terrible putter to really appreciate some of the functions of these types of balls. I will however, survive.

Guys I used to smoke off the tees are now slamming their drives by me. Even Chief, who uses his high tech weapon with a Lady Precept, loves to harangue me for his lengthy shots. I am a man who usually does not lack self-confidence, but being out-driven by more people due to technology is a severe blow to my golfing psyche. The whining must stop and I need to do something about it. Skill can only take me so far today.

My 7-year-old TaylorMade 8.5-degree loft 510 model driver is an antique like my inherited collection of 1953 year Britain's Limited lead army soldiers. The size of the head is still substantial but it looks like a Mini Cooper car compared to the up-to-date Cadillac Escalade versions of Nike, Callaway, and other TaylorMades. It has become necessary for me to upgrade my driver so I can get back on track. My plan for the year 2012 is to improve driving prowess and wipe Chief's smirk off his face.

Three hundred now seems to be the number. I see golfers attaining this drive length when they never had one iota a chance in the past. Where does the importance of swing plane, timing of thrusting hip movements, and technology begin when attempting to achieve the new demarcation line of 300? I can hit 300 on occasion but I have to slip a couple of vertebrate to do it. The new technology I plan to purchase next should help this aging man keep up with the other competitors. It just seemed harder to master the game decades ago.

The driver used to be just one club in a set. Today, a whole monster industry has been created by companies that focus on selling them. TaylorMade, for example, was originally known for marketing and selling only drivers. The cost of one of these babies could be more than a set of irons. Such behemoth drivers allow golfers to keep up with the Joneses and nothing, I mean nothing, can replace the feeling of absolutely uncorking a mammoth drive. This type of high has an addictive feeling that filters from your head, to your hands, and throughout the rest of your body.

A well-struck three-iron is much more difficult to hit and sometimes more satisfying, but people want length and it is length you get with these R9s, FTIs and other mechanical marvels. Golf manufacturers know about ego and they feed the frenzy of desire for distance to those who had thus far seen 300 as being unobtainable and an urban myth. The eager sharks are circling and ready to produce their substantial chequebooks after such brainwashing. Golfers will then venture to the nearest big-ticket golfing emporium or source eBay for that special prey. They must have it to feed their habit.

Jack Nicklaus, Greg Norman, and John Daly were all known as PGA's biggest drivers of the ball during their peak playing years. Two-fifty blended into 300 yards. But the next generation of PGA stars like Bubba Watson, Gary Woodland, and Dustin Johnson are now pushing the envelope to the 350 zone and, sometimes miraculously, further. Four hundred yards when conditions are right. Incredible! Where is it all leading? I just hope all the great traditional courses are not dwarfed by this relentless march of technology and rendered obsolete. The Luddite Commish would then frown.

Three hundred is now the new 250. I have to get over the earlier days when I was part of the small privileged group who could hit it 250.

More people, especially due to superior golf equipment, better balls, and improved course conditions can achieve this special number. My blessing goes out to those who want to upgrade their equipment. Get the set that helps your game but don't get too obsessive about it and forget that this is a game. I might recommend though, that you invest in good golf balls. Purchase a pack of Titleist Pro V1s, NXTs, TaylorMade Pentas, or another high-grade ball and at least try them out so you know what true quality is. They may be more expensive but often comprise a potent combination of length and tremendous feel and stopping power on greens. You will understand this sound advice after you play them. Feel balls are better than those harder Pinnacles and Ultras.

Revolutionary breakthroughs offered by the golf industry are good for the game but sometimes my ego gets bruised. I will purchase a new big-assed driver and crunch out another drive with Pro V1s. Perhaps I can replace the 1977 "rock" classic "Hotel California" by The Eagles that I hummed in the past with a catchy tune by the cutting-edge group Arcade Fire. It will be a symbolic admission that I have caught up with the times. Vinyl to digital. Persimmon to metal wood. The modern world!

Hole No. 22, Par 3. Would you Edinburghians like a sip from our Cup?

The Edinburghians were grossly unprepared for what hit them. The sudden and unexpected sight was a shock of epic proportions to their cultural system. A formidable group of vocal Colonials, in high spirits, were parading down the main thoroughfare of this beautiful and historical city with a hoisted Cup. Our blazers and slick pants (no kilts were available at the time) disguised the informality of such a raucous bunch. We were jubilant and that special feeling was not going to soon dissipate. It was imperative, we felt, to share the spoils of war with the club-goers and sightseers. Stale, warm beer swished around in the monstrous bowl of The Verma Cup as we raised this symbol of comradeship. We delightfully anticipated who our next victim would be to sip the liquid gold. What a great trip we had just completed, which included golf at the venerable Old Course with a dedicated caddie, eating deep-fried Mars bars in a St Andrews fish shop, and concluded with whisky-sipping and beer-draining in Edinburgh. How much better could it get than spending our last night in this manner after experiencing our remarkable golf trip to Scotland?

In the 8 brilliant days we explored parts of Scotland, I had not heard or witnessed any raising of voices or hollering from the indigenous people. There was a close call, however, when an elderly lady at Gullane No. 2 course admonished Chief for his overly boisterous and piercing "Yeeoww!!!" when he sank a 10-foot par putt for the win on the 8th hole. She did not yell, but her curt words were enough to subdue our larger-than-life colleague. It was close but no cigar in this Scottish challenge.

William Wallace and his clan would doubtless have been dejected to see the tranquil nature of his people, so we took it upon ourselves to make Braveheart proud and pick up our own 21st century club, the Cup, and rally the troops. Many of us have Scottish ancestry and we passionately desired to share our triumph with our fellow Scots. So that was our mission, to crank up the volume, have tremendous fun this night, and entice young people to drink from the golden chalice. By all accounts, they loved our version of a Canadian invasion!

How did we end up in this magnificent city and hometown of the knighted Sean Connery? (He's an avid golfer, as most of his fans know.) The 2008 Scottish trip was ending tonight in Edinburgh and, by gosh, we were going out in style. Our group enjoyed a classy night held at the Edinburgh Whisky Society. We sampled different single-malt Scotches, exchanged laughter, indulged in great food, projected memorable pictures taken during the week onto the screen, and made heartfelt speeches about the importance of spending time together in the heartland of golf. This was the culmination of our inaugural Verma Cup match play championship between two fiercely proud teams.

I was the losing captain as our team got pummelled. But I was also the Commish for the tournament and the fun of the matches needed to supersede this unfortunate fact. At least, that is my justification for being the losing skipper . . . I was supremely proud of the guys and how well everything worked. No one came to blows over a slight or a bypassed rule of golf, even in the clubhouses and pubs after one too many celebratory pints.

As Canadians from a hockey-crazed country, we thought it was appropriate to entice the local Scots to drink from our Cup. It was not the illustrious Lord Stanley's Cup but the pewter was still an impressive symbol for a prestigious championship. We thought this intimate gesture would be a great way to say thank you to the kind people of Edinburgh and Scotland as a whole. The lads felt it was important to show gratitude for the remarkable excursion we had in playing the Old Course, Gullane, Carnoustie, and other fine golf courses. Call it breaking bread or, in this case, sharing the suds between a proud nation of Sherwood and Victoriaville hockey sticks with an equally proud and older nation of mashie and hickory sticks.

Very few of the young Edinburgh folk we approached refused to partake of this sip of grandeur. The indigenous folks were quite tickled and honoured. Some of them mistook us for Americans but we quickly dispelled them of this egregious error and announced that we were proud Colonials: We are hearty Canadians and we are your loyal cousins. I don't know for sure if that helped to tip the balance in our favour but the smiles were contagious and positive comments abounded. They respected our creative celebration. Perhaps they soon understood that the mistake of calling us American was as sacrilegious as calling a Scotsman an Englishman. And we know what often results with such a dangerous miscue with respect to heritage. I remember hearing an old adage: "Call me a Scot, call me an Irishman or call me a Welshman but don't call me an Englishman!" My English brother-in-law cringes when he hears this well-worn phrase . . .

Even usually mild-mannered Scugog participated in this raucous performance. He happily convinced young and well-dressed lady nightclubbers who were waiting in line at their favourite watering hole to have a swig from the Cup. Free of charge, my young lasses! Some snapped blackmail pictures in this friendly atmosphere and stored them for future use. We headed for more action fuelled by liquor and the high of an experience of a lifetime.

The trip was a monumental undertaking of planning by four of us and many things could have gone wrong. But they didn't. Even the gods were kind to us by providing us with 8 days of no rain during our golf rounds. Can you imagine that? People still shake their heads in disbelief when I tell them of such glorious luck. Mother Nature provided winds but of the tolerable kind and the sun was a constant, welcome ally. Some of the players on this trip still grumble to me because their high-end Gore-Tex rain gear was not suitably battle-tested by fierce Scottish horizontal sheets of rain and hurricane force winds. I raise a Spockian eyebrow and tell them to stop their whining.

By the end of the night, the boys were slowly running out of petrol. We found out that pubs close earlier than we expected. Without the fuel of ales to kindle the fire, the group's energy was waning. Our more advanced age and the week of golf and nights of fun were taking their toll. Flights were leaving in the morning and we had a long day ahead of us. Hangovers were inevitable but they would be worthwhile badges of honour for such a festive occasion.

Back at the quaint old Edinburgh hotel with its claustrophobic elevator, we exchanged handshakes and accolades. Memories of Scotland and our competition for the Verma Cup would not be forgotten. Friendship bonds were stronger and those who had not previously known each other well now had better connections. We were comrades in arms with our common weapons being Pings, TaylorMades, and Callaways. And sipping from the Cup, of course.

To any historians, traditionalists or passionate seekers of golf, I highly recommend you find colleagues who would like to share the sights of Scotland. It staggers the mind when you realize you are playing on golf courses that are hundreds of years old. Nothing compares to hitting shots over stone walls or driving blindly over mounds with sheep as targets. The feeling of striking such shots is foreign and sometimes awkward because it is like speaking a new language or learning a new job in a different field. Maybe feeling uncomfortable is something you should seek. Forget about the unblemished, lush fairways found in North America and discover brown links grass and low-to-the-ground golf shots. Soak in the way that true links golf should be played. The warmer beer in true pint glasses is fabulous too!

The next big question that lingered in the air for the group was: "When is the next scintillating trip?" Such a query is a real compliment to us for organizing this odyssey. The boys definitely wanted to repeat an adventure of this magnitude. Would it be to the west coast of Scotland to play Turnberry, Prestwick, and Troon, to the highlands of Scotland to play Royal Dornoch and Cruden Bay, or perhaps to play Ballybunion, and Lahinch in Ireland? When would this take place? More importantly, could the Irish or Scottish people sustain another onslaught of Canucks celebrating and sipping from the Verma Cup?

We decided that playing legendary southwest Irish links courses like Ballybunion Old Course, Lahinch, and Waterville and the new visually stunning Old Head at Kinsale in May, 2011 would whet our ever-growing appetites for culture, golf, food, and craic (fun). I will have to write about this Verma Cup 2 Irish Adventure and our corresponding antics in my next book . . .

In the end, the choice of destination is inconsequential. Any trip with these men is bound to be fantastic. Because wherever we go, the distinguished adults revert to being kids again. Golf, the eternal fountain of youth!

AFTER THE ROUND: REFLECTIONS

If there is one lasting thought that I hope I've impressed upon you, it is for you to respect the integrity of the game. This goal should be an honourable and mandatory pursuit for all golfers and I am one of the proud torch-bearers of this prestigious flame. Funky shirts with no collars and large-headed drivers that you can land a plane on can provide change in golfing culture but the underlying attitude of playing golf the right way needs to survive. It must.

I, the Commish, am passionate and emphatic about protecting the sanctity of this statement. Rules, sportsmanship, traditions, and etiquette have to be upheld like a code of chivalry on all courses that are played. The game is greater than all of us. And the way you play golf, in all its facets, will be indicative of your conduct as a businessman, a family member, a friend, and as a participant of the human race. Old Tom Morris, Bobby Jones, Tom Watson, Gary Player, and Jack Nicklaus would all concur.

Continue to take advantage of all the joys golf gives to you. Don't take it too seriously so that it dilutes the fun. Yoda, Chewie Open, Folded Arms, and St Andrews. These are some of the key words from this book for you to retain. If you remember them, how can you go wrong enjoying golf with your friends and acquaintances in the future?

Feel free to email your comments about *Golf Shorts and Plus Fours* to wayne.morden@rogers.com. Perhaps I could design a second course if you provide me with intriguing ideas for new holes!

Cheers,

Wayne T. Morden ("the Commish")

Reading List

Bamberger, Michael. *To the Linksland.* New York: Penguin, 1992.

Bowden, Tripp. *Freddie & Me.* New York: Skyhorse, 2009.

Brown, Robert. *The Way of Golf: Reconnecting with the Soul of the Game.* Short Hills: Burford Books, 2000.

Coyne, Tom. *A Course Called Ireland.* New York: Penguin, 2009.

Coyne, Tom. *Paper Tiger: An Obsessed Golfer's Quest to Play with the Pros.* New York: Gotham Books, 2006.

Daley, Paul. *Golf Architecture: A Worldwide Perspective.* Glen Waverley, Victoria, Australia: Full Swing Golf Publishing, 2002.

Dodson, James. *A Son of the Game.* Chapel Hill: Workman, 2009.

Dodson, James. *Final Rounds.* New York: Bantam Books, 2006.

Dodson, James. *The Dewsweepers.* New York: Dutton, 2001.

Feinstein, John. *Moment of Glory.* New York: Back Bay Books, 2010.

Frost, Mark. *The Match.* New York: Hyperion, 2007.

Garrity, John. *Ancestral Links.* New York: New American Library, 2009.

Greig, Andrew. *Preferred Lies.* London: Weidenfeld and Nicolson, 2006.

Jack, Zachary Michael. *Let there be Pebble.* Lincoln: University of Nebraska, 2011.

James, Mark. *Into the Bear Pit.* London: Virgin Books, 2000.

Kilfara, Darren. *A Golfer's Education.* Chapel Hill: Algonquin Books of Chapel Hill, 2001.

Konik, Michael. *In Search of Burningbush.* New York: McGraw-Hill, 2004.

Lazarus, Adam, and Steve Schlossman. *Chasing Greatness: Johnny Miller, Arnold Palmer, and the Miracle of Oakmont.* New York: New American Library, 2010.

Links, Bo. *Follow the Wind.* New York: Scribner, 1996.

Martin, Scott. *The Intelligent Golfer.* New York: Universe Publishing, 2011.

Mott, Billy. *The Back Nine.* New York: Knopf, 2007.

Murphy, Michael. *Golf in the Kingdom.* New York: Compass, 1997.

Nicklaus, Jack. *Jack Nicklaus: Memories and mementos from golf's Golden Bear.* New York: Stewart, Tabori & Chang, 2007.

Peper, George. *St Andrews Sojourn.* New York: Simon & Schuster, 2006.

Peper, George, and Malcolm Campbell. *True Links.* New York: Artisan, 2010.

Pressfield, Steven. *Legend of Bagger Vance.* New York: William Morrow, 1995.

Roberts, Jimmy. *Breaking the Slump.* New York: Harper, 2009.

Rubenstein, Lorne. *This round's on me: Lorne Rubenstein on golf.* Toronto: McClelland & Stewart, 2009.

Westrum, Dexter. *Elegy for a Golf Pro.* Short Hills: Burford Books, 1997.

Answers to Cart Girl and Nineteenth Hole Visits

Cart Girl Visit #1 on Outward Nine

1. They all shot 59s in professional tournaments.
2. They all holed out shots with irons to defeat Greg Norman on the last hole. Tway holed a greenside bunker shot to win the 1986 PGA at Inverness. Mize chipped in from off the green on the eleventh hole (2nd playoff hole) to win the 1987 Masters. Gamez jugged a 176-yard seven-iron from the middle of the green at the difficult closing hole at Bay Hill to win the 1990 Nestlé Invitational. David Frost holed out a bunker shot at the 1990 USF&G in Louisiana to win. Snake-bit (or Shark-bit)!

Cart Girl Visit #2 on Outward Nine

1. Ben "The Hawk" Hogan. Also known as the Wee Ice Mon after winning at Carnoustie.
2. Tom Watson during the final round at Turnberry. Also famously called "The Duel in the Sun" at the 1977 Open Championship where Watson defeated Nicklaus by one stroke. Weekend rounds for Watson were 65-65 while Nicklaus was 65-66. Amazing golf!

Cart Girl Visit #3 on Inward Nine

1. Queen, Queen Mother, and Jack Nicklaus.
2. Lee Trevino.

Cart Girl Visit #4 on Inward Nine

1. Notah Begay. All teammates on Stanford golf team.
2. Royal Montreal, Royal Quebec, and Toronto Golf Club (which is actually in Mississauga, Ontario!)

Nineteenth Hole and Refreshment Hut #1

1. Bobby Jones played these courses to win the Grand Slam. The second four courses are the ones Tiger played to win the Tiger Slam.
2. They all won U.S. Amateurs.
3. Tom Watson, Steve Pate, Davis Love, and Craig Parry.

Nineteenth Hole Following the Round

1. A turkey farm.
2. Ben Hogan and the eccentric Canadian Moe Norman.
3. Johnny Miller.

ABOUT THE AUTHOR

Wayne T. Morden has passionately pursued golf since he was 5 years old. He played varsity golf and graduated from Queen's University. He is fondly known as "The Commish" by his golfing cohorts. Originally from Woodstock, Wayne presently lives in Port Credit (Mississauga), Ontario with his wife Alison and their cat Squeaky. This is his first book.

CPSIA information can be obtained at www.ICGtesting.com
Printed in the USA
LVOW062127090312

272481LV00001B/3/P